ALL SOLUTIONS
ARE WITH THE PROPHET'S PROGENY

BY
DR. MUHAMMAD AL-TIJANI AL-SAMAWI

Translated by
Abdullah al-Shahin

IN THE NAME OF ALLAH,
THE BENEFICIENT, THE MERCIFUL

CONTENTS

Introduction	7
Preface	11
This is the True Islam	17
The Ahlul Bayt are the Natural Continuity of the Mission of their Grandfather	22
Keeping to Religion in the Past and the Present	32
Is Islam Difficult so that People Cannot Comply with it?	42
Does Islam accept Development?	48
The Political Problems Created by Civilization	61
Enjoining of Good and Forbidding of the Evil	65
Modern Man and the Lenient Religion	69
The Shia in Brief	90
The Shia in the Qur'an	90
The Shia in the Prophet's Traditions	92
Today, I have Perfected for You Your Religion…	96
Eid Al-Ghadir	96
Striving to remain firm on Guidance	122
The Shia are the Followers of the Sunnah, But…	134
Every Day is Ashura and Every Land is Karbala	138
The Shia and the Prayer	144
The Shia and the Friday Prayer	153
Smoking in the Places of Prayer	157
I bear Witness that Ali is the Friend of Allah	167
Epilogue to the Previous Chapters	176
The Shia and the Sunni Refute the Wahhabis	189
Kharijites' Doubt in the Past and Wahhabis' in the Present are the same	201

Discussion with one of the Wahhabi Ulama	209
Wahhabism Refuted by the Prophet (S)	217
The Companions Seek the Blessing of the Prophet's Hair	219
Companions and Caliphs Seek Blessings in the Prophet's Belongings After His Death	221
An Important Point	222
The Prophet Allowed Seeking Blessing and taught it to His Companions	225
Muhammad is a Human Not Like Other Humans, but as Corundum Among Gems	227
Seeking Healing by the Prophet's Blessing	231
Wahhabism has Historical Roots	235
Wahhabism Prohibits Visiting Of Graves	239
The Ahlul Bayt and a Modern Muslim	241
The Solution is in the Ahlul Bayt's School	243
To Relieve from Hardship	243
This is the Wudhu'	245
This is the Prayer	247
This is the Zakat	251
Temporary Marriage and its Importance	255
Woman is Wronged among us	259
Temporary Marriage is the very Solution	266
Temporary Marriage was Legislated for Woman's Welfare	272
Temporary Marriage and its Benefits	276
This is Al-Mahdi	282
"Then I Was Guided" is the Ahlul Bayt's Book	285
"Then I Was Guided" in the Court	289
Reference Books	298

INTRODUCTION

In the name of Allah, the Beneficent, the Merciful

Praise be to Allah - the Lord of the worlds and the best of blessings and purest of greetings be on the one who was sent as His mercy to all creatures, our master and guardian Abul Qasim Muhammad ibn Abdullah (s), the last of prophets and messengers and on his immaculate progeny - the leaders of guidance and lanterns in darkness, the Imams of the nation and Saviors of mankind.

Allah has, by the grace of Muhammad (s) and his progeny (peace be on them), favored me with the guidance to know the Truth beyond which there is nothing except deviation. He made me taste the sweetness of the fruit that had ripened in the six books[1] - *Then I was Guided, To be with the Truthful, Ask Those Who Know, The Shia: The Real Followers of the Sunnah, Fear Allah, Know the Truth,* - in order to inform people of that concealed truth. As a consequence many truthful people, who are always in search for the pure truth, turned to follow the way of the immaculate Ahlul Bayt (as) and became Shia.

Such people cannot be counted. In fact, only Allah the Almighty knows their real number:

And none knows the hosts of your Lord but He Himself.

[Qur'an, 74:31]

However, many letters that come to me in Paris and in Tunisia from all over the world made me happy and hopeful that the deliverance of Allah is imminent and that His promise is true. Thus, I quote this verse that reads:

Or do you think that you would enter the garden while yet the state of those who have passed away before you has not come upon you; distress and affliction befell them and they were shaken violently, so that the Messenger and those who

---
[1] Earlier books written by the author

believed with him said: When will the help of Allah come? Now surely the help of Allah is nigh. [Qur'an, 2:214]

Through the reading of these letters, I feel that goodness does not and shall never stop at all. The truth prevails and it is not overcome. Allah the Almighty says:

Nay! We cast the truth against the falsehood, so that it breaks its head, and lo! it vanishes. [Qur'an, 21:81]

Since it is Allah who casts the truth against the falsehood, I do not and will never hesitate at all in announcing that what I believe is the truth - until Allah judges between me and those fanatics who approve of nothing except that which they have been accustomed to, even if it is false and deny nothing except that which they have ignored even if it is truth. Nevertheless, I pray Allah to endow them with guidance and success, for it is He who guides whomever He likes to the Right Path.

And since I communicate with a great number of readers and researchers through letters or direct reviews during the lectures that I give on different occasions, I have found that some people see what I have written (in my books) as the truth. Yet they often say: we are in no need to provoke these problems that may be against the unity of Muslims at a time when the West and the East have gathered together to do away with the Muslims.

I see an acceptable logic and reasonable opinion in their saying because they are trying their best to narrow the cycle of disagreement and to unite the rows (of Muslims). Therefore, I have followed their request obediently and accepted their advice with gratitude, calling to the mind a saying of Ameerul Mu'minin (as):

> *"Let the most beloved of affairs to you be the most moderate in truth, the most comprehensive in justice, and most thorough in the satisfaction of the subjects, because the dissatisfaction of the public annuls the satisfaction of the upper class and the*

dissatisfaction of the upper class is forgiven by the satisfaction of the public..."[1]

For these reasons I have put before dear readers this book '*All solutions are with the Prophet's Progeny*' in which I have tried my best to avoid the sensitive issues that may provoke some people and then take them away from truth, and thus the purpose of guiding them becomes in vain.

In fact, I think that the provocative manner which provokes high souls, on which I have depended upon in my previous books, has given fruitful and wonderful results. Nevertheless, it is no problem for me to follow a peaceful, lenient manner that may convince many more people, and here the fruits become more delicious and more appetizing. Thus, I follow the two manners together as shown in the Holy Qur'an which has followed the manner of both reward and the warning - to take the greedy to the Paradise and save the fearful from the Hell.

Since we cannot achieve the position of Imam Ali (as) who did not worship Allah out of the greed for His Paradise nor out of the fear of His Fire and who even if the veil to Truth was removed from him, would not have been any more certain than he always was, so we ask Allah the Almighty to favor us with His mercy and join us with the righteous.

Muhammad al-Tijani al-Samawi

---

[1] Imam Ali's letter to Malik al-Ashtar when (he) Imam Ali appointed him as the Governor of Egypt.

PREFACE

We have tried our best in our previous books to convince Muslims of the necessity of adhering to the Holy Qur'an and the immaculate progeny of the Prophet (s) and to keep them together to ensure guidance and the deliverance from deviation. This is according to what the Prophet (s) had confirmed and reliable narrators had narrated in their true books of Hadith of the two sects, the Shia as well as the Sunni altogether.

Aa we think, we have carried out the research on this subject fully and did not spare any effort in explaining this fact in the different ways that the research required and took us to it, whether willingly or unwillingly, until some people thought that we were trying to defame the Prophet's companions, hurt their dignities or deface their honesty.

We swear by Allah the Almighty that we did not want anything but to exalt the Prophet (s), who represents the whole of Islam and deem him far above every defect, and to exalt and deem his progeny who are equivalent to the Qur'an, far above every defect. Whoever knows them knows the Qur'an and whoever ignores them ignores the Qur'an. This is as the Prophet (s) often declared.

By the assistance of Allah the Almighty, we shall uncover in this book that a contemporary Muslim, who lives in the civilization of the twentieth century and faces different challenges, cannot abide by the Islamic Sharia[1] correctly unless he keeps with the Immaculate Progeny of the Prophet (s).

The fact that cannot be overlooked is that the Holy Qur'an and the Prophet's *Sunnah* have been liable to misinterpretation and distortion. The verses of Qur'an have been interpreted into different meanings away from the actual concepts of the Sharia, and the Prophet's *Sunnah* has been distorted by adding fabricated traditions to it - such that the Prophet (s) was free from.

---

[1] The Islamic code of religious law based on the teachings of the Qur'an and the traditional sayings of the Prophet Muhammad (s).

All the *tafsirs*[1] that we have in our hands nowadays are not free from some Israelite fables and false interpretations or some personal opinions of interpreters who say that some verses have been abrogated. The same is said about the books of Hadith that underwent fabrication, insertion and distortion. It can thus be said that no book has remained untouched. Therefore, Muslims have to revert to the infallible imams of the Prophet's progeny as they are the only ones who can correctly interpret and explain the revelation of Allah and purify the Prophet's traditions from all blemishes and distortion.

If the final goal of Muslims today is the call to go back to the righteous first companions to take the two sources of legislation from them only as they were the best of people, as most of Muslims believe - then we have to ask these people what their argument is. We can ask them for a convincing evidence and inevitable proof from which no Muslim can turn here or there. This would make any Muslim submit satisfactorily while his heart is certain. Just trusting in someone or even his righteousness and good conduct do not make it certain that he has sound perception or infallibility.

Imam Ali (as), the Gate to the Prophet's City of knowledge, referred to this point when he said:

> *In the hands of people there is truth and falsehood, truthfulness and untruthfulness, abrogating and abrogated (rulings), general and special (rulings), clear and ambiguous, memorizing and supposition. There was fabrication against the Messenger of Allah (s) in his time itself until he made a speech saying, 'Let him, he who intentionally fabricates against me - take his seat in the Fire...'*

> *In fact, those who convey to you such speech are four kinds of men, and there is no fifth one.*

> *First is a hypocrite man who shows faith, pretends Islam, does not refrain from sins or feel shy and fabricates intentionally against the Messenger of Allah (s), may Allah have blessing and peace on him and his progeny. If people knew that he is a*

---

[1] Books of interpretation and commentary on the Qur'an.

hypocrite and liar, they would not accept from him or believe what he says. Instead they said, 'he is a companion of the Messenger of Allah (s), may Allah have blessing and peace on him and his progeny, that he (the hypocrite) has seen him - the Prophet (s), heard from him, and taken from him'.

And so people accepted him even though Allah has informed you about the hypocrites with what He has informed and described them to you with what He has described. They followed him after the Prophet, peace be on him and approached the leaders of deviation and the inviters to the Fire with falsehood and fabrication. They entrusted them with posts and made them rulers over the necks of people, and consumed with them this worldly life. Surely, (most of) the people are with rulers and the worldly life except those whom Allah has preserved. So, this is one of the four men.

And then there is a man who heard something from the Messenger of Allah (s) but did not memorize it as it was and he was uncertain of it and did not intend to tell lies. Thus, this (saying of the Prophet) is in his hands and he narrates and acts according to it and says, 'I heard it from the Messenger of Allah (s), may Allah have blessing and peace on him and his progeny'. If Muslims knew that he was uncertain about it, they would not accept from him and if he himself knew that it was so, he would deny it.

And a third man is one who heard from the Messenger of Allah (s) something that he - the Prophet (s) ordered people to do, and then he ordered them not to do it, but the man did not know this. Or he heard the Prophet (s) forbid something and then he permitted it, but the man did not know, so he memorized the abrogated thing and did not memorize that which was forbidden and allowed subsequently. If he knew that it had been abrogated, he would deny it, and if Muslims when hearing from him knew that it was abrogated, they would deny it.

And a fourth man is one who fabricated neither against Allah nor against His Messenger (s). He hates lying for fear of Allah and for glorification of the Messenger of Allah (s), may Allah have blessing and peace on him and his progeny. And he was not uncertain, but he memorized what he heard as it was. He narrated exactly what he heard with neither increase nor decrease. He memorized the abrogating ruling and did according to it, and memorized the abrogated thing and avoided it. He knew the general and special (rulings) and the clear and the ambiguous, so he put everything in its right place.

A speech of the Messenger of Allah (s), may Allah have blessing and peace on him and his progeny might have two aspects – a special meaning and a general meaning. One may hear it and not know what Allah the Almighty has meant nor what the Messenger of Allah (s) has meant by it - and so the hearer interprets it without knowing its actual meaning, purpose and reason.

Not all companions of the Messenger of Allah (s) asked and enquired from the Prophet (s) nor did they wish a nomad or a foreigner to come forward and ask him so that they would hear (the answer). But nothing from him passed by me except that I asked the Prophet (s) about it and memorized it. These are the aspects that people are in disagreements about and have defects in their narrations.[1]

From this speech of Ameerul Mu'minin (as) it becomes clear that a great difficulty surrounds us in order to arrive at the real concepts and meanings of the Sharia.

Since this was Imam Ali's analysis at his very time when there was no more than twenty-five years that had passed after the Prophet's death, he was available and most of the Prophet's companions were alive to revise and purify the Prophet's traditions, then what can be said about the state of Muslims after the passage of fourteen centuries - when the nation has disagreed and divided into different sects and cults? For all that, a researcher has to be fully cautious before he judges a certain sect and considers it true or turns against another and deny it.

As we have mentioned in our previous books through scientific historical studies that the 'Twelver Shia' is the group with salvation

---

[1] *Nahjul Balaghah*, Sermon 208.

representing the right Islamic line. This judgment was not the result of the conditions and circumstances that I had lived with and then reacted accordingly. Rather it is a fact proven by the Qur'an and the *Sunnah*. This has also been proven by true history which is free from distortion and fabrication. In fact, it is easy to get to this clear fact through reason endowed by Allah along with the ability to argue and distinguish through evidence. Allah the Almighty says:

...therefore, give good news to My servants, who listen to the word, then follow the best of it; those are they whom Allah has guided, and those it is who are the men of understanding. [Qur'an, 39:17-18]

Allah also says about those who set their reasons aside and therefore deserve torment:

And they shall say: Had we been wont to listen or have sense, we had not been among the dwellers in the Burning Fire. [Qur'an, 67:10]

In spite of all this and in spite of all the clear arguments and irrefutable proofs that have been mentioned in my previous books, some people - may Allah forgive them - do not read with their minds and hearts but with their emotions. They only read what pleases their feelings and inclination. They have learnt to be against all what may oppose their beliefs and to despise all what may disagree with their wishes.

Since we are from the faithful who love goodness to be for all Muslims and try the best to guide them to the right path, which we think, is the Ship of Deliverance, we do not become desperate. We continue to invite them to goodness and happiness that is to be found nowhere except in the Garden of Bliss, until the last of our lives.

Ameerul Mu'minin Imam Ali (as) says:

May Allah have mercy on a man who sees truth and assists it, or sees injustice and denies it and assists against the doer of injustice with truth.

He also says:

> *I hate for you to be revilers, but you may describe their deeds and mention their conditions and it would be more correct in saying and more effective in excusing. You may say instead of abusing them: O Allah, spare our bloods and their bloods, and reconcile between us and them and guide them from their deviation until those who have ignored the truth know it and those who have attached themselves to aggression and enmity refrain from it.*[1]

In my six previous books, I have followed this style which Imam Ali (as) had advised his followers to follow. I was not a reviler, but I described their[2] deeds and mentioned their conducts, so that those who ignored the truth would know it. Yet, what shall I do for those who do not accept even to describe and mention the deeds and conducts of those companions? And what shall I do when the truth cannot be shown except in this way?

Here in my seventh book, I try my best not to mention the conducts of those companions or describe their deeds. Instead I try to prove the right of the Ahlul Bayt (as) and their followers in a new manner which may please most of people. Although I think that the satisfaction of all people is an unreachable goal, I pray to Allah the Almighty to make me successful in doing what He may please, to make all Muslims successful in doing everything good and guide them and us to the truth, make us not die except on the Right Path, and make our end the best.

Longing for his Lord's mercy
Muhammad al-Tijani al-Samawi

---

[1] *Nahjul Balaghah*, sermon 204.
[2] The companions were men of authority in the first stages of Islam who had committed some errors and injustices and who had been taken as a role model by a great number of Muslims.

THIS IS THE TRUE ISLAM

This was the title that I chose for the lecture I gave two years ago in the mosque of my Sunni brothers in the city of San Francisco, California, the United States of America. That day, there was a great crowd of men and women from different nations and countries - people from Africa, Turkey, Afghanistan, and Egypt attended the lecture and most of them left satisfied after a free and purposeful debate.

An academic Egyptian, who had recently received his doctorate, objected to me during the debate saying, "How could Shiism be the true Islam, whereas the well-known thing is that the Sunni are the group with Salvation on the Day of Resurrection as the ones who kept to the Qur'an and the *Sunnah* altogether, while the other sects were in deviation?"

Very calmly, I answered him and directed my speech to all present in attendance, saying, "O brothers, I loyally swear that if I found one group from the Sunni or other than them practicing their religion according to a creed ascribed to Abu Bakr - I would say: Well blessed! Abu Bakr was a great companion and he was one of the first Muslims. He accompanied the Messenger of Allah (s), was the second of the two in the cave, and was the first of the (four) orthodox caliphs. I would be satisfied with that and be one of that sect.

And if I found a group of the Sunni practicing their religion according to a creed ascribed to Umar ibn al-Khattab, I would say: Well blessed! Our master Umar was a great companion. He was the Farouq, who differentiated between the truth and falsehood, by whom Allah had strengthened Islam. He was from the first Muslims, and he was the second orthodox caliph. Then, I would be satisfied and would follow this group.

And if I found a group of the Sunni or any other than them practicing their religion according to a creed ascribed to Uthman ibn Affan, I would say: Well blessed! Our master Uthman was from the first companions, and he was one of the two lights of whom angels felt shy. He was the third of the orthodox caliphs, and it was he who had gathered the Qur'an (in one written book). Then, I would be satisfied and follow this creed.

However, I did not find any group of the Sunni, nor from other than them claiming that they followed a creed belonging to one of these three caliphs or any one of the first companions. On the other hand, I found one group practicing their religion according to a creed ascribed to Ali ibn Abi Talib (as), and this group is the Twelver Shia.

The other sects of Muslims follow Abu Hanifah, Malik, Al-Shafi'e, or Ahmad ibn Hanbal. These scholars, in spite of their high positions, great knowledge, and piety - had never accompanied the Messenger of Allah (s) for even one day, nor had they seen him at all. They all lived after the great sedition that spread over them from its darkness and they all had been affected by its bad effects.[1]

---

[1] Ibn Khaldun in his *Muqaddimah* (p. 411), shows the cause of the difference between the first companions and the imams (of the Sunni) who came later by saying, "The new events are not covered by the (religious) texts, and for what is not clear in texts, it is required to turn to other (texts) when there is similarity between them (events). And all these things cause disagreement which necessarily takes place."

It is clear that there came widespread dispersal of the companions and the second generation that came after them in different countries and towns. Some of them were appointed as judges or were in charge of giving fatwas. It led to differences in their theories and ijtihad (personal reasoning in giving a certain fatwa on a certain event). These differences arose depending on the situation of the country they lived in and the personality of the jurisprudent himself when facing different questions. As a result, two schools came to light for them.

First, the School of Opinion that was famous among the Iraqis. The most prominent one of this school were Abu Hanifah an-Nu'man ibn al-Munthir in Kufa and his disciples and adherents. This school had some characteristics. One, they used branchings and then violated them - even the imaginary and abstract things. Therefore, they would often say, "what do you think if it was so", then they asked about a contradictory situation, and then derived a ruling for that situation. Then, they turned the question over and over - upside down considering all its possible aspects, until they were called by the scholars of Hadith as Ara'aytiyyun (in Arabic, '...do you

And if we divested Imam Ali (as) of everything and did not acknowledge any preference or virtue as due to him, even then he would always remain the great companion and the first Muslim who spent all his life beside the Messenger of Allah (s). So I adjure you all by Allah, that if you gave up fanaticism and emotion, made reason your judge in order to please your Lord before anything else and then to please your conscience, whom would you choose to follow and obey?"

Most of them cried out, "Imam Ali (as) is the worthiest to be followed…"

---

think…' is 'a ra'ayta'). Secondly, they narrated and trusted in a few traditions and only according to certain conditions. So, only a few traditions were accepted by them, some of which were so excessive in nature, that it was thought not to depend on Prophet's traditions at all. Their argument in this was that they suspected the narrators of Hadith and there was much doubting in traditions about narrators.

Second was the <u>School of Hadith</u> whose characteristics were - one, they very much disliked to ask about situations because the source for them was Hadith, which was limited. They disliked giving personal opinion (on these matters). They disliked being asked about an event except when it had actually happened. They often criticized the Iraqis for their discussion of possible situations. Secondly, they depended on all traditions, even the weak ones. They were not strict about the conditions for accepting traditions and they preferred this to the giving of one's opinion. Refer to *Fajr* (dawn of) *al-Islam* by Ahmad Amin, p.243.

The disagreement and dispute between the two schools was so strong that they abused, reviled, and accused each other of impiety and disbelief. In fact, some of them fabricated false traditions. It was narrated from Abu Bakr and Umar that they approved and reproved the acting according to Hadith.

The same was narrated from ibn Mas'ud. Some scholars overexerted themselves to reconcile the contradictory sayings of the disputing schools. Therefore, the truth and honesty was not observed and Allah the Almighty was not feared. For more details, refer to the book *Know the Truth*, p. 96-98, and *Fear Allah*, p. 67-72, by the author of this book.

I said, "What if I added to these reasons the traditions of the Messenger of Allah (s) that have been mentioned by the Sunni in their books of Hadith (Sahihs and Musnads), like the following ones:

I am the City of knowledge and Ali is its gate.[1]

Of whomever I am a guardian; here Ali is to be his guardian.[2]

Ali is with the truth and the truth is with Ali. It turns with him wherever he turns.[3]

Ali to me is as Aaron was to Moses.[4]

Ali explains to my nation what they shall disagree on after me.

Ali is with the Qur'an and the Qur'an is with Ali; they shall not separate until they come to me at the Pond in Paradise.[5]

If Muslims know these facts after having acknowledged their reasons to follow Imam Ali (as) just for his companionship with the Prophet (s), then no doubt shall remain that the true Islam is the Islam adopted by the Twelver Shia who are also called *Refusers* (*rawafidh*) because they refuse to follow anyone else other than Imam Ali (as)."

After having given answers to the questions and discussing calmly through the scientific, historical research, many in attendance came to me - congratulated me and kissed me, and praised Allah, the Almighty for the guidance. They asked me to give them all my books and to lead them to some books of the Shia.

From among these people was the imam who managed the mosque. He was crying while I was talking to him about the tragedy of the Ahlul Bayt (as). He was an Egyptian physician who loved the Ahlul Bayt (as) too much. He said to me, "Be delighted my brother! I

---

[1] *Mustadark al-Hakim*, vol.3, p. 126

[2] *Sunan Tirmizi*, vol.5, p. 633, *hadith* no.3713

[3] *Ihqaq al-Haqq*, vol.5, p. 623. *Tarikh Baghdad*, vol.14, p. 321

[4] *Kanz al Ummal*, vol.11, p. 603, *hadith* no. 32915

[5] *Mustadark al-Hakim*, vol.3, p. 124. *Mu'jam al-Awsat Tabarani*, vol.5, p. 455, *hadith* no. 487

did not think that you would convince us so easily. I was warned about you by some fanatic persons who did not like you, but by the grace of Allah and by your influential and truthful speech, you could affect their hearts…yes by Allah!"

THE AHLUL BAYT ARE THE NATURAL CONTINUITY OF THE MISSION OF THEIR GRANDFATHER

When we say 'the Ahlul Bayt', we mean the twelve Imams of the immaculate progeny of the Prophet (s) whom we have studied in full in the previous books. The Shia and the Sunni have agreed that the Messenger of Allah (s) said:

The Imams after me are twelve; all of them are from (the tribe of) Quraysh.[1]

The tradition mentioned in the Sahih al-Bukhari reads:

This matter (caliphate) shall remain in Quraysh even if (only) two people remain alive.[2]

We know necessarily that Allah the Almighty has chosen Adam, Noah, the family of Abraham, and the family of Imran and preferred them - a progeny of one from the other - to the rest of mankind. The Prophet Muhammad (s) has taught and declared to us that Allah the Almighty chose him from among all the Hashimites, who were the choicest of choices. In the Sahih of Muslim - the book of 'Virtues', chapter of 'The preferring of our Prophet to all Creation' - it is mentioned that the Prophet (s) has said:

Allah has chosen Kinanah from the children of Ishmael, the Quraysh from Kinanah, the Hashimites from Quraysh and me (the Prophet) from the Hashimites.[3]

---

[1] *Sahih al-Bukhari* vol.9, p. 78, vol.4, p. 218, Book of Rulings (*Ahkam*), Chapter of 'The Emirs from Quraysh'; *Sahih Muslim* vol.3, p. 1451, *hadith* no. 1818 and 1822, Book of Emirate, Chapter of 'People are Followers of Quraysh and the Caliphate is in Quraysh'.

[2] *Ibid.*

[3] *Sahih Muslim* vol.4, p. 1782, *hadith* no. 2276

The meaning of this tradition, as understood by every reasonable person, is that the Hashimites were a family that had been chosen and preferred among all mankind. Allah chose Muhammad (s) from the Hashimites to be the best of all mankind. This shows that the Hashimites came second after the Prophet Muhammad (s) in preference with no separation.

Likewise the Prophet Muhammad (s) chose Ali and his progeny from all of the Hashimites[1] to be his successors by the command of the Revelation, and made it obligatory on all Muslims to pray to Allah to send His blessings on them. We have found that the most *tafsirs* (commentaries) mention their names and confirm that it is they who are referred to in the Qur'anic verses of '*Purification 33:33'*; *'Love, mawaddah 42:23'*; *'Guardianship, wilayah 5:55'*; *'Choosing and bequeathing of the Book 35:32'*; *'The people of remembrance 16:43'*; *'Who are firmly rooted in knowledge 3:7'* and the *Surah of al-Insan (or 'hal ata') 76*.[2]

As for the Prophet's traditions that have been agreed upon as true traditions by all Muslims and in which the Prophet (s) has referred to the Ahlul Bayt (as) with preference and virtues saying that they were

---

[1] The Prophet (s) meant a specific group of people from the Ahlul Bayt (s). The Qur'anic verses and prophet's traditions on different occasions confirm this fact. Otherwise could the Prophet (s) mean some people whom the nation did not know or could not be led to? Could the nation get to these people who were not known - whether in names, description, or place? The Hashimites were too many and they had spread everywhere in the land so that no country or town was empty of them. So, those whom the Prophet (s) meant were the nine imams after Ali, al-Hasan, and al-Husayn (peace be on them) – they were the Ahlul Bayt (s) only on the basis of traditional and intellectual proofs. He declared them as the second weighty (important) thing beside the Qur'an, so that the nation would not miss a match to him in any age, and that the nation would not miss a guide with whom if they adhered, they would not go astray...

[2] We have mentioned in brief some Qur'anic verses which the Sunni scholars acknowledge that they were revealed concerning the Ahlul Bayt (s), whereas ibn Abbas said that one third of the Qur'an had been revealed to talk about their virtues.

the Imams of guidance, are too many. So, here we mention just two of them.

The first tradition was mentioned by Muslim in his Sahih, the book of *Virtues,* chapter of *The Virtues of Ali ibn Abi Talib.* The Prophet (s) said:

> *O people, I am but a human being. The messenger of my Lord (Death) is about to come and I shall respond. I am leaving among you two weighty things - the first of them is the Book of Allah in which there is guidance and light. So follow the Book of Allah and keep to it. The second is my Household. I remind you to obey Allah by being dutiful to my progeny (Ahlul Bayt), I remind you by Allah not to forget my progeny, I remind you by Allah to remember my progeny.*[1]

The second tradition was mentioned by Muslim in the same book narrated by Sa'd ibn Abi Waqqas from his father, that the Messenger of Allah (s) had said to Ali:

> *You are to me as Aaron was to Moses, except that there shall be no prophet after me.*[2]

For brevity, these two traditions are enough to prove that Imam Ali (as) was the chief of the Prophet's progeny and he protected the Messenger of Allah (s) and continued on his way. The Messenger of Allah (s) for emphasizing the same point said:

> *I am the city of knowledge and Ali is its gate*

Surely, this saying alone is enough to show that the whole of nation cannot enter this city of Muhammad's knowledge except when entering through the gate of Ali (as), because Allah the Almighty has ordered His people to enter houses through their doors.

Here, we must point out that Imam Ali (as) had acquired his knowledge from the Prophet (s) who had brought him up since childhood. He accompanied the Prophet (s) all through his life. The

---

[1] *Sahih Muslim* vol.4, p. 1873, *hadith* no. 2408

[1] *Sahih Muslim* vol.4, p. 1873, *hadith* no. 2404. It has also been mentioned in *Sahih al-Bukhari,* the book of Maghazi (battles), the Battle of Tabuk.

The Natural Continuity of the Message

Prophet (s) taught Imam Ali (as) the knowledge of the past and the future where he said:

Gabriel did not pour anything into my chest except that which I poured it into the chest of Ali.

Imam Ali (as) said about that:

If the rug was folded to me (to sit on),[1] I would judge among the people of the Torah according to their Torah, among the people of the Gospel according to their Gospel and the people of the Qur'an according to their Qur'an.[2]

He often said:

Ask me before you shall miss me.[3]

All the companions and all Muslims throughout history witness that Imam Ali (as) was the most knowledgeable of all people in the affairs of religion and the world, and that he was the most pious, most abstinent, most patient with calamities, the bravest in wars and the most forgiving.

For better understanding, we have to read what Imam Ali (as) said about the relation between the Prophet (s) and his progeny. He said:

They are the place of his secret, the recourse in his affairs, the sack of his knowledge, the resort for his wisdom, the den of his books, and the mountains of his religion. By them he has made erect the bending of his back and driven away his fear.[4]

He said:

By Allah, I have been taught the knowledge about missions, carrying out of promises, and all words and there are doors of wisdom and light of all affairs with us the Ahlul Bayt ...[5]

He said:

---

[1] If I was allowed to judge among people...
[2] *Al-Manaqib*, by Khawarizmi, p. 47
[3] *Ibid.*
[4] *Nahjul Balaghah*, sermon 2.
[5] *Ibid.*, sermon 11.

...where are those who claim that they are deep-rooted in knowledge other than us – claiming falsely and oppressively against us. Allah has exalted us and lowered them, given us and deprived them, included us and excluded them. Guidance is looked forward to through us and thereby blindness is recovered...the Imams from Quraysh have been sowed in this set of Hashim so that imamate does not fit other than them and chiefs from other than them shall not be fit.[1]

He said:

...surely the example of the progeny of Muhammad, may Allah have blessing and peace on them, are like the stars of the sky – when one star sets, another star shines. As if the virtues from Allah have been perfected in you (the Ahlul Bayt) and He has given you what you hoped for.[2]

He said:

...no one from this nation can be compared to the progeny of Muhammad, may Allah have mercy on him and his progeny and no one on whom their favor has been bestowed can be equaled to them at all. They are the foundation of religion and the pillar of certainty. The oppressed resort to them and followers join them. The specialties of the right of guardianship are for them and among them is custodianship and inheritance...[3]

He said:

...and surely I am on the clear way that I picked up, picking it from between the ways of deviation and confusion. Observe the progeny of your prophet, cling to their way and follow trace of their footsteps for they will not take you away from guidance, nor will they take you back to be perished. If they keep silent, you have to keep silent and if they rise, you have to rise. Do not precede them lest you go astray and do not lag behind them lest you perish...[4]

---

[1] *Ibid.*, sermon 142.
[2] *Ibid.*, sermon 99.
[3] *Nahjul Balaghah*, sermon 2.
[4] *Ibid.*, sermon 96.

He said:

They are the life of knowledge and death of ignorance. Their discernment informs you of their knowledge and their silence tells of the wisdom of their logic. They do not contradict the truth, nor do they disagree on it. They are the pillars of Islam and the associates of those who resort to them. Through them, the truth has come back to its rightful place and falsehood has been kept away from its position and its tongue has been severed from its root. They have understood the religion with reason and care, not with the understanding of hearing and narration because the narrators of knowledge are too many, but its caretakers are few.[1]

These passages quoted from *Nahjul Balaghah* and said by Imam Ali (as) give us a real picture about the firm relation between the Prophet (s) and his progeny and make them the only continuity of his mission, and that they are the only ones who can inform of what he has announced for all mankind throughout ages and for all nations and cultures.

Imam Ali (as) was not satisfied with showing of the high rank of the immaculate progeny and their position to Muslims only. He showed that he himself was the axis of the quern and chief of the immaculate progeny. He showed his role - that which he had been entrusted with by Allah and His messenger to manage people and not to let them go astray. He said:

...whereto do you go and how are you diverted while the banners are being raised, signs are clear and the light stands are set up? So to where do you go astray, or how are you blind when amongst you there are the progeny of your Prophet (s) who are the reins of truth, leaders of the religion, and the tongue of truthfulness? So observe them in the best positions of the Qur'an, and hasten to them as the hastening of extremely thirsty ones (to the drinking fountain).

O people take it from the Messenger of Allah (s), may Allah have blessing and peace on him and his progeny, he said that: 'One of us dies, but he is not dead, and one of us is decomposing,

---

[1] *Ibid.*, sermon 236.

but he is not decomposed.' So, do not speak of what you do not know because most of the truth is in what you deny and excuse the one against whom you have no argument, and that person is me.

Did I not act among you according to the Major weighty thing (the Qur'an) and I left among you (after me) the Minor weighty thing (the Ahlul Bayt - at that time Imam al-Hasan and al-Husayn)? I fixed among you the banner of faith, showed you clearly the limits of the lawful and the unlawful, dressed you with soundness of my justice and spread to you the favor of my saying and doing. I showed to you the noblest of morals from myself. Therefore, do not use (your own) opinion in that whose insides cannot be perceived by the sight, nor can be penetrated by thinking.[1]

If you, dear reader, ponder on the saying of Imam Ali (as), you shall find in it the interpretation of the tradition of *Thaqalayn* (the two weighty things) that has been narrated by the Sunni from the Messenger of Allah (s) who said:

I have left among you the two weighty things - the Book of Allah and my progeny. If you keep to them, you shall never go astray after me at all.

Imam Ali (as) also said:

Did I not act among you according to the Major weighty thing (the Qur'an) and I left among you the Minor weighty thing (the Ahlul Bayt)?

This saying of Imam Ali (as) is a clear proof that Imam Ali (as) managed people according to the rulings of the Holy Qur'an, whose reality no one could understand except him. Also he left among them the Minor Weighty things, who were the infallible Imams from his progeny so that each one of them would carry out the same role that the Prophet (s) carried out in his nation.

If we ponder on the saying of the Prophet (s): "*I am leaving among you the two weighty things*" and the saying of Imam Ali (as): "*did I not act among you according to the Major weighty thing*" - we

---

[1] *Nahjul Balaghah*, sermon 86.

understand that the role of the immaculate progeny is to explain and declare the Book of Allah to the nation lest they disagreed after the death of the Prophet (s).

What confirms this fact is this saying of the Prophet (s):

In every generation of my nation there are just men from my progeny who protect this religion from distortion of deviants, fabrication of liars, and misinterpretation of the ignorant. Surely, your Imams are your delegation to Allah, so be careful to whom you delegate.[1]

He also said:

Stars are security for the people of the earth from drowning and the people of my house are security for my nation from disagreement. If a tribe from the Arabs disagree with them (the Ahlul Bayt), they shall disagree among themselves and become the party of Iblis.[2]

He also said:

Surely, the example of my progeny among you is like the Ark of Noah; whoever rode on it would be rescued and whoever lagged behind it would drown.[3]

Through this brief study, the guidance becomes clearly distinguished from error to us, and we can say that the Twelver Shia is the true sect, because it is the only sect that has kept to the two weighty things, boarded the Ship of Rescue and clung to the Rope of Allah. The Shia neither precede the Ahlul Bayt (as) nor do they turn away from them, but they follow and imitate them. Therefore, they are guided by their guidance and they follow their path.

"Here is the Qur'an that you can ask to speak out, and it shall not speak out but what I tell you about. It has the knowledge of what shall come; it speaks about the past, the healing of your ailments, and the managing of you.[4]

---

[1] *As-Sawa'iq al-Muhriqah* by Ibn Hajar Al-Shafi'i, p. 90, 148.
[2] *Mustadrak al-Hakim*, vol. 3 p. 149.
[3] *Ibid.*, vol. 3 p. 151, *as-Sawa'iq al-Muhriqah* by Ibn Hajar Al-Shafi'i, p. 184.
[4] *Nahjul Balaghah*, sermon 156.

Keep to the Book of Allah, for it is a firm rope, clear light, advantageous cure, satiating drink, a resort for those who seek and a rescue for those who cling. It never bends to be set right, nor does it errs to be blamed. The much reciting and listening to it do not make it old. Whoever speaks with it is truthful, and whoever acts according to it wins.[1]

Prophet (s) left to you what other prophets had left for their nations so that they did not leave them to go astray without showing clear way or a raised banner.

The Book of your Lord is among you showing His lawful and unlawful things, obligations and favors, abrogating and abrogated things, permissions and necessities, special and general rulings, lessons and examples, absolutes and finites, clear and ambiguous things, interpreting its statements and explaining its obscurities.

There are some verses in Quran whose knowledge is obligatory and others whose ignorance by people is not forgivable. And there is that which is fixed as obligatory in the book, but its abrogation is known in the Prophet's Sunnah, or there are those which appear obligatory in the Sunnah, but in the Book it is permitted to be given up.

And, there are other verses which were obligatory in its time but not so in future (with passing of its time). There are verses of His different prohibitions for major sins - for which He has threatened of His Fires, or minor - for which He has promised forgiveness, and there are those verses which are accepted in small portion (in reciting of the Qur'an) and permitted for leaving its big portion."[2]

---

[1] *Ibid.*, sermon 154.
[2] *Nahjul Balaghah*, sermon 1.

KEEPING TO RELIGION IN THE PAST AND THE PRESENT

It is well known that Islam, with which the Prophet Muhammad (s) had been sent by Allah, is the last of religions in the matter of Divine Legislation. Allah the Almighty says:

Muhammad is not the father of any of your men, but he is the Messenger of Allah (s) and the Last of the prophets. [Qur'an, 33:40]

Since Muhammad (s) is the last of the prophets and messengers and his Book is the last of the Books revealed by Allah, so there shall be no Divine Book after the Holy Qur'an. Islam is the basic religion to which all the divine religions have been fused. Allah says:

He it is Who sent His Messenger with the guidance and the true religion so that He may make it prevail over all the religions; and Allah is enough for a witness. [Qur'an, 48:28]

After the advent of Muhammad (s) as prophet, it has become obligatory on all human beings to turn from the previous religions whether Judaism, Christianity, or any other religion and embrace Islam to worship Allah the Almighty according to the Sharia of Muhammad (s), because Allah will not accept any religion other than Islam since then. Allah says:

And whoever seeks a religion other than Islam, it shall not be accepted from him, and in the hereafter, he shall be one of the losers. [Qur'an, 3:85]

We understand from this that the Jews and the Christians however much they claim that their laws and legislations are true and that they follow the Prophet Moses (s) or the Prophet Jesus Christ (s), the reality requires that they must follow the Prophet Muhammad (s) since the moment Allah sent him as a messenger. A Christian has no right to say that he wants to remain on his religion, nor does a Jew.

The fact is that Muhammad (s) was sent as a prophet to all mankind and as a mercy to all people with their different races and beliefs. This does not mean that we condemn the previous divine religions, but Allah the Almighty knew that His people had distorted His laws. They made lawful what was unlawful and unlawful what was lawful for the sake of their own desires. Therefore, they went astray and made those who came after them go astray.

So the advent of Muhammad (s) the last of the prophets was a mercy to all mankind in order to allow them to restore themselves again and go back to the truth so that they would win the Paradise. However, most of people detest the truth. Desires, fancies and fanaticisms play with them and devils occupy them so that they become excessive in their deviation.

Allah says in this concern:

Those who disbelieved from among the followers of the Book and the polytheists could not have separated (from the faithful) until there had come to them the clear evidence; a messenger from Allah, reciting pure pages, wherein are all the right ordinances. And those who were given the Book did not become divided except after clear evidence had come to them. [Qur'an 98:1-4]

It is also not sufficient that a Jew or a Christian says, 'I believe in Muhammad, but I will remain on my religion', as I myself have heard from some Arab Christians. We say to such people that Allah does not accept from them except when they actually follow him. Allah says in this concern:

Those who follow the Messenger-Prophet, who can neither read nor write, whom they find written down with them in the Torah and the Gospel (who) enjoins them good and forbids them evil, and makes lawful to them the good things and makes unlawful to them impure things, and removes from them their burden and the shackles which were upon them; so (as for) those who believe in him and honor him and help him, and follow the light which has been sent down with him, these it is that are the successful. [Qur'an 7:157]

This invitation from Allah the Almighty was not limited to the Jews and the Christians, all of whom represented "the People of the Book", but it included all human beings with no exception.

Allah the Almighty says:

Say: O people! surely I am the Messenger of Allah (s) to you all, of Him Whose is the kingdom of the heavens and the earth, there is no god but He; He brings to life and causes to die; therefore believe in Allah and His messenger, the Prophet, who can neither read nor write, who believes in Allah and His words, and you follow him so that you may walk in the right way. [Qur'an 7:158]

The Holy Qur'an is too clear in stating the obligation of following the Prophet (s) and not just believing in his prophethood. This is the wisdom of Allah in sending the messengers. We have never heard in all the history of humankind that Allah has sent a messenger to say to people: remain on your religion which you have inherited from the messenger that had come before me.[1]

---

[1] Therefore, the Jews turned out to be racists by not accepting any as leader except those whose blood was Jewish. Thus, they gathered together their dispersed lot claiming that they were "the chosen people of Allah" and any other than them were not human. This was on the basis of Torah that was lost and ruined after the Babylonian Captivity at the hands of the Babylonian king Nebuchadnezzar who occupied Jerusalem in the year 586 BC.

The Jews, who were not killed, remained captives in Babylon until the year 457 BC when they could go back to Palestine by the assistance of Cyrus the great king of Persia. After their returned to Palestine, a man called Ezra collected and reformed the books of the Old Testaments, which is the Torah of today.

From this, we know that between the loss of the Torah and its recollection, there were more than 125 years. During this period, most of the memorizers of the Torah had been killed or died in prison where they were forbidden to practice any religious activity. Therefore, the Torah had to have human interventions. So it is now full of fables, contradictions, untruths, distorted events and unrealities...etc.

All of the prophets have called for belief in all the messengers of Allah, so that no one might harm their prophethood or be excessive about their real position and give them the position of a deity.

Allah the Almighty says:

The messenger believes in what has been revealed to him from his Lord and (so do) the believers; they all believe in Allah and His angels and His books and His messengers; We make no difference between any of His messengers; and they say: We hear and obey, our Lord! Thy forgiveness (do we crave), and to Thee is the eventual course. [Qur'an, 2:285]

If we know that Islam is the last religion that Allah the Almighty has endowed His faithful people with, so its laws and rulings are valid for every time and every place, because there is no prophet to come after Prophet Muhammad (s) and no divine book to come after the Holy Qur'an according to this saying of Allah:

This day have I perfected for you your religion and completed My favor on you and chosen for you Islam as a religion. [Qur'an, 5:3]

However, some Muslims, if not most of them, do not abide by the laws and rulings of Islam. They claim that these are difficult to carry out and that most (ordinary) people are unable to carry them out.

The same thing happened to Christianity; the four Bibles were not written down at the time of Jesus Christ (as). The oldest one, which is "The Gospel of Mark", was written down forty years later in Rome. Therefore, it was subject to distortion like the Torah at the time of Augustine who mixed between idolatry and the statements of the Bible.

The idolatry on which the idolaters of India, China, and old Egypt agreed on such as, the belief in Trinity and the ascribing of vices to the prophets (as) and even to Jesus Christ (as) influenced this. Moreover, they annulled the main purpose of all religions, which is to guide the human beings, when they claimed that Jesus Christ (as) had redeemed the criminals and sinners, so there was no necessity for any guidance after him or to send other prophets. For more details, refer to *"The School Journey"* and *"The Guidance to the Religion of al-Mustafa"* by Sheikh Muhammad Jawad al-Balaghi.

Some others, who are learned people, say that it is necessary to develop the rulings according to the requirements of the modern life. They see *ijtihad*[1] to be necessary in everything and claim that *ijtihad* is one of the virtues of Islam and one of its prides. These learned people may influence the minds of many young students, especially as they pretend that they love Islam too much and are too careful to apply its rulings.

These people justify the underdevelopment and deterioration of Muslims as they have not developed their religion from where it had been established fifteen centuries ago at a time where there was no means of transport except for mules and donkeys.

These people say that as for today we live in the age of rockets - whose speed exceeds the speed of sound, telephone, fax, and computer - through which man can contact with any place in the world within a few seconds. So we cannot remain looking at the Qur'an with that superficial sight where we judge against a thief by cutting his hand or a criminal by cutting his head by the sword...they often say so and have odd philosophies in this regard.

Once, I was talking with a university professor about this. In my talk with him, I said that the Messenger of Allah (s) has said:

> *There is no magnanimous young man except (like) Ali, and no sword except Dhul Faqar."*

He laughed at me and said, "O doctor, do not say like this again. It was valid at the time of the Prophet (s) when the sword had a role in winning the battles and it was the only weapon which the heroes had pride for in their poems. Now we are in the age of the machine guns that shoots seventy bullets in a second and the jet fighter that can destroy an entire city in few minutes. In fact, we are in the age of the atomic and nuclear bombs that can destroy a continent in some moments. Are you ignorant of all this and are you still talking about the sword and the courage of Imam Ali ibn Abi Talib?"

I said, "This does not refute that or contradict it, and every occasion has its own context. Do you not see that when Allah talked

---

[1] Using of one's (usually a mujtahid) effort to form a judgment on questions concerning the Sharia and religious affairs.

about weapons, He included in one word all means of destruction when He said in brief:

And prepare against them what force you can and horses tied at the frontier. [Qur'an, 8:60]

Thus, the Qur'an connected what military means the people at the time of the Prophet (s) had to win battles with what the people of this time have. So, this statement of Qur'an -

'And prepare against them what force you can'

can be understood by everyone according to the language of their time. The source and meaning of "*force*" is the same to the all, and this is like the saying of Allah:

...and We have made the iron, wherein is great violence and advantages to men... [Qur'an, 57:25]

Therefore, all weapons, whether the simple ones like the sword or spears or the developed ones like tanks, machine guns, and bombs are defined as means of "violence". Similarly, all means of ease and comfort such as cars, airplanes, ships, televisions, and others are defined as "advantages to people". Glory be to Allah Who has created iron and made it of use for people and taught them what they did not know.

Thus, the Holy Qur'an is in the hands of all kinds of people that every generation can understand it by the language of its age. And as for your saying "we cannot look at the Qur'an with a superficial view - that we judge against a thief by cutting his hand or a criminal by cutting his head by the sword", if you try to replace the laws of Allah with manmade laws whose makers claim that they are more beneficent and merciful to people than their Creator is to them, then this can never be acceptable. It is undoubtedly clear disbelief.

And, if by "development" you mean the development of the means of execution against a criminal or the means of cutting a thief's hand, this can be discussed, because these are minor things that the Islamic Legislation did not concentrate on. Rather it concentrated on abiding to laws by carrying out the sentences determined by Allah the Almighty concerning "retribution". Allah says:

O you who believe! retaliation is prescribed for you...And there is life for you in (the law of) retaliation, O men of understanding, that you may guard yourselves against evil. [Qur'an, 2:178-179]

As for cutting the hand of a thief by a sword, a cleaver, or a modern tool, the legal ruler (judge) or the religious authority can give his opinion in the matter (by deriving it through the legal proofs).

What is important dear Sir, is that we do not replace the laws of Allah by the so-called positive laws that were agreed to by the European systems that have abrogated the death sentence against criminals however extreme their crimes were.

Allah says:

And there is life for you in (the law of) retaliation, O men of understanding... [Qur'an, 2:178-179]

The meaning of the saying of Allah here is that if we abrogate the laws of Allah and abolish the law of retaliation, our life shall be without safety and security and the criminals shall corrupt everything. Then, life shall become like hell with no goodness or peace.

This university professor debated saying, "Evil is not to be treated with evil. Statistics has proven that some of those who were sentenced to death for the accusation of a crime were innocent."

I said, "With my respect to you professor, but by your saying "evil is not to be treated with evil" you have made yourself more aware than Allah the Creator of everything and this is not your right. And as for your saying that some of those, who were sentenced to death, were innocent, this is another matter. To your knowledge, I say that Islam does not punish just for suspicion or accusation, but after evidence, witnesses and confession." The debate came to no use, because each one of us clung to what we believed to be right.[1]

---

[1] The likes of this professor are those who have westernized and live with the complex of the yielding before the masses of iron and bricks amassed even if by stealing and assassinating other people or even entire humankind.

It would be better thus to end this section with what Imam Ali (as) has said about the Prophet Muhammad (s) and about Islam. He said:

He (Allah) has sent him with the shining light, the clear proof, the right method, and the guiding Book. His family is the best of families and his tree is the best of trees; its branches are straight with its fruits hanging loose. His birth was in Mecca and his immigration was in the Good City where his mention was high and his call reached too far. He has sent him with a sufficient argument, curative breach and preventive invitation (that prevented every corruption of the pre-Islamic age).

The Nazis, for example, since they felt that they had some arms, adopted the slogan of "the Aryan race". Under this banner of racism, they destroyed civilizations and killed tens and millions of people in two destructive wars within time frame of no more than a quarter of a century. And the allies were not better than them. They invaded the different nations as colonists and tore those nations into pieces in order to be able to rule them and control their treasures and resources. In this way, they built their false civilization on bloods, sweat, and efforts of the suppressed peoples.

In the same way as the Nazi model, the American tyranny succeeded in blackmailing different countries and adopting the illegitimate child "Israel". It secretly and openly brought up and assisted it by all means until it became a pit of the worst criminals and blood-suckers in the world.

Whereas, Ali ibn Abi Talib (as) had come to enliven the humanity inside a man following the true Mohammedan Islam and saying, "A strong man is weak before me until I take the right from him, and the weak is strong to me until I take back the right for him." He liberated man when he fought against the enemies of humanity. He said to Malik al-Ashtar when appointing him as the governor over Egypt, "...and do not be as predatory beast over them...for people are of two kinds; either your brother in religion or your equal in creation." He also said, "Do not be a slave to another while Allah has created you free."

So man whatever he is - black, poor, or weak – all walk under the banner of Ali ibn Abi Talib (as) that carries the high values of liberation and human rights. On the other hand some people become mean and weak before technology which is possessed by the traders of wars and the suckers of peoples' bloods.

He (Allah) has declared through him - the Prophet (s) - the unknown laws, suppressed through him the irrelevant heresies and explained through him the decisive judgments. So whoever seeks a religion other than Islam, his misery becomes certain, his firm hold is broken, his fall becomes great and his end comes to eternal sadness and severe torment...[1]

This is exactly as what has been declared by the Holy Qur'an:

And whoever desires a religion other than Islam, it shall not be accepted from him, and in the hereafter he shall be one of the losers. [Qur'an, 3:85]

I think that after this explanation, no argument or excuse shall remain for those who flatter their Jewish and Christian friends and say to them: We and you are on the truth as long as we all believe in one God Who has sent Moses, Jesus, and Muhammad and if we are different as to the prophets, we have agreed on the One Who has sent them to us.

Allah says:

Say: Do you dispute with us about Allah, and He is our Lord and your Lord, and we shall have our deeds and you shall have your deed and we are sincere to Him. Nay! do you say that Abraham and Ishmael and Jacob and the Tribes were Jews or Christians? Say: Are you better knowing or Allah? And who is more unjust than he who conceals a testimony that he has from Allah? And Allah is not at all heedless of what you do. [Qur'an, 2:139-140]

---

[1] *Nahjul Balaghah*, sermon 159.

IS ISLAM DIFFICULT SO THAT PEOPLE CANNOT COMPLY WITH IT?

This is a false claim that has no basis in truth at all. Anyone who says so is ignorant and knows nothing about Islam. Or, he is biased intending to alienate people from their religion to give up its laws and rulings. Or, he is an excessive puritan who has no regard except for the opinions of the puritan clergymen who forbid people to worship Allah in any way other than their own way and make themselves the guardians of Allah's religion. Therefore, they regard things lawful or unlawful according to their own reasons or the only traditions that have reached them.

The first thing that comes to mind in this concern is this saying of the Messenger of Allah (s):

Make it (the affairs of religion) easy and do not make it difficult! Bring good tidings and do not constrict (make people alienated from religion).[1]

Do not be hard against yourselves, lest Allah be hard upon you as He did to the Children of Israel.[2]

The Prophet (s) often said before his companions:

I neither wish for you misery and worries nor humiliation and disgrace. Allah has sent me as a facilitating teacher.[3]

It is well known that the Prophet (s) was not made to choose between two things, except that he chose was from the order of God.

The Prophet (s) was not a legislator as some people think incorrectly when they read this verse of Qur'an:

...and whatever the Messenger gives you, accept it, and from whatever he forbids you, abstain (from it). [Qur'an, 59:7]

---

[1] *Sahih al-Bukhari*, vol.1, p. 27, vol.8, p. 36.

[2] *Kanz al Ummal*, vol.3, p. 35, *hadith* no. 5346

[3] *Sahih Muslim*, vol.2, p. 1105, *Sunan Abu Dawood*, vol.4, p. 276, hadith no. 4904

Is Islam Difficult?

The commanding and forbidding of the Prophet (s) did not come from himself. He only conveyed what was revealed to him by his Lord. He did not do anything except what Allah ordered him to do with not a bit more and not a bit less. Therefore, all the commands and prohibitions are from Allah the Almighty, though they are not recorded in the Holy Qur'an.

Allah says about the Prophet (s):

Nor does he speak out of desire. It is naught but revelation that is revealed. [Qur'an, 53:3-4]

Since it is so, let us come to the Qur'an to see if Islam is so difficult that people cannot comply with it - in order to see whether this claim is true or false, so that we can be on a clear proof as to our affairs.

Allah says in the Qur'an:

He has chosen you and has not laid upon you a hardship in religion. [Qur'an, 22:78]

Allah does not want to put on you any difficulty, but He wishes to purify you and that He may complete His favor on you, so that you may be grateful. [Qur'an, 5:6]

Allah wants ease for you and He does not want for you difficulty... [Qur'an, 2:185]

This concerns the Muslim nation that has embraced Islam and abides by its laws and rules in matters of worship and behaviors. Of course, the mercy of Allah has also included all His people with their different religions. Allah has been merciful to all of them imposing no any hardship on anyone.

Allah says:

Of a small seed; He created him, then He made him according to a measure. Then (as for) the way, He has made it easy (for him). [Qur'an, 80:19-20]

So, the way of Allah that man follows to return to his Lord is an easy way with no difficulties or hardships. Allah the Almighty has repeated this meaning five times in the Qur'an. He says:

Allah does not impose upon any soul a duty but to the extent of its ability. [Qur'an, 2:286]

We do not impose on any soul a duty except to the extent of its ability. [Qur'an, 6:152]

And (as for) those who believe and do good We do not impose on any soul a duty except to the extent of its ability. [Qur'an, 7:42]

And We do not lay on any soul a burden except to the extent of its ability, and with Us is a book which speaks the truth and they shall not be dealt with unjustly. [Qur'an, 23:62]

From all this, we understand that Allah the Almighty has not imposed anything on any man except that which is within his capacity since the time of our father Adam (as). If there has been any difficulty or hardship in any one of the divine religions, it would be a result of those who interpreted the purpose of religion according to their personal opinions, or that there might be some people torturing themselves hard because of their many sins, looking forward to the forgiveness of Allah or in order to be nearer to Him. Therefore, they invented some things that were not from the religion and bound themselves to them, but they failed in bearing them.[1]

---

[1] Monasticism comes true in two ways: First is a serious monasticism that runs by itself in order not to be touched by any harm and be saved by itself (Muhammad Baqir as-Sadr, *Trends of History in Qur'an*, p. 103) And this is from the view that "Stopping on the hill is more safe". Consequently, the way is cleared before different claims and excuses that a ruler gives or the fabricated traditions that assist his creed and rule.

Second is a false monasticism where one pretends he is from the *ulama* to warn people against the injustice of a tyrant. And soon the falseness of these untrue claims and pretenses is uncovered for example, the justification that "it is not permissible to disobey the ruler or turn away from congregation", as they did to Imam Husayn (as) when he offered himself and family to save

Allah the Almighty says:

...and monasticism they innovated - We did not prescribe it to them - only to seek Allah's pleasure, but they did not observe it with its due observance... [Qur'an, 57:27]

Here we see the tradition of the Messenger of Allah (s):

Do not be hard against yourselves, lest Allah be hard upon you as He did to the Children of Israel.[1]

And in the same way, we interpret this Qur'anic Verse concerning the Prophet Muhammad (s):

...he enjoins them good and forbids them evil, and makes lawful to them the good things and makes unlawful to them impure things, and removes from them their burden and the shackles which were upon them. [Qur'an, 7:157]

The burden and shackles, which were on them - were made and imposed by them, and they themselves had bound themselves.

We conclude from this analysis that Islam is a religion that has no difficulty, hardship, overburden or shackles. It is a religion of ease, mercy, and leniency where the weaknesses of man in all his psychological and bodily aspects are fully cared for. Allah says:

Allah wants that He should make light your burdens and man is created weak. [Qur'an, 4:28]

---

the true religion and in the same way to the Alawid and Talibid revolutions that followed him.

Similar to that in our present time is the falseness of the monks of churches who serve the rulers and noblemen. They become a cause for ordinary people to disbelieve and turn away from religion where it is hardly tried to separate it from politics. And we still see many rulers and their mercenary (clergymen) preachers encourage the state of ignorance and underdevelopment among Muslims with their fatwas. These keep the Muslims away from modernity and from meeting and uniting with other Muslims.

[1] *Kanz al Ummal*, vol.3, p. 35.

...this is alleviation from your Lord and a mercy. [Qur'an, 2:178]

We shall see inshallah, in the coming chapters that Islam, as known by the Ahlul Bayt (as), is the religion that is without the opinions of opinion mongers, the excessiveness of the excessive, or the falsehood of fabricators. Then, we shall know that the Muslims of the present age can abide to the Sharia without any difficulty or hardship.

DOES ISLAM ACCEPT DEVELOPMENT?

Yes and there is no doubt that Islam is the very development, progress and renewal. It is the highest code that humanity has ever reached since its beginning. In the Holy Qur'an, there are many verses encouraging knowledge, learning and inviting man to follow reason and to try the best in all fields of life in order to reach the highest levels even in the space. Allah says:

O community of the jinn and the men! If you are able to pass through the regions of the heavens and the earth, then pass through... [Qur'an, 55:33]

This encourages man to develop and progress. When he is not satisfied within the limits of the earth, he looks towards the sky, the planets, and stars in order to make use of them, as long as Allah has given him all powers and informed him that he is preferred to all other creatures, which are for his benefit. Allah says:

Allah is He Who made subservient to you the sea that the ships may run therein by His command, and that you may seek of His grace, and that you may give thanks. And He has made subservient to you whatsoever is in the heavens and whatsoever is in the earth, all from Him; most surely there are signs in this for people who reflect. [Qur'an, 45:12-13]

Do you not see that Allah has made what is in the heavens and what is in the earth subservient to you and made complete to you His favors outwardly and inwardly? And among men is he who disputes in respect of Allah though having no knowledge nor guidance, nor a book giving light. [Qur'an, 13:20]

How can the Muslim who reads in the Book of his Lord that all what there is in the heavens like orbits, planets, suns, moons, stars, galaxies, air, clouds, rain, snow and all that is there in the earth, such as rivers, seas, oceans, mountains, forests, jungles, beasts, animals, treasures, minerals, plants - everything has been made subservient to him, remains sitting on his hands until knowledge, progress, and invention comes to him from the West? If he acts so, he disavows his duty and obligation, degrades himself and loses so greatly because the Qur'an that has been revealed by Allah has all things and lacks nothing.

Allah says:

We have not neglected anything in the Book. [Qur'an, 6:38]

The Prophet Muhammad (s) often said:

Seek knowledge from your cradle until grave.[1]

The Prophet (s) encouraged Muslims to get to their highest when he said:

If the determination of the son of Adam turns toward what is beyond the Throne, he will get it.

Thus, Islam does not see anything impossible in the field of knowledge, sciences and development. We avoid expatiation here as we may go far away from the theme of this book; otherwise, we could write an independent book on this subject. However, we ask scholars to refer to the scientific sources and books in this regard.

This is in answer to the title of this chapter where development is meant to concern the scientific and technological development in the fields of industries and inventions that have invaded the minds and houses of people from Europe, the United States of America and Japan especially. Anyhow, Muslims are indifferent to all that, and some of them have been affected by the civilization and the scientific inventions that have come from other than Muslims. Therefore, they think that Islam is the cause of the underdevelopment, especially the ones who are influenced by communism that says: "*Religion is opium for the people*".[2]

These people are ignorant, and if they are somehow fair, they will say that Islam is the incentive to people for their renewal and development. Indeed, Islam created a nation from nothing in the Arabia which conveyed to the entire world a civilization and many sciences and inventions, until some scholars wrote: "*The sun of the*

---

[1] *Nahjul Fasaha*, p. 218

[2] Famous quote of German philosopher and economist Karl Marx

Arabs shines over Europe", acknowledging that the Arabs after embracing and applying Islam, were precedent in every goodness, every discovery and invention.[1]

---

[1] Reinhart Dozy, an orientalist from Holland, writes, "In all Andalusia, there was not one man illiterate, whereas no one was able to read and write in Europe except the highest class of priests."
Muslims were prominent in Europe in different sciences:
1. *Geography:* There were the around-the-world travellers like ar-Razi, Abu Ubaydah al-Bakri, al-Ghurari, al-Idrisi, ibn Jubayr, ibn Batuta, and others. Al-Idrisi had made a great silver ball representing the terrestrial globe and it is still kept in Berlin. The Arab scientists drew maps by which the people of the West guided on their way to India and other places in the world.
2. *Astronomy:* Muslims had observatories in Toledo, Cordoba, Baghdad, Damascus, Cairo, Samarqand, and Persia. Draper says, "The Arabs knew the size of the earth by measuring the degree of its surface, and they defined the eclipse of the sun and the moon. They made correct tables for the sun and the moon, estimated the year and knew the two equinoxes…"
3. *Geometry:* Gustave Lebon says, "Europe took from the Arabs the details in embellishment and it was found on some churches in France as figures of Arabic letters sculptured on stone."
4. *Mathematics:* the orientalist Sidio* says, "…and the Arabs paid much and special care for all sciences of mathematics. Indeed, they were our teachers in this field." Leonard Albizi (Blussy)* wrote about 1200 theses in Algebra that he had learned from the Arabs. Hitti said in his book 'the History of the Arabs', "…and the zero that has solved many problems in the mathematical operations had come to Europe from Andalusia. And the 'zero' is still but an Arabic word."
From among the geniuses in mathematics were al-Hasan ibn al-Haytham, ibn Sina (Avicenna), al-Khawarizmi, ibn al-Banna', and others. The book of al-Khawarizmi on mathematics has been translated into many European languages.
5. *Physics:* Light - ibn al-Haytham was very expert in the science of light (optics), and he had written a book called 'al-Manadhir' in seven volumes, and tables of Arabic names of the parts of the eye translated into foreign languages and are still used with their Arabic names.
The compass - Sidio* and Sarton confirm that it was the Arabs who invented the compass. The pendulum - the Muslims called it 'al-Mawwar' which was invented by ibn Younus al-Misry (the Egyptian) who died in 399 AH-1009

However, if by 'development' it is meant what the western world in Europe and America presents as the indecorous fashions of clothes, the absolute freedom given to the clubs of the naked, sodomy, the practice of sexual intercourse in public places, legislating of inheritance for dogs and other animals, and all what is shown in the TV of immoral programs...all these can never be recognized by Islam, nor does it comply with it. Surely Islam fights against all these immoralities and tries to do away with them.

On the other hand there are also some extreme practices by some Muslims who claim they are in keeping with the Prophet's *Sunnah*,

---

AD. It was used to count the periods during the observations of stars. Scientist Smith pointed out in his book 'The History of Mathematics' that ibn Younus had preceded Galileo in knowing and inventing the pendulum.

Note*: I apologize to readers that some foreign names may be written unlike their origins. I tried my best, but I could not arrive at a result.

6. *Chemistry:* The Arabs were expert in dyeing, tanning, mineral industries, and blending of perfumes. Gustave Le Bon says, "It was the Muslims alone who had invented the gunpowder as an explosive propellant to shoot bullets and England took this invention from them followed by the rest of Europe ..."

7. *Industry:* Philip Hitti says, "Paper is one of the great utilities that Islam had offered to Europe and the entire world." In Andalusia, pottery became very flourishing, besides colored mosaic and textiles. Among the other crafts that were passed to Europe were metalwork, glass making, and different industries of pottery.

8. *Agriculture:* Muslims were expert in the characteristics of soils and the suitable fertilizers for each to an extent more than any others were.

Medicine: Philip Hitti says, "...in the middle of the eighth century A.H. - the fourteenth century AD - when plague spread in Europe, the people there remained seated on their hands before it was considered as a fate from Allah. At this very time, the physician ibn al-Khateeb al-Ghernati wrote his book '*Haqeeqatus Sa'il wa al-Maradhul Ha'il* - The fact for the enquirer about the frightful disease' to confirm it was a matter of infection and provde it..."

It is not unknown that the books of Abu Bakr ar-Razi (850-932 AD) and Avicenna such as the books 'al-Qanoon' and 'ash-Shifa"remained until recently as major references in medicine.

This is just a brief glimpse of some sciences of Muslims and their influence on the European renaissance until the present age.

These are from among the Salafists in particular. They have long beards flowing to their chests, putting on a long shirt, having a walking stick in their hands, standing at the gate of the mosque while brushing their teeth with a teeth cleanser (*siwak*) and rubbing them left and right, spitting sometime and puffing out at another. If you sit with them at a meal, they will refuse to sit at a table. They refuse to use a spoon and a fork while having food. They do not eat except with their fingers claiming that the Messenger of Allah (s) did so.

Extremism made some of them prohibit the tape recorder and loudspeaker in calling out of *azan*, claiming that it was a heresy to use when these were not available at the time of the Prophet (s).

Extremism reached its peak with some of them when they imagined themselves as the guides who could force and make people adopt this *Sunnah*, which they thought of as the true religion. Therefore, you see them scold whoever laughs loudly saying that the Messenger of Allah (s) just smiled and did not laugh loudly, or kick whomever they find sleeping on his abdomen saying that it is the sleeping of Satan. Once, I was present when one of them beat his daughter because she offered some drinks to the guests not beginning from the guest on the right. He scolded and insulted her before the guests so that they would know that he kept to the *Sunnah*.

What *Sunnah* is this that makes others detest it especially when it is practiced in western societies and before people who bear grudge against Islam and Muslims? Instead of presenting before others a beautiful picture about Islam and the Prophet (s) of Islam and to endear this religion to everyone, such people make them look down upon Islam because of their wrong and bad practices.

The strange thing is that when you try to talk with them and make them understand that when the Prophet (s) used to brush his teeth with the tooth cleanser (stick of *siwak*), there was no brush and tooth paste as there is today, they are not satisfied. They dispute that the *siwak* stick of that certain tree is better than all the modern invented things, because it has salts and so on and so forth. And if you talk to them about all the modern inventions and tools that can clean the teeth and sterilize the mouth, they will remain in preference of that piece of wood which they insert in their pockets and take out from time to time after having been red because of the blood from the mouth. They move this piece of wood right and left inside their mouths while repeating this saying of the Prophet (s):

Had I not thought it difficult for my Ummah, I would have commanded them to use the Miswak (tooth-stick) before every prayer.[1]

Unfortunately, these people do not understand anything from the Prophet's *Sunnah* except what is on surface and apparent. They do not penetrate deep into the spiritual and scientific dimension of the Prophet's deeds and sayings.

It is odd too that they stick to such deeds in a blind imitation with no proof or perception. They only repeat what they hear from their sheikhs and imams. Most of them are illiterate and they may often insist on the illiteracy of the Prophet (s) that he could not read and write, and thus they are the proud of the fact that they imitate the Prophet (s) in everything!!![2]

---

[1] *Sahih al-Bukhari* vol.2, p. 299

[2] As for the Salafiyah phenomenon - you have read before about the contradictions and disagreements between the school of opinion and the school of ijtihad.

Since Islam is a universal mission for all mankind, so it has what pleases the European man who has been involved in his laboratory and technology, as well as the nomad man and that man who lives in the unexplored areas of Africa. As Islam is the religion of nature, it is perfect in all its laws from the simple aspects of life like the brushing of teeth to the greatest decisions about managing the humanity.

Our ancestors conquered the land of the Romans in the year 17 A.H., Persia in 56 A.H., and Spain in 93 A.H.. They did not take with them tents and sticks of siwak but as Victor Robinson said in his comparison between the Islamic civilization and the conditions of Europe, "Europe was in a terrible darkness after the sunset, while Cordoba was lit by lanterns in the public places. Europe was dirty, whereas one thousand public bathhouses were built in Cordoba. Europe was covered by vermin, while the people of Cordoba were the example of cleanness..."

On one hand we, the Muslims, enrich and refine other civilizations and on the other hand, there are some people, who according to the fatwas of some

One day, I debated with some of them in the Umar ibn al-Khattab Mosque in Paris. I said to them, "If you actually keep to the Prophet's *Sunnah* and deny everything new that you say: '*the worst of things is the new of them, and every new thing is a heresy, and every (man of) heresy shall be in fire*', then why do you offer your prayers on the moquette which is artificial that comes to us from the western countries and we do not know from what material it is made, and certainly the Prophet (s) did not know such things nor did he offer prayer on them?"

Some of them replied, "We are in the land of emigration and our ruling is like the ruling of an obliged one. Do you not know that '*necessities permit prohibited things*'?"[1]

---

schools, have reached the top of extremism besides the negligence of Sufis and keepers of hospices. And, between this and that - there are moderate people.

Some may be fanatic with some things that do not reach the degree of disbelief and unlawfulness, like the imitation of the great leaders and companions and make that seem as the whole Islam. For example, some Salafi persons say: 'what do you have to do with books? You can take knowledge orally!' or they make some challenges with dentists on the basis of the importance of the siwak, or something like that.

Until this far, there is no problem – but as expected and that some of which has actually happened - some agents of intelligence may sneak into these groups and incite them to give a fatwa on burning of books, clinics of dentists, or pharmacies because they are from heresies and deviations in faith - as they think. However, they forget that they make use of the latest technologies. They travel to the west by airplanes, whereas the Prophet (s) traveled on camels!!!

They neglect the great issues of the nation, and busy themselves with trivial things.

[1] From the results of the Sunni jurisprudential school, it is for the lack of seriousness toward the matter of ijtihad that a Sunni may interpret an important question according to their personal thoughts. Therefore, we often see that some of them practice a thing that is quite unlike the reality, and herein lies the great calamity!

They may put into effect a rule in other than its actual place, and consequently, they fall into unlawful things and major sins because

I said, "Which necessity? You can remove this moquette and offer the prayer on the ground as the Messenger of Allah (s) did, or you can bring with you some stones to prostrate on."

Their imam looked at me and said mockingly, "I knew that you were a Shia since the moment you came into the mosque and put a piece of paper in the place of prostration."

I said, "Do you deny this? Can you convince me with the true *Sunnah* which you claim to follow?"

He replied, "We have been forbidden from debating and especially with the Shia, besides we are not ready to listen to you. Your religion is for you and our religion is for us."[1]

"necessities permit prohibitions". They may, when are obliged especially in the western countries and without considering or piety, eat without knowing how the meat has been served or if the fried foods have been cooked in the pig's fat, or the refreshments have alcoholic liquor or not.

All that is not a problem, but the problem is when one does not use the siwak, not let his beard reach his chest, or when he prostrates on what has been permitted to prostrate on imitating the Prophet (s) who prostrated on the stones and earth of the Qabaa Mosque!!! Yes, this is considered by these people as heresy and polytheism!!!

[1] Let us review here some matters. One day, Abu Hanifa saw one of his companions in ragged clothes. He put in his hand one thousand dirhams and whispered to him, "redress yourself!" The man said, "I am in no need of this. I am rich enough, but I seek asceticism in this life." Abu Hanifa said, "Allah pleases to see the effect of His blessing on His servant." Refer to *The condition of Ijtihad* by Dr. Abdul Aziz al-Khayyat, p. 16.

Metonymically, we say, "You have observed one thing, but missed many things!"

It is like that sheikh who interpreted this tradition of the Prophet (s), "Simplicity of clothes is from faith" as 'raggedness of clothes' and followed it out of his ignorance and stupidity." In fact, the Prophet (s) often said, "Clean your clothes and better your mounts until you become as a mole (prominent) among people." Mentioned by al-Hakim in his book - *al-Jami' al-Kabeer*, p. 152 from Sahl ibn al-Handhaliyyah.

The worst of that is the lack of seriousness and the daring in ijtihad that may lead to contradict the Book of Allah. Allah says: ***O children of Adam! attend to your embellishments at every time and place of prayer.*** [Qur'an, 7:31]

These are some notes that we must mention, so that it would be clear to the learned Muslims that the Prophet's *Sunnah* does not contradict the scientific and civil development and does not forbid man or woman from wearing any dress fitting him or her. The important thing is that this dress must cover man and woman's body in the way as Islam requires. The Prophet (s) says:

Allah does not look at your clothes or figures, but He looks at your hearts and deeds.[1]

The Prophet's *Sunnah* does not forbid man from sitting at a table and having his meal with a knife and a fork. What is important is that one should be polite and well behaved and not make others feel that he is in a fight like a beast with its prey, especially when he lets his moustache and beard participate with him in having his meal.

The Prophet's *Sunnah* does not forbid man from cleaning his mouth and teeth with a brush and toothpaste or any modern product made for this purpose. The Prophet's *Sunnah* does not forbid man from cleaning his apparent and hidden body, shaving the hair of his armpits and the pubic hair, using perfumes, putting in his pocket a handkerchief for his saliva or other uses. But as for those who claim they stick to the Prophet's *Sunnah* while their smells are unpleasant with whatever they use as musk because their bodies are unclean especially in summer, with the long hair of their armpits and with their bad behavior that you find them blowing their noses with their fingers, throwing their nasal mucus wherever they like paying no any attention to the passersby and then wiping their hands with their sleeves… such people are too far from the Prophet's *Sunnah*.

The Prophet's *Sunnah* does not forbid Muslims from making use of the modern tools like tape recorders or loudspeakers to let call of *azan* reach further and further. It does not forbid the use of TV and videos sets even in the mosques to show religious lessons and Islamic films at times other than the prayer times.

Moreover, Islam calls for smoothing of moustache, trimming of beard, plucking of the hair from the armpits, adorning oneself on Fridays…etc. Thus, we must be a good example of our clean, pure religion, but not vice versa.

[1] *Sahih Muslim* vol.4, p.1987, *hadith* no. 2564

The Prophet's *Sunnah* does not forbid a Muslim from making water in water closets in railway stations, airports...etc., that have been designed in a special way especially in the western countries, while standing up but what is important is that he should hide his private parts and not to impure his body or clothes.[1] Allah says:

...surely Allah loves those who turn much (to Him), and He loves those who purify themselves. [Qur'an, 2:222]

The Prophet's *Sunnah* does not forbid a Muslim woman from using the modern disposable tissues during her menstruation, or forbid her from driving a car or going to markets, but the important thing is that she should veil herself and observe the Islamic laws and rulings.

In brief, the Prophet's *Sunnah* does not forbid any development or progress as long as it is for the welfare of man, which leads to his ease, happiness and protection from any harm.

Allah says:

Say: Who has prohibited the embellishment of Allah, which He has brought forth for His servants and the good provisions? [Qur'an, 7:32]

Surely, the Prophet's *Sunnah* just prohibits impurities, filth, and everything which the souls detest by nature such as - bad smells, filthy fingernails, unkempt hairs and impure heels. It is said:

Allah is beautiful and He loves beauty.

We see that adorning oneself is a natural instinct in man and animals. No man, whether faithful or unfaithful, goes out of home, except that he looks at himself first in the mirror to adorn and refresh himself. And today, you cannot see even one house that has no mirror inside it. Since men do so, then why do we forbid women from doing it? It is preferred for woman to adorn herself, but on

---

[1] To make water while standing up is not unlawful, but it too is hated or disapproved due to our mujtahids.

condition that she should not unveil herself or use cosmetics before *non-mahram* men.[1]

People are enemies of that which they do not know.[2]

In my youth, I liked to kohl my eyes every Wednesday. In in spite of the fact that all the Sunni books mention that the Prophet (s) used kohl and encouraged people to use it, each time I used kohl, I felt that men and women disapproved of it as if I had committed a sin. Therefore, I gave it up unwillingly.

Some Arab men of the deserts pierced their earlobes and hung earrings in them. This is famous among some Arab tribes.

However, if we see today a man from the west with an earring in his earlobe, we find it strange and say that he is effeminate. It is the same when we see a man with long hair, though history proves that men lowered their hairs like women. Some companions narrated that the Prophet (s) had plaits of hair. The important thing is that we should recall the sayings of the Prophet (s):

Surely, Allah does not look at your dresses or figures, but He looks at your hearts and deeds.[3]

Allah curses men who imitate women and women who imitate men.[4]

Sticking to what the Prophet (s) did fourteen centuries ago and prohibiting everything new and modern is something unacceptable and very odd.

What for is all this extremism in the religion of Allah? What for is all these ties that have shackled us and made us feel that our religion is full of difficulties and hardships? Surely, Allah is free from all that when He says:

---

[1] The Islamic laws for socialization with *non-mahram* males are available at: https://www.al-islam.org/code-ethics-muslim-men-and-women-sayyid-masud-masumi/rules-related-socializing

[2] *Nahjul Balaghah*, saying no.438

[3] *Sahih Muslim* vol.4, p.1987

[4] *Musnad Ahmad*, vol.1, p. 227

...and He has not laid upon you any hardship in religion. [Qur'an, 22:78]

His messenger (s) is also free from all that when he says:

Make it easy (in religion) and do not make it difficult, bring good news (to people) and do not make them alienated from the religion.[1]

In the end, we say to all these people whether they are Salafi, Sunni, or Shia that be lenient and moderate to yourselves and to others and do not make it difficult for Muslims, lest they detest the religion and turn away from Islam, instead of endearing Islam to them. Do not forget the saying of the Prophet (s):

If Allah guides one man by you, it would be better to you than the entire world and what there is in it.[2]

Yet, if you want to be negatively puritan, then you have to ride on donkeys and mules and go back on them to your countries, because the Messenger of Allah (s) used to ride on them and he had never seen any motor vehicle or airplane in all his life. If you do not do, and certainly you shall not do, then you fear Allah about your behavior to your brothers and speak kindly to them. If you refuse to progress, at least do not regress![3]

---

[1] *Sahih al-Bukhari* vol.1, p. 27, vol.2, p. 36

[2] *Musnad Ahmad*, vol.5, p. 333

[3] Our problem today is that the means have changed to be the purpose. We have neglected the major and common matters that face not only the Muslims but all people. Non-Muslim nations may have many habits and traditions that Islam invites us to accept and adopt. Unfortunately though and indeed unfortunately, many Muslims sanctify men and what they say and make them as the whole of Islam. They consider everything other than that as falsehood, polytheism and atheism. For example, Abu Hanifah sees that the reciting of surahs of the Qur'an after the imam in the congregational prayers is forbidden, while Al-Shafi'i sees it as obligatory. Al-Maliki, for example, sees that lowering the hands in the prayer is right as the Shias think. To them, these opinions represent the opinions of their owners and they reached these opinions through ijtihad. Yet how terrible it is that some Muslims think themselves as the only true Muslims and their creed as the only true creed, they beat and abuse a praying Muslim when they see him

doing so in his prayer and they say to him: 'Do not offer the prayer like the dogs'!!! If someone passes in front of them while they are offering the prayer, or if they see a new Muslim convert putting on some gold ornaments, or see someone reciting the Qur'an while lying down, holding the Qur'an in some way that they feel incorrect or not using the sticks of siwak...etc., they raise the Devil and raise the Devil!! Thus, they brush aside the teachings and morals of Islam, and get outside of humanity by shouting, roaring, reviling, and making trouble. By this way, they try to replace a dislikeable thing with an unlawful act and a less corrupted thing with a more corrupt one.

THE POLITICAL PROBLEMS CREATED BY CIVILIZATION

When the Messenger of Allah (s) ordered his companions to emigrate, he said to them, "*Go to Abyssinia, for there is a king near whom no one is treated unjustly at all.*"[1] He did not give them passports, nor did he request visas for them from the government of Abyssinia, nor were they forced to change the currency that was available there.

All these procedures were not known or followed at that time, but the land of Allah was vast. When a man's own country became constrained to him, he rode on his mount and intended the mercy of his Lord. Wherever he went, he found what he sought with no inspectors to watch his coming and going. No custom-houses would ask him to pay customs and taxes or send him back if he had no documents of vaccination or ask him to show the documents for possession of his mount, in case it might have been stolen or the dues of the road had not been paid.

Yes civilization, or may we say that managing greater masses of human beings has required for these procedures. The earth has been divided into nations, and then into many countries. Every country or all people who speak the same language made a government and every government took a special flag, marked its borders in the land and the sea and put guards at the borders so that no one unwanted could enter their country.

When the number of people increased more and more and one became greedy for what the other had - they exploited each other and colonized each other. Revolutions and crimes increased. The developed societies were obliged to define every citizen. Therefore, newborn children and dead people were counted. Every person had his/her own birth document, identity card and passport. The borders were controlled so that no one from one country would enter another except after getting the permission of that country and agreeing to abide by the conditions imposed by that country.

---

[1] *Tarikh Ibn Athir*, vol.2, p. 74

I, like many other young Muslims, when my country became limited to me, tried to immigrate to another country, but I found that all the doors were closed before me, especially that of the Arab and Muslim countries.

I was very confused when I recited this saying of Allah:

Surely (as for) those whom the angels cause to die while they are unjust to their souls, they shall say: In what state were you? They shall say: We were weak in the earth. They shall say: Was not Allah's earth spacious, so that you should have migrated therein? So these it is whose abode is hell, and it is an evil resort. [Qur'an, 4:97]

I said then to myself that the earth is Allah's without doubt, but the servants of Allah have possessed it, divided it among themselves and not permitted it for others.

If I tried to find an excuse for the non-Muslim countries like France, England, Germany, or the United States of America, in this context, I might find one, but what would be the excuse for the Arab and Muslim countries?

And if I tried to find an excuse for the Arab and Muslim countries that they had submitted to the international system for the sake of reciprocating, then what would be the excuse for the rulers of Mecca and Medina who imposed on Muslims visas for going to perform the Hajj and umrah besides the taxes that must be paid to enter this land?

I also was confused when I recited this saying of Allah:

Surely (as for) those who disbelieve, and hinder (men) from Allah's way and from the Sacred Mosque which We have made equally for all men, (for) the dweller therein and (for) the visitor... [Qur'an, 22:25]

If the inviolable Mosque (the Kaaba) that Allah has made as safe and sanctuary for all people, the residents and non-residents, now becomes a property of a certain country that permits some and prevents others from visiting it, then we must review our Islam, Qur'an, and all concepts!

I remained for a long time confused between different thoughts and obsessions that at some times I talked with my Lord saying: "O my Lord, You have said and Your saying is the truth:

Was not Allah's earth vast, so that you should have migrated therein? [Qur'an, 4:97]

You have also said:

And proclaim among people the Pilgrimage: they will come to you on foot and on every lean camel, coming from every remote path. [Qur'an, 22:27]

Yet at present Your vast land has been prevented from entry by people and Your House has been possessed and its gate has been closed, so what do we do then?

One day, while I was reading some sermons of Imam Ali (as) in *Nahjul Balaghah* when he talked about the Qur'an, one statement attracted my attention and I reread it many times. I found in it what I sought for a long time. It was the only answer that solved the riddle and removed my obsessions.

Imam Ali (as) said in the first sermon when talking about the Book of Allah, *"...and between a thing that is obligatory at its time and that shall be null in its future..."* I understood from this speech that such verses Qur'an, which were possible at the time of the Prophet (s) would not be possible in the future because of the prevailing of the unjust and the tyranny of disbelievers.

Thus, if someone shall say to his Lord on the Day of Resurrection: 'I was disabled on earth', Allah the Almighty - Who is aware of all things, will know that this man is from late people. So Allah will not say to him: your abode is Hell and it is an evil resort!

And if someone shall say to his Lord on the Day of Punishment: 'I was prevented from going to perform the pilgrimage to Your Inviolable House', it shall be said to him: 'I had said to you that if you *can* afford the journey to it. So your excuse is accepted, and the one who prevented you from that, is responsible for it.'

May peace be upon you O my Master on the day that you were born, on the day when you died and on the day when you shall be restored to life.[1]

---

[1] While the Zionists have occupied Palestine and Jerusalem, most of the Muslim countries have been occupied by the agents and officials of the international Freemasonry. One of these countries is Hijaz - I mean Saudi Arabia. I went from Iraq and Jordan to Saudi Arabia to perform the hajj. I saw with my eyes how an applicant for hajj was treated in the medical centers and the passport control departments, until he reached the airport of Jeddah. I remained there for seven hours until some people slept there itself and many others spoke loudly. This inconvenience was besides the bad and rough treatment by the airport officials and the impolite policemen towards all hajjis. As if they wanted to say - we are rich and in no need of you. Hasten to the hot tents and deserts! It would be expected that these places would be planted with trees and flowers. They would have comfortable buildings and services for the hajjis. There would be laws and systems to manage the affairs and ease of the hajjis from their (hajjis) own monies! However, these monies, in addition to good shares of petrol, go to increase the welfare of the American people and the Zionists and to support the French Franc!

ENJOINING OF GOOD AND FORBIDDING OF THE EVIL

Selfishness and man's being busy with himself without caring for others, as long as he is at ease and not needy is one of the serious problems that civilization has created in societies. This is more dangerous than any disease.

When people are selfish, the society is afflicted with paralysis and the welfare of the nation is suspended. Its fate is played with so that there is no one who can offer anything for reprieve. Then, the values of magnanimity, heroism, sacrifice for others, altruism and the fight against injustice and corruption die. In such a case, religion and conscience shall wither away and become weak.

The Prophet (s) said:

Either you enjoin the good and forbid the evil or Allah will impose upon you the worst of you. Then the best of you shall pray to Allah and it shall not be responded to.[1]

"The enjoining of good and the forbidding of the wrong" is such a necessary matter in the life of a nation that some of the imams have considered it as one the pillars of Islam. Therefore, you see that the first motto that the modern Islamic movements adopt is "the enjoining of the good and forbidding of the wrong". However, civilized societies today object seriously to this matter through the institutions created recently in the democratic societies such as the Assembly of the Human rights, the Assembly of Women's rights and even the Rights of animals.

If a government is not responsible for the "enjoining of the good and forbidding of the wrong", it will be impossible for a group or individuals to undertake it by themselves. Today, you see wrong and corruption everywhere and you cannot change anything. It is very easy for any girl to bring a suit against you, and in the best condition it shall be said to you - do not interfere in what does not concern you! If you say that you just enjoin the good and forbid the wrong,

---

[1] *Musnad Ahmad* vol.5, p. 391, *Al-Sunan al-Kubra*, vol.10, p. 93

the answer shall be - 'and who are you? And by which right you permit yourself to do so? And who has given you this authority?'

I myself have tried these experiments, as have many other Muslims. We got bitterness of weakness and failure out of those experiments. I remained confused between beliefs that forced me to carry out this duty and threatened me if I did not. The reality that we live in prevented me from this right, and threatened me if I tried to do it again.

I remember that once a governor said to me, "Are you the Messenger of Allah that Allah has sent with a new religion to reform people?" I said, "Certainly not." He said, "Then be satisfied with yourself and family and keep us away from your evil. It is we who are responsible for the safety and peace of people. If we leave the matter for every nosy one to enjoin and forbid, there shall be anarchy."[1]

I knew my worth and stopped at the boundaries! I was afraid, and my soul incited me to venture forth at one time and to retire at another. I remained so for some years until a tradition of the Messenger of Allah (s) attracted my attention. In this tradition, the Prophet (s) said:

> *Whosoever of you sees an evil let him change (reform) it with his hand, and if he cannot do so - let him do it with his tongue, and if he cannot do so then let him do with his heart, and this is the weakest of faith.*[2]

---

[1] Because we are Arabs or in fact underdeveloped nomads, we let our learned men and thinkers solve the social, economic and political problems of the country. Only recently, we became free from regency and the mandatory rule. Therefore, we have little choice but to keep silent and obedient to keep pace with the movements and clubs of nudism and perversion. And so we announce, like in the west, our need for some girls to act in a licensed film for wages. Of course, then they go on their way. Why should we remain nosy? Otherwise, the tongue of every nosy person who wants to be an obstacle in the way of development and prosperity must be severed! Long live the civilization!

[2] *Sahih Muslim*, vol.1, p. 69, *hadith* no 78. Chapter of "the forbidding of evil is from faith..."

The Prophet (s) said:

No prophet that Allah has sent for his nation before me, except that he had from his community disciples and companions who followed his Sunnah and obeyed his commands. Then after them their successors came who said what they did not do and they did what they were not ordered to do. Whoever resists them with his hand is faithful, whoever resists them with his tongue is faithful, and whoever resists them with his heart is faithful, and anything else than that is not from faith inasmuch as a grain of mustard.[1]

I praised Allah the Almighty that He has not imposed on us that which we have no capacity to bear. Thus, the Prophet's traditions explained the Book of Allah, and because Allah knows all things in the past, present, and future, so He knew that a time would come to people where a Muslim would be unable to reject the evil. Therefore, He made it easy for Muslims and imposed on them only what they could bear. Therefore, the saying of the Prophet (s), "*Whoever of you sees an evil let him change (reform) it with his hand, and if he cannot do so, let him do with his tongue...*" is a proof on the changing of the Muslim society from a state of powerfulness into the state of weakness. Besides that, it is a proof that the legal obligation changes from a state into another.

So the duty of one, who is powerful, is to reform the evil by power which is represented by the "hand" in the tradition, and the one, who is powerless, has to reform the evil through speech and breaches which are represented by the "tongue". And the one, who is certain that his speech shall cause him harm and trouble, has to deny the evil in his heart without announcing his opinion openly and this shall be his legal duty.

Glory be to Allah Who does not impose on a soul except what it can bear, and blessings and peace be on the Prophet (s) of mercy who

---

[1] *Sahih Muslim*, vol.1, p. 70, hadith no 80. Chapter of "The forbidding of evil is from faith..."

was more merciful to the believers than they themselves were and on his generous, immaculate progeny.[1]

---

[1] Unfortunately, we find among foreigners and in the western countries attentive listeners, but we do not find them in our Arab and Muslim countries. In fact, attentive listening is forbidden here!

MODERN MAN AND THE LENIENT RELIGION

There is no doubt that the goals of the divine religions are firstly to make man know his Creator and keep him away from idolatry and all kinds of polytheism and deviation. Secondly, it is to manage his life socially, economically and politically. These goals can be summarized into two things: faith and action. We mean true faith and good deeds, because not every faith or every deed can be accepted by Allah the Almighty. Man may believe in doctrines that contradict Islam and what Allah has revealed to His Prophet (s). Or he may reject a belief inherited from ancestors - that even if it is right, it can be changed and replaced.

Allah the Almighty says:

And when it is said to them: Believe in what Allah has revealed, they say: We believe in that which was revealed to us, and they deny what is besides that, while it is the truth verifying that which they have. [Qur'an, 2:91]

Man may do many things that he thinks are for the welfare of humanity, whereas they cause harms and damages. Allah the Almighty says:

And when it is said to them: Do not make mischief in the land, they say: We are but peacemakers. Surely, they themselves are the mischief makers, but they do not perceive. [Qur'an, 2:11-12]

Man may do great deeds that are very useful to mankind, but if he does not intend the contentment of Allah, he is just seeking fame and prominence, and so his deeds are: ...*like the mirage in a desert, which a thirsty man thinks to be water; until when he comes to it, he finds it to be nought.*

Allah says:

And We will proceed to what they have done of deeds, so We shall render them as scattered motes. [Qur'an, 25:23]

Religion is the landmark, by which man is guided and exalted. Wherever man is living, religion is found there too since the beginning of humanity. Excavations and scientific studies have proven that primitive man did not know many things until after several ages, but he did know about temples since the beginning of his time. Thus, we can certainly say that civilization is the extract of the divine religions. Since it is so, then Islam that has been revealed to the Prophet Muhammad (s) is the most advanced civilization, and humanity cannot overlook or precede it.

This century has recorded a very strange change in the modern man who suffers different woes because of atheism, disbelief, absence of spiritual values and mental emptiness that come out of being non-religious. Today, man is searching for his identity and lost personality and trying to come back little by little into the laps of a lenient religion. Allah says:

Then set your face upright for religion in the right state; the nature made by Allah in which He has made men; there is no altering of Allah's creation; that is the right religion, but most people do not know. [Qur'an, 30:30]

Today, we see a great Islamic awakening in all settings, whether learned or otherwise. We see that the change has influenced all people of different races and nationalities.

In the atheist milieu that used to adopt the theory of human rights and absolute freedom, we see that they have begun retreating and changing their theories. They prevent man from drinking alcohol while driving his car, in spite of the Christians' claim that their religion permits them to drink alcohol and that Jesus Christ (s) himself made wine for them. They have passed such a law after the increase in accidents on the streets because of drinking. Statistics shows that twenty thousand people are killed every year in France only because of such accidents.

If we review the laws that have been enacted by the most advanced civilizations in the most developed counties and compare them to the laws of Islam, we shall see as great difference between the two as there is distance between the earth and the sky.

With one look at the epistle[1] of Imam Ali (as) to Malik al-Ashtar when he appointed him as the governor (*Wali*) of Egypt, we shall clearly see the precedence of Muslims in all fields. Imam Ali (as) said in his epistle to Malik:

In the name of Allah, the Beneficent, the Merciful. This is what the servant of Allah, Ali Ameerul Mu'minin, orders Malik ibn al-Harith al-Ashtar in his covenant to him as he appoints him the Wali over Egypt - (ordering him) to collect its revenues, fight its enemies, manage its people's affairs and to improve the country. He is ordered to fear Allah, obey Him and to follow what Allah has ordered in His book of obligations and norms which state that no one will be prosperous other than by following and no one will be wretched other than by denying and missing.

And, he is asked to support Allah (by supporting the right) with his heart, hand and tongue because Allah has promised to support whoever supports Him and glorify whoever glorifies Him. He is ordered to control his soul's fancies and to subdue his soul if it wants to err because the soul often incites towards evil except those whom Allah has mercy upon.

O Malik, know that I have sent you to a country that had experienced just and unjust rulers before you. The people will think of your deeds as you thought of the deeds of the Walis who preceded you, and they will talk about you as you talked about the Walis that ruled before you. The virtuous men will be known by what is said about them by the people (by the favor of Allah). Let the loveliest provision to your self be the benevolent doing. Control your fancy and prevent yourself from what is not legal to you because controlling one's self is the very fairness to it in what it likes or dislikes.

Fill your heart with mercy, love and kindness towards your people and do not be with them like a beast, waiting for an opportunity to eat them because people are of two kinds - either a brother to you in religion or an equal to you in humanity. They fall into mistakes and may be incited by the slips. They may

---

[1] *Nahjul Balaghah*, letter no. 53 to Malik al-Ashtar.

commit sins on purpose or unknowingly. So you are to forgive them as you like Allah to forgive you.

You rule over them and the responsible guardian rules over you and Allah is the Ruler upon the one, who appointed you. Allah tries you by managing your people's affairs, so do not be in a war against Allah (by trespassing His Sharia and by wronging His people) because you are unable to put up with His wrath and you cannot do without his forgiveness and mercy. Do not regret when you forgive someone and do not boast when you punish someone. Do not be angry about something that you may find an excuse for it. Do not say: 'I am the superior. I order and I must be obeyed' for it corrupts the heart, destroys the religion, and approaches to the others (the opponents).

If your high position gives a sense of splendor or pride, you are to think of the supreme power of Allah over you and His ability to act upon you what you can never put up with. This will lessen your vanity, prevent your sharpness and restore what is missed by your reason for you.

Beware not to compare yourself with Allah in His greatness or to imitate Him in His supreme power, because Allah degrades every arrogant and demeans every haughty one.

Be fair before Allah and do not prefer yourself, your relatives or your close companions to people. If you do not follow this advice, you will wrong; and whoever wrongs the people, Allah will be his opponent and when Allah becomes the opponent of someone, He refutes his excuses and that he will be in a state of war against Allah until he dies or he repents.

Nothing leads to change the blessings of Allah and to hasten His wrath more than to persist in oppression, because Allah hears the prayer of the oppressed and He always waylays the oppressors.

Let the loveliest thing to yourself be that which is moderate in rightness, more general in justice and widely accepted by people. Know that the discontent of the public removes the content of the upper class and that the discontent of the upper class will be excused by the content of the public.

No one is more dependent upon the Wali during ease, less helpful during distress, more reluctant of justice, more insistent on gifts, less grateful when gifted, less indulgent when prevented and less patient during misfortunes than the upper class. Whereas the pillar of the religion and entire nation of Muslims - always ready to stand up against the enemy - are the public of the ummah. So let your inclination be with them and let your attention be to them.

Let him who looks for defects of other people, be the furthest one from you and the most odious to you, because people have defects and the Wali is the first one, who has to cover them. Do not try to disclose what is hidden of those defects, but you have to purify what is apparent to you and Allah decides upon what is unknown for you. Cover the defects (of people) as much as you possibly can and Allah will cover of your defects just as how you like to cover your people's defects.

Remove every grudge from the people's hearts by behaving fairly with them and keep away from all that may cause enmity. Overlook whatever is not clear to you and do not hasten to believe any slanderer, because a slanderer is deceitful even if he imitates the sincere people.

Let neither a miser participate in your consultation because he makes you be away from virtue and frightens you of poverty if you want to spend, nor a coward because he disheartens you, nor a greedy one because he graces greed for you with wrongfulness. Miserliness, cowardliness and greed are different instincts but they participate in one common thing, which is distrusting in Allah.

The worst of your viziers are they, who were viziers of the wicked rulers before you and who participated in their sins. So do not let them be of your retinue, because they were supporters of sinners and brothers of the unjust. You will find better than them, who have the same experience but without sins and guilt and who haven't helped the unjust in their injustice, nor the sinners in their sins. They will be less burdensome on you, more helpful for you, more kind-hearted to you and less intimate with other than you (the opponents).

So you depend on such people in your retinue and then let the most preferable one to you be the one who is most truthful in saying the bitter truth to you and the least helpful when you do what Allah hates for His guardians to do whether it agrees with your fancy or not. Stick to the pious and truthful people and inure them not to praise you or make you feel proud about something that you have not done, because much praise leads to vanity and arrogance.

Do not consider the benevolent and evildoers as equal, for you will discourage the benevolent to do benevolence and encourage the evildoers to commit more offenses. You have to reward every one according to his doing. Know that nothing makes the ruler think much of his people better than to be kind to them and to lessen their burden and not force them to do what they are not able to do.

Let you do that which causes mutual trust between you and your people, because their confidence will keep you away from many troubles. As long as you do good to them, they will confide in you and as long as you do evil to them, they will distrust you.

Do not break a good tradition followed by the leaders of this ummah, upon which the ummah agreed unanimously and that which was a cause of the people's virtuousness. Do not create a tradition which will oppose some of those previous traditions, so that the merit will be for those who enacted those traditions and the sin will be upon you because you oppose them.

Always discuss with the ulama and wise men to affirm what improves the affairs of your state and to revive what had rectified the people before you.

Remember that people are composed of different classes. The progress of one is dependent on the progress of the other and none can afford to be independent of the other. From among them, there are the soldiers of Allah (the army), clerks and civil officers, judiciary, revenue collectors and public relations officers, the people of land taxes and jizya[1] of Muslims and Zimmis,[2] merchants and craftsmen, and the lower class of the needy and the indigent. Allah has prescribed for each his share (rights), and determined His penalties (on violations) in His Book or the Sunnah of His Prophet, may Allah have blessing on him and his progeny - a covenant from Him that is observed near us.

The soldiers, by the will of Allah, are like a fortress to the people, dignity to rulers, glory of religion, and means of peace and safety. Without them, the state cannot stand. And, they cannot stand without the support of the revenue that Allah gives by His grace, by which they become strong to fight their enemy and rely on it to satisfy their needs.

Then, these two kinds - the military and the civil population - cannot stand without the third category of judiciary, workers and clerks, who run the transactions and dealings among people and those who are entrusted with the private and general affairs. And all these cannot do without the tradesmen, the merchants and the craftsmen, who run the market and offer their services to the others who may not be able to do by themselves. Then, there is the lower class of the poor and the needy, who deserve to be helped and assisted. Allah has given an appropriate opportunity of living to all.

The rights of all of these classes are to be under the charge of the Wali and nothing will acquit the Wali of his charge except by carrying out his charge fairly with full care after praying to Allah to support him. And he (the Wali) has to accustom himself to keeping to the truth and being patient with it whether it is light or heavy to him.

So appoint (in important posts) from your soldiers those, who in your opinion, are most faithful to Allah and His Apostle, most loyal to your imam, most honest, and most patient of them, who restrain themselves at anger and calmly accept (others') excuses,

---

[1] Jizya is an attribute taken from non-Muslims who live under the Islamic rule.

[2] The free non-Muslims, who live under the Islamic rule by paying *jizya* (tax).

are kind to the weak and strict to the strong, who will not be incited by the violent provocation and who will not falter at any task.

Keep to those of good reputation, integrity and glorious past and those of courage, bravery, magnanimity and generosity. This is because they are the bases of liberality and branches of benevolence. Care for them as parents care for their children and do not exaggerate what you have done to them. Do not let any little kindness to them make you think that it might be worthless. For, any kindness towards them will lead them to confide in you and to offer you their sincere advice.

Do not give up caring for their little affairs, relying on their big ones, because the little of your favor has a place that they benefit from, and the big (of your favor) has a position that they cannot do without.

Let your commander in chief be the one, who helps his men and gives them from his wealth what suffices them and suffices the families they left behind so that their concern will be the only concern in their jihad against the enemy. Your being kind to them will turn their hearts towards you.

The best delight of the Wali's eye is spreading of justice in the country and the expression of the people's cordiality. They do not express their goodwill except when their hearts are content. They will not be sincere unless they are willing to safeguard their Walis and are content with their rule and are hopeful of their goals. Therefore, try to achieve their hopes and keep on praising them and mentioning their good deeds, because praising the good deeds inspires the brave and encourages those who lag inshallah.

Keep every one's right and do not ascribe someone's excellence to another. Do not belittle one's great deed. Do not let someone's nobility lead you to glorify his slight deed, and do not let the meanness of someone lead you to belittle his great deed.

Turn to Allah and to His Prophet for guidance whenever you face a hardship and feel uncertain about what you have to do. Allah has said to some people, whom He wished to guide:

O you who believe! obey Allah and obey the Messenger and those in authority from among you; then if you quarrel about anything, refer it to Allah and the Messenger. [Qur'an, 4:59]

Referring to Allah means to obey His Book, and referring to the Prophet means to follow his Sunnah - which calls for unity and warns of division.

Choose, for judging among people, the best of them – one who is not obsessed by distresses, does not become importunate before the opponents, does not keep on making mistakes, does not miss reason, does not hesitate to follow the truth when he finds it, does not think of greed, does not satisfy with the least perception without looking for the farthest, the most pondering on the unclear matters, the most dependent upon evidences, the least bored in inspecting the opponents, the most determined when the truth appears, who is not affected by praise, who is not incited by any temptation, and these are very few.

Observe his (the judge) judgments always and be openhanded to him to satisfy his needs so that he shall not be in need of people. Give him a position in your court so high that none can even dream of coveting it and so high that neither backbiting nor intrigue can touch him. Think of this so much, for this religion was captive under the control of the evildoers, doing with it according to their fancies and using it as a means to obtain the vain pleasures of this worldly life.

Then, think about your officials, and employ them after trying. Do not appoint them as a favor or autocratically, because these ways compound injustice and treason. Seek after the experienced and coy men of the benevolent families having precedence in Islam because they are more honest, less greedy, noble, and more prudent.

Then supply them with sufficient living, for it helps them to purify themselves and prevents them from seizing what is there under their control. It will be evidence against them if they break your order or betray the trust. Then, check their jobs and send truthful and sincere inspectors to watch them. Watching them secretly leads them to be honest and loyal in doing their jobs and to be kind to people. And beware of assistants. If one of them betrays the trust, you will be informed of that by your spies. This will be enough witness to let you punish, disgrace, defame, and girt him with the shame of the guilt according to what he commits.

Take much care of the revenue, so as to prosper the producers because their prosperity leads to the prosperity of the others. There is no prosperity without them, because all people are dependent upon them. Let yourself think of reclaiming the lands more than to think of getting the revenue. Whoever seeks after revenue without reforming shall ruin the country and destroys people. His rule shall not last long.

If the farmers complain of deficiency or lack of water (in rivers or rains) or that their farms are damaged by floods, you have to aid them with what may lessen their sufferings. Do not be vexed about what you give them to relieve their distress, because they will, in return, recompense in prospering your country and strengthen your rule besides getting their goodwill and being delighted by spreading justice among them. They will join their power to yours and will confide in you after receiving your favors and being fair to them.

One day if something happens, you may charge them with a heavy burden and you find that they undertake it willingly. Prosperity bears whatever you burden it with, but the destruction of the land comes out of the indigence of its people, and the indigence of people comes out of the eagerness of the Walis to heap up monies for themselves and of their distrust about remaining in their positions and that they have not learned from the previous examples.

Then think about your clerks. Trust your affairs to the best of them. Trust your special books, in which you put your plans and secrets, to the one who is honest, who does not pride upon his position so that he may dare to stand against you in front of people when there is a disagreement between you and him, who does not ignore to inform you of the correspondences of your officials in the different countries or to reply to the received books correctly instead of you, who does not weaken a contract *he concludes for you and is not unable to cancel an ineffective contract, who is not ignorant of his ability in dealing with the affairs because he who ignores his own ability, is more ignorant of the others' abilities.*

Let your choosing them not be according to physiognomy and confidence, because people feign before the Walis so that they may think well of them. In fact though, there is nothing of truth and fidelity behind that. You have to try them with what they did to the just Walis, who ruled before, you and then choose the best in serving the public and the most loyal among them. This will show your sincerity to Allah and to him, who has entrusted you with the position you hold.

Appoint for each of your affairs the one who is not defeated before great difficulties, nor is he lost among the many problems when facing him. If you ignore any defect available in your clerks, you will be responsible for it.

Take much care of merchants and the craftsmen, the residents and the ones travelling through the countries. And, take much care of laborers because they are the source of the welfare and the means for bringing devices and utensils from one place to another, on the land and in the sea, from plains and mountains where people cannot reach.

They (merchants and craftsmen) are peaceful people, who do not cause troubles or calamities. Care for their affairs in your country and about it. And know nevertheless that many of them are cruel in dealing, with stinginess, monopolizing of the utilities and controlling of the deals. This is a disadvantage for the public and a defect for the Walis.

Prevent monopoly, because the Messenger of Allah (s), peace be on him and his progeny, had prohibited it. Let dealing be lenient and fair, and with fair prices for the two parties; the seller and the buyer. If someone monopolizes something after being forbidden, then you have to punish him severely but without exceeding the limits of justice.

For the sake of Allah, take much care of the lower class - the poor, the needy, the destitute and the handicapped, who have no way to earn their living. Among this class, there are the beggars and those who are in serious need but do not beg. Obey Allah with what He may have entrusted you of their rights. Assign for them something from the treasury and something from the yields of the Muslims' booty lands in each country. The far and the near of them have equal right and you are responsible for the right of every one of them. Do not be careless about them because you shall not be forgiven when wasting the slight thing for the sake of achieving the great thing. Do not be ignorant about their affairs and do not be proud before them.

Seek for those, whose news does not reach you because people scorn and hate to look at them. Order some of benevolent and humble people to seek for the destitute and to inform you of their affairs and then you are to do to them what Allah may forgive you for when you meet Him, because this class of people is in need of fairness more than any others. Anyhow, you have to give everyone his right.

Attend to the orphans and the old people, who are helpless and do not demean themselves by begging people. This is too heavy for the Walis and the whole righteousness is heavy, but Allah may make it easy for those who hope for the good end by being patient and believing in what Allah has promised them of.

Assign some of your time to the plaintiffs. You sit humbly with them in a public meeting and keep your guards and soldiers away from them, so that they may talk frankly without any fear. I had heard the Messenger of Allah (s) (s) saying more than a time: "A nation will not be sanctified if the right of the weak is not taken back from the powerful without threatening or frightening." Tolerate their severity and ineloquence. Do not show them intolerance and disdain, so that Allah spreads upon you his mercy and rewards you for your obedience to Him. If you give, give willingly and if you deny, deny kindly and with apology.

There are certain things that you have to do yourself. You have to answer your governors when your clerks are not able to. You have to answer the people's wants as soon as they reach you, since your assistants may delay them.

Achieve every day's duty in time, because each day has its own duties. Choose for yourself the best time to be with Allah. Know that the greatest of your doings, although that they all are to be for the sake of Allah, are those that you do with good will and those you do for the sake of your people.

Let the best thing with which you worship Allah sincerely, be the offering of obligations, which are for Allah alone. Tire your body for your Lord during your day and night. Approach to Allah sincerely with all what you do for the sake of Him without any shortage or hypocrisy whatever you become tired.

When you lead the people in offering the prayer, try neither to lengthen it nor to lose anything of it, because among people there are some who are ill, and some who have things to do. Once, I asked the Messenger of Allah (s) (s), when he had ordered me to go to Yemen, about how to lead people in offering the prayer and he said, "Offer it like the prayer of the weakest of them and be kind to the believers."

Do not hide too long from your people, because the hiding of Walis from people is a kind of distress and ignorance of their affairs. Hiding from people prevents them from knowing why they are kept away and so the great thing will be insignificant for them and the insignificant thing will be great, the good things will be bad and the bad will be good and the truth will be confused with falsehood.

A Wali is but a human being. He does not know what is hidden of the people's affairs and the righteousness has no signs by which one can distinguish between the truth and the falsehood. You (the Wali) are but one of two. Either you are a man with a liberal character who follows righteousness. Then why do you hide from a right duty that you have to do or a deed of munificence that you are to offer? Or, you may be a man of stinginess. Then you will find that how soon people will despair of asking you for anything, in spite of the fact that most of people's wants are about complaining about injustice or asking for fairness of a conduct - neither of which cost you anything.

A Wali has a retinue and close companions. Among these there are some persons who are selfish, impudent and unfair when dealing with people. Cut off this thing by cutting off the reason that encourages them to be so. Do not donate to anyone of your retinue or relatives a donation. Let them not expect from you to possess any property, which will harm other people of their watering or a shared act. They (the Wali's retinue or relatives) enjoy it at the expense of the others, and hence the benefit will be for them whereas, the blame will be upon you in this life and in the afterlife.

Make every one submit to the truth whoever he is whether it be from your retinue or relatives or not. Be patient and tolerant in applying that, irrespective of whatever effect it has upon your relatives and close companions. Care for its result however heavy it is to you, because the result of that will be good.

If people suspect you of doing injustice, come out to them with your evidence to refute their suspicion. Through this, you will accustom yourself to justice. Be kind to your people when showing your evidences to achieve your aim in rectifying them according to their rightness.

Do not refuse the peace your enemy invites you to if it pleases Allah, because peace will bring your soldiers comfort, make you safe from your troubles and bring security for your country. But be extremely careful of your enemy after the peace, because the enemy may approach you under the pretense of peace, in order to attack you unexpectedly. So be resolute and doubt your enemy's good will.

When you conclude an agreement with your enemy or you promise of something, you have to keep your agreement with fidelity and keep your promise with loyalty. Make yourself the safeguard of what you have promised, as none of Allah's obligations that people agree upon, in spite of their different thoughts and fancies, is better than to glorify fulfilling of promises. Polytheists, rather than the Muslims, kept to their promises among them when they saw the bad results of perfidy. So do not betray your agreement, do not break your promise and do not cheat your enemy, for no one dares to disobey Allah but the miserable ignorant.

Allah made His promise as safety that He spread between His people with His mercy and made it as a sanctum to whose power people resorted to and to whose protection they hurried. So never let thwarting, cheating or forging be with your promises. Do not conclude an agreement that you may use confused statements in order to find a way that you may cheat with it and do not depend upon a solecism as an excuse after certifying your promise.

Let no distress lead you to annul your promise unfairly, because tolerating a distress so that you expect its relief and good result is better than cheating so that you fear its bad consequence. Besides that Allah will ask you about His right of fidelity that you broke, and then He will bless neither your life nor your afterlife.

Avoid and avoid shedding of blood unjustly and without any right cause leading you to it. Nothing leads hurriedly to wrath, to evil consequence, to transience of blessings and cessation of life worse than shedding of blood unrightfully. Allah the Almighty will judge among His people, first of all, about shedding of blood on the Day of Resurrection.

Do not try to firm your rule by shedding haram (unlawful) blood, because this will weaken and enfeeble your rule, or in fact, it will remove your rule and transfer it to others. Neither Allah nor I will forgive you for an intended killing, because it must have a penalty. If you face a wrongdoing, let your whip, sword or hand not exceed in punishment because a blow may cause a killing. Let your rule not make you proud that you did not give the guardians of the killed one their right.

Avoid self-conceit; do not confide about what you like of yourself and do not wish to be praised, because this is the best opportunity for Satan to crush the benevolence from inside the benevolent.

Do not mention the favors you do to your people. Do not exaggerate your deeds and do not promise your people and then you break your promise, because mentioning the favors done by you void benevolence, exaggeration puts out the light of rightness, and breaking the promise brings detestation of Allah and people. Has Allah said:

(It is most hateful to Allah that you should say that which you do not do). [Qur'an, 61:3]

Do not give your judgment about matters before their time and do not be indifferent when they occur. Do not insist upon dispute when matters are not clear and do not be indifferent when they become clear. Put everything in its place and every order in its place of concern.

Do not distinguish yourself with what people are equal in and do not ignore your duties when they become clear for people, because what you take unrightfully will be taken from you to others, and soon your affairs will be uncovered and then the rights of the wronged ones will be extracted from you.

Control your passion, intensity, power and sharpness of your tongue. Be away from all that by preventing your tongue from setting about and by delaying your power until your rage calms down, and then you have the option to decide. You will not control yourself until you worry yourself with recalling that you will meet your God in the next world.

You have to remember what preceded you of a just government, a virtuous norm, a tradition of our Prophet (s) or an obligation in the Book of Allah. Then, you have to follow what we have done according to that and to try your best to follow what I have entrusted you with in this charter. I have quitted myself from anything you may protest with later on and lest you find any excuse when you hasten after your fancy.

I pray to Allah, with His infinite mercy and great power of granting every wish, to grant me and you success to do what pleases Him and His people with the rightful conduct, and to make us worthy of people's good will and to offer beneficial achievements to the country. I pray Allah to grant us blessing and dignity and to conclude my life and yours with happiness and martyrdom. To Allah we will return. Peace be upon the

Messenger of Allah (s) and Allah may bless him and his pure progeny with great peace and blessing. With salaam.[1]

If one studies deeply this epistle that Imam Ali (as) had written to his Wali, he shall find the highest meanings for humanity in it – the like of which the civilization of the twentieth century has not yet reached. It includes all fields of life, such as social, economic, political and cultural besides worship, ethics, psychological education and human nature.

If I feel sorry, my sorry is for most Muslims who neglect the *Nahjul Balaghah* of Imam Ali (as) and the Gnostic treasures and scientific facts it has, and they run after the western writings and theories, thinking that they may thus reach the convoy of the false civilization which has brought woes and calamities to weak societies and peoples.

If I say to one of them that in Islam and in the Islamic personalities there are great and good examples for all humanity, he would answer that if this was true, then Muslims would not remain underdeveloped while others developed and progressed. Such people and their likes ignore a regrettable fact that Islam remained but a theory without being applied. The great Islamic personalities, who tried to apply it, were fought with, exiled and killed or they were abused and reviled from minibars. Their work and book remained unknown under the intellectual siege, different accusations and rumors.[2]

Western scientists in America, Germany, and England made great use of the facts of Islam, while the Muslims are still indifferent. Allah the Almighty says:

But there came after them a generation, who neglected prayers and followed lusts, so they will meet perdition [Qur'an, 19:59]

---

[1] *Nahjul Balaghah*, letter no. 53 to Malik al-Ashtar.
[2] Refer to the books *'What has the world lost by the decline of Muslims?'* by an-Nawawi, *'The Arabian man and civilization'* by Anwar ar-Rifa'i, *'The excellences of our civilization'* by Dr. Mustafa as-Siba'i, and *'Islam and the Arab civilization'* by Muhammad Kurd Ali, and many other books.

One day, someone said to me, "If you mean by 'the Islamic personalities' - the twelve Imams of the Ahlul Bayt – then why the Shia, as mentioned in your books, who have believed in their imamate, obeyed and followed them in the affairs of life and religion, remained underdeveloped like the rest of Muslim, and have advanced neither in a science or invention?"

I said to him, "The Shia, who had believed in the twelve imams were a minority like a white spot on a black dress. They feared for their lives - their blood was shed, their honor (women) was violated, and they were tortured severely throughout the ages. In such conditions, could the Shia, who were all the time busy with their grief and distress and were afraid of being killed at any moment, advance or develop?"

It is well known that when man becomes needy and hungry, his mind becomes busy, before everything, with assuring his living, which is the cause of his survival and continuity. Then, how it is if the means of his living and the living of his family and all who he resorts to or support him are prevented? However, if the means of good living and ease are available to man and he enjoys the pleasure of life, he becomes very ambitious and his reason and intellect go high and higher. Therefore, you see that governments regard the people of knowledge and sciences very highly, prepare for them all means of living and ease, spend great monies on them, prepare for them libraries and laboratories equipped with all modern tools. In these conditions, how would they not advance and invent?

Nevertheless the Twelver Shia, in spite of all poverty, expelling, torturing, and killing they suffered, were the first in all fields of knowledge and sciences, because they had drunk from the springs of the school of the Ahlul Bayt (as) from which the best of scientists and scholars in different fields of knowledge had graduated. Imam Ja'far bin Muhammad as-Sadiq (as) taught besides jurisprudence and *tafsir* (interpretation of the Qur'an) the applied and theoretical sciences such as mathematics, medicine, physics, chemistry, astronomy and other sciences whose importance did not appear except after the industrial revolution and in the recent centuries.

Here, I mention just some of that which western scholars had acknowledged and some of the facts that orientalists have mentioned about Imam as-Sadiq (as) in their scientific meeting held in the year 1968 A.D. in Strasburg University in France when discussing the scientific and civilizational history of the Twelver Shia. More than twenty scientists from the United State of America, England, Germany, France, Belgium, Switzerland and Italy attended this meeting.[1]

These scientists spoke in detail about Imam Ja'far as-Sadiq (s) and his disciple Jabir ibn Hayyan who had left behind one thousand and five hundred theses from the lectures of his teacher on chemistry, medicine and philosophy as mentioned by ibn an-Nadeem in his book *al-Fihrest* and by ibn Khillikan in his book *The News of Imam as-Sadiq*.

The participants in that scientific meeting all agreed upon that Jabir ibn Hayyan could apply many scientific theories and prepare chemical matters and compounds that have a great role in making bombs and explosives. They also said that he could discover the secrets of chemistry that was called "San'ah craft" which is the transmutation of poor metals into expensive ones like gold, silver, and others. In this concern, Jabir ibn Hayyan said, "My teacher Ja'far ibn Muhammad had taught a branch of knowledge that if I wanted, I could change all the earth into gold with it."[2]

Dr. Muhammad Yahya al-Hashimi (a today-scholar) has written a book called *'Imam as-Sadiq, the Inspirer of Chemistry'*. He says in this book, "That which increases our admiration is the claim of Jabir ibn Hayyan that this secret (the transmutation of metals and the changing of matters) has a role in all operations. And if we think deeply, in the present time, we shall see from the discovery of radioactive elements that one element of a matter changes into another and destroys the atom. This has led not only to the atomic

---

[1] *Imam as-Sadiq as Known by the Western Scientists*, translated into Arabic by Dr. Nooruddeen Aal Ali.

[2] For introduction to scientific contribution of Imam Sadiq (as), please visit: https://www.al-islam.org/articles/imam-jafar-al-sadiqs-contribution-sciences-hasnain-suchedina

bomb, but also to find new sources for power that had never come to man's mind before."[1]

In addition to all of that, the Twelver Shia were the first in all sciences, whereas the rest of Muslims were limited to jurisprudence, *tafsir*, and ethics in which the Shia had already reached the top, because of the vast knowledge they had inherited from the Ahlul Bayt (as). We, as history confirms, see that the Shia were the first of creators and first of inventors.

For more details, researchers can read the book '*The Shia and the Arts of Islam*', or the introduction of '*The Origin of Shiism and its Principles*' to be certain that the Shia had preceded all other sects in all fields of knowledge and sciences under the guidance of their infallible Imams (as) who had penetrated all knowledge. Really, they are the true propagandists of knowledge. Imam Ali (as) said:

...*but I contain a hidden treasure of knowledge that if I reveal, you shall be confused like the confusion of ropes in a deep well.*[2]

---

[1] *Imam as-Sadiq; the Inspirer of Chemistry*, by Dr. Muhammad Yahya al-Hashimi, p. 156.
[2] *Nahjul Balaghah,* sermon 5.

THE SHIA IN BRIEF

The talks about the Shia in the last years, especially after the victory of the Islamic Revolution in Iran, have been so widespread. The western information and its media spread everywhere in the world, focused on the Iranian Shia, describing them as 'the fool of Allah' one time and 'terrorists' another time.

This included the Lebanese Shia as well after they had threatened the American and western interests in Beirut. They were described as 'excessive and extreme'. Not long after this, these descriptions were ascribed to all the Shia in the world. In fact, they included the Islamic movements everywhere in the world even if they were Sunni movements having nothing to do with the Shia.

It does not matter to us what the western information and enemies of Islam say or the false justifications and fabrications they follow, for 'you may hope for the friendliness from every enemy, except the enemy of your religion'. What does really concern us is that which some Muslims say about the Shia. You hear from them wonders and wonders! It is too odd that they do not have any evidence, clear proof or irrefutable argument in their false accusations, but they only repeat what their ancestors used to say without any analysis or verification.

In addition to the actual definition of Shiism we have mentioned in our fourth book "*The Shia are the People of the Sunnah*", we see that we must show the Muslims, who seek the mere truth and do not fear a blame in the way of Allah, the sayings of Allah and His messenger (s) about the Shia. Then, we shall be able to discuss the sayings of some approving and disapproving scholars and thinkers.

THE SHIA IN THE QUR'AN

Allah the Almighty says:

As for those who believe and do good - surely they are the best of men. [Qur'an, 98:7]

Jalaluddin as-Sayuti says in his commentary (*tafsir*) of the Qur'an called *Al-Durr al-Manthur fit Tafsir al-Ma'thur*, "Abu Hurayra narrated that the Prophet (s) said:

> *Do you wonder at the position of the angels to Allah? I swear by Him, in whose hand my soul is, that the position of a faithful servant to Allah on the Day of Resurrection is greater than the position of an angel. If you want, you can read this verse:*

As for those who believe and do good, surely they are the best of men. [Qur'an, 98:7]

Aa'ishah narrated, "*Once, I said, 'O Messenger of Allah (s), who is the best of people to Allah?*' He said:

> *O Aa'ishah, do you not read:*

(As for) those who believe and do good, surely they are the best of men)?

Jabir ibn Abdullah narrated, "One day, we were with the Prophet (s) when Ali (as) came and then the Prophet said:

> *(I swear) by Him, in whose hand my soul is, that this (Ali) and his Shia (followers) shall be the winners on the Day of Resurrection.*

Then, this Verse was revealed:

(As for) those who believe and do good - surely they are the best of men.

Whenever Ali (as) came, the Prophet's companions said, '*The best of men has come.*'"[1]

Abu Sa'eed narrated that the Prophet (s) said:

> *Ali is the best of men.*[2]

Ibn Abbas narrated, "When this verse was revealed

---

[1] *Al-Manaqib Khwarizmi* p. 62

[2] *Al-Durr al-Manthur fit Tafsir al-Ma'thur* vol.8, p. 589. *Tazkiratul Khawas*, p. 18.

As for) those who believe and do good - surely they are the best of men, the Messenger of Allah (s) said to Ali:

Surely, you and your Shia (followers) shall on the Day of Resurrection be pleased and be pleased with (by Allah).[1]

Imam Ali (as) said, "The Messenger of Allah (s) said to me:

Have you not heard this saying of Allah:

(As for) those who believe and do good, surely they are the best of men?

It is you and your Shia, and your appointment and my appointment shall be at the Pond (in Paradise). When nations shall come for reckoning, you shall be called 'ghurral muHajjalin - honorable and marked with lumosity.[2]

The Sunni scholars, who have mentioned this interpretation when interpreting this verse, are too many. Besides Jalaluddeen as-Sayuti, we can mention at-Tabari in his *Tafsir*, al-Hakim al-Hasakani in his *Shawahid at-Tanzeel*, al-Shawkani in *Fath al-Qadeer*, al-Aaloosi in *Roohul Ma'ani* and al-Manawi in *Kunooz al-Haqa'iq*.

We can also mention al-Khawarizmi in his *al-Manaqib*, ibn as-Sabbagh al-Maliki in *al-Fusool al-Muhimmah*, ibn Asakir in *Tarikh Damashq*, ash-Shabalanji in *Noor al-Absar*, Ibnul Jawzi in *Tazkiratul Khawas*, al-Qandoozi al-Hanafi in *Yanabee' al-Mawaddah*, al-Haythami in *Majma' az-Zawa'id*, al-Mutaqqi al-Hindi in *Kanzol Ummal*, and ibn Hajar in *al-Sawa'iq al-Muhriqah*.

On this firm basis, researchers cannot be satisfied with the opinions, which suppose that Shiism did not appear except after the martyrdom of Imam Husayn (as).

THE SHIA IN THE PROPHET'S TRADITIONS

The Messenger of Allah (s) many times talked about the Shia. Each time he confirmed that the followers of Ali (as) would be the

---

[1] *Ibid.*

[2] *Al-Durr al-Manthur fit Tafsir al-Ma'thur* vol.8, p. 589. *Tazkiratul Khawas*, p. 18.

winners, because they supported the truth and kept away from and let down the untruth. He also confirmed that the followers of Ali (as) were the followers of the Prophet (s) himself.

Here, we mention the following tradition that has been mentioned by Ibn Hajar in *as-Sawa'iq al-Muhriqah* and other Sunni scholars.

The Messenger of Allah (s) said to Ali:

Are you not pleased that you shall be with me in the Paradise, and al-Hasan, al-Husayn and our progeny after us, our wives after our progeny and our Shia (followers) to our left and right sides?

Many times, the Prophet (s) said about Ali (as) and his followers:

By Him, in whose hand my soul is, this (Ali) and his Shia are certainly the winners on the Day of Resurrection.[2]

It is very natural that the Prophet (s) praised the followers of the truth and distinguished them with a sign by which they would be known throughout the ages, so that Muslims would know the suppressed truth and be guided to it through the nearest way.

Because of the Prophet's praise and continuous instructions, a group from the best of his companions became adherents to Imam Ali (as). They were famous for their love and support to him after the death of the Prophet (s). Among these great companions there were Salman al-Farsi, Abu Dharr al-Ghifari, Ammar ibn Yasir, Huzayfah ibn al-Yaman and al-Miqdad ibn al-Aswad. Thus, the word "*shia*" became a surname for these men.

Dr. Mustafa Kamil ash-Shaybi mentions this fact in his book '*The Relation between Sufism and Shiism*', and the same is mentioned by Abu Hatim in his book *az-Zinah* when saying, "The least name of a creed that appeared in Islam was the "Shia" and this was a surname of four companions who are Abu Dharr al-Ghifari, Ammar ibn Yasir, Salman al-Farsi, and al-Miqdad ibn al-Aswad."

This shows clearly that the orientalists and some of Muslim researchers, who had quoted from those orientalists, were not truthful when they said that Shiism was a political phenomenon that came

---

[1] *As-Sawa'iq al-Muhriqa* by Ibn Hajar, p. 161.
[2] *Al-Manaqib* by Khawarizmi al-Hanafi, p. 62.

out as a result of the circumstances after the martyrdom of Imam Husayn (as). It also clearly demonstrates the falsehood of those who tried to attach Shiism to the Persians. In fact, these people just reveal their own ignorance and fanaticism.

How would these biased people justify the existence of Shiite states in the Arab land in north Africa like Morocco and Tunisia and in the east like Egypt and Halab (in Syria) centuries before the appearance of Shiism in Persia? The state of the Idrisids (Adarisah) in Morocco was in the second century of hijra and the state of the Fatimids was in Tunisia at the end of the third century of hegira. The Fatimids also ruled in Egypt in the middle of the third century of hegira. The Shiite state of the Hamadanids ruled Halab (Syria) and Iraq in the fourth century, whereas Iran turned to be Shia in the tenth century of hegira at the hand of the Shah Ismael.

Those, who try in a way or another to attach Shiism to the Persians, will never be able to prove that whatever they try to do.

As I have mentioned before in my book *'Then I was guided'*, most of the Sunni scholars and imams who were Persian, were not Shia! In fact, they were very puritan and fanatic against the Shia and Shiism. Some historians mention that the people of Persia used to abuse Imam Ali (as) on their minbars even after Umar ibn Abdul Aziz, the Umayyad caliph, had prohibited it (the abusing of Imam Ali).[1]

If we know that the first and most famous interpreter az-Zamakhshari was Persian, the great traditionists al-Bukhari and Muslim were Persian, Abu Hanifah the Greatest Imam, as called by the Sunni, was Persian, the master and most famous of scholars Seebwayh was Persian, the master of theologians Wasil ibn Ata' was Persian, the master of linguists al-Fayrooz Abadi the author of al-*Qamus al-Muhit* (Comprehensive Dictionary) was Persian. Imam al-Ghazali, ar-Razi, Avicenna, and Ibn Rushd all were Persian... and all of the mentioned above men were from the scholars and heads of the Sunni, then would those fabricators and agitators turn to reason and let alone the true scholars and researchers conclude and arrive at the

---

[1] *The Present Islamic World*, vol. 1 p. 191, quoted from al-Khawarizmi.

truth derived from the true history through their reasons and not emotions and fanaticism?

TODAY, I HAVE PERFECTED FOR YOU YOUR RELIGION...

Would that all Muslims have converted to Shia on that day!

Eid Al-Ghadir[1]

Eid al-Ghadir is the greatest and most important eid to Allah.

All Muslims in the east and the west of the earth celebrate two eids; the first is the Eid al-Fitr after the end of Ramadan, and the second is Eid al-Adhha immediately after performing the Hajj.

Muslims, since the beginning until now, keep on celebrating these two eids everywhere in the world. They call the first eid as 'the minor eid' and the other one as 'the major eid'.

However and unfortunately, Muslims have disagreed on the third eid, which is the greatest of all eids and called Eid al-Ghadir. It is the day when Allah the Almighty declared to have perfected the religion and completed His favor on Muslims.

One, who studies history, can undoubtedly discover that this disagreement has come out of the political situation of the *men of the Saqifah* within the first moments after the Prophet's death. They permitted themselves to behave unlike the clear texts of Qur'an and Prophet's traditions[2] and impose their will on Muslims by force.

---

[1] For details of Eid al-Ghadir, visit: https://www.al-islam.org/ghadir/

[2] Besides that, they contradicted many occasions on which the Prophet (s) often declared and announced his successor clearly and openly. Allama Sayyid Muhammad Husayn Tabataba'i, in his book *'The Shia in Islam'*, p. 24, says, "It is impossible for the leader of a revolution, and in its first days, not to assign one of his companions as vizier or successor to him over the others, and not introduce him to the most loyal of his close companions and supporters...or keep him away from the responsibilities of vizierate and succession!!

Because of this, Imam Ali (as), who had been appointed as the caliph after the Prophet (s) according to many clear texts, was kept away from caliphate and replaced by another one chosen by Quraysh[1] based on their desires and ambitions. Thus, this was the first relapse that afflicted the Muslims soon after the death of their prophet, paving the way for the quarrel of untruth against the truth and of *jahiliyyah* (ignorance of the pre-Islamic era) against Islam.

There is no doubt that the following verse of Qur'an has a direct relation with the Eid al-Ghadir:

And Muhammad is no more than a messenger; the messengers have already passed away before him; if then he dies or is killed will you turn back upon your heels? [Qur'an, 3:144]

The Messenger of Allah (s) celebrated the Eid al-Ghadir when Allah the Almighty ordered him to appoint Ali (as) as the caliph after him and introduce him to the nation. The Messenger of Allah (s) called out, "*Allahu Akbar*" when the present Muslims finished paying their homage to Imam Ali (as) and Gabriel came to the Prophet (s) revealing this verse to him:

This day have I perfected for you your religion and completed my favor on you and chosen for you Islam as a religion. [Qur'an, 5:3]

The Prophet (s) said:

Allah is Great. Praise be to Allah for perfecting the religion and completing the blessing and the contentment of the Lord with the guardianship of my brother and cousin.

On the same day, the Prophet (as) held a meeting to congratulate Imam Ali (as) and there was not one of the Muslim men and women present on that day, who did not come to Imam Ali (as) to congratulate him on that guardianship.

However, it did not last long! Only two months after the celebration of that great eid, the nation disavowed and denied the eid and the hero of the eid, and chose someone else against the will of

---

[1] Quraysh was the biggest tribe in Mecca of great power and authority.

Allah claiming at one time that Ali was too young and then at another time that the Hashimites had already had the honor of the Prophethood and so they should not get the position of caliphate as well. And, a third time it was said that the people of Quraysh would not agree on the one who had killed their heroes, defeated their brave knights, and crushed their pride.

Ali ibn Abi Talib (as) had no guilt in all that at all, except that he had sold his life for the contentment of Allah and sacrificed everything he had for supporting the religion that his brother and cousin had received from the heavens, never minding any blame in the way of Allah and nothing of this worldly life's vanities could turn his determination away.

I cannot account Imam Ali's virtues or show his qualities. I know certainly that:

If the sea were ink for the words of my Lord, the sea would surely be consumed before the words of my Lord are exhausted.

It sufficed him as pride and honor that Allah the Almighty had perfected the religion with his imamate, completed His favor with his caliphate, and been pleased with the Muslims who believed in his guardianship. And it sufficed him as glory and virtue that the Messenger of Allah (s) had made him as the Imam (Chief) of the pious, the master of Muslims, the leader of the honorable and enlightened ones and the head of people in religion.

I am in no need of showing a proof on the fact of the Eid al-Ghadir or proving the narrations and historical events on it, for the *ummah* has agreed unanimously on the reality of this event, whether the Shia, who celebrate it every year, or the *Sunnah* who try to misinterpret it.

We have read the sayings of the celebrators as we have read the sayings of the misinterpreters. We have read the sayings of the adherents, who have understood from those texts, traditions, and celebrations that imamate is a fundamental principle of the religion.

We have read the sayings of the dissenters who have misinterpreted the texts as to be no more than a personal opinion that Muhammad adopted about his cousin and husband of his daughter to endear him to the hearts of haters and enviers.

After that, we know the situation of the adherent supporters who were few, poor and disabled. And we also know the situations of the disappointing opponents who were in great numbers, wealthy and arrogant. Therefore, they violated the sanctity of the Prophet's household, beginning with the Chief of all women of the world - Fatima (sa). Then they broke out many wars against Imam Ali (as) - the master of all guardians; al-Jamal, Siffin, and then an-Nahrawan were fought until at last they assassinated him in the *mihrab* during his prayer. He prostrated thereafter, to thank Allah for all that!

However, they were not satisfied with all this until, they killed the two Masters of the youth of the Paradise - Imam al-Hasan (as) with poison and then Imam al-Husayn (as) by sword in Kerbala along with his family and loyal companions.

From all this, we know that the Eid al-Ghadir was the trial for this nation, which disagreed and was divided and separated like the Jews and the Christians as the Prophet Muhammad (s) had predicted.[1] We also knew that the holy imamate, which is one of the fundamental principles of religion, was suppressed and subdued. Its people had nothing to do, except to be patient and submissive. This divine imamate was replaced with false emirate that was "a slip away from whose evil Allah had kept Islam and Muslims safe".

Until after that time, the *tulaqa'* (prisoners set free) and the profane wished for, but no one rode on the ship of rescue that Muhammad (s) had made except for a very few loyal companions. The current of this worldly life and the love of power swept away the rest of Muslims, who turned their backs to the infallible Imams of guidance and followed creeds they themselves invented. It had a proof neither in the Book of Allah nor in the *Sunnah* of His messenger.

This is, in brief about the event of Eid al-Ghadir, the Hero of al-Ghadir, and the plot that was born after the Day of al-Ghadir. For more details, I suggest for readers to read my book '*To be with the Truthful*'.

---

[1] *Sahih al-Bukhari*, vol. 4 p. 144, vol. 8 p. 151.

Today, we have to know that both the Sunni and the Shia are victims of the false history or in fact, the victims of the plots and transgressions that had been done by other than us. Surely, these are the results of the crimes that our ancestors had committed, and Allah knows that we are free from them. We are just followers and nor heretics. We have been created on nature and our parents were the cause of our being Shia or Sunni, guided or deviant.

We still have to know that the deviation, which has been ongoing for fourteen centuries, cannot be reformed in a few years. Whoever believes in this just deceives himself and wishes for the impossible.

It goes without saying that the infallible Imams (as), from Imam Ali (as) to Imam al-Hasan al-Askari (as), spared no any effort to unite the nation and guide it to the right path. They sacrificed their lives and the lives of their children to keep the Religion of Muhammad (s) untouched, but most of people were unfaithful and resistant to the Truth which they detested terribly.

We also have to know that efforts of faithful and truthful reformers failed and the hope of unity was broken against the rock of the blind fanaticism and offensive ignorance. Hills and mountains of nationalities and races besides governments stood in the face of these hopes. Behind all of these, there were and are those who were enemies to us, whose friendliness could not be wished for. They were active since the beginning of the Mission until today. They have spared no effort to put out the Light of Allah. Besides these, there are many opportunists who do not think except of their own benefits, which the unity of Muslims seriously threatens.

In addition to all those, there is the cursed Iblis about whom Allah the Almighty has said:

He said: As Thou has caused me to remain disappointed I will certainly lie in wait for them in Thy straight path. [Qur'an, 7:16]

We have to know too, that time has elapsed. Fourteen centuries have passed while we have been sleeping, bewildered, drunken and confused. The ornaments and embellishments of this life have intoxicated our minds, and many incurable diseases have gnawed our bodies. In the same time, our enemies worked and are still working day and night for scientific and technological development.

It was due to this that they were able to colonize our countries, subdue us, and suck our blood and treasures - claiming that we were underdeveloped nations which should be developed, or that predatory beasts must be tamed. They controlled every way and closed every door before us. They began counting our breaths so that if anyone of us sneezed, even one sneeze at the end of every century - they counted it against him and asked him to prove the source of that flu, fearing infection for their own selves, which might result in unpleasing outcomes.

They took much from Islam and did according to it, whereas we turned away from much of what Allah had ordered us to do. Here, there is no need of more explanations and details, because "*a word is enough for a wise man*".

Today, we have woken up from our lethargy and have begun clapping and dancing to the tunes of unity. Each one of us has claimed to be the hero of this unity. We have imagined that this was a simple matter and that we would unite the nation overnight by calling out some slogans and holding some conferences.

Since I have opened my eyes towards this life, I have heard of "unity". In my first school I learned songs of unity whose meaning flowed with my blood in my veins. I grew up and every day I dreamt of unity. Now, I am more than fifty years of old, but I have not seen any sign or even ghost of this unity.

After being desperate for the unity of Muslims, and even of the unity of the Arabs, I was satisfied with a minor unity between two neighboring countries. In the morning, I was very delighted for that unity and in the evening of the same day that it was born, I wept for it. Two people who were twins had nothing that separated them except that which was called - "the government verdicts".

By that time, I knew that the destinies of people was in the hands of a few persons who controlled them as they liked; if they liked, they would unite them, and if they liked something else, they would set them against each other and throw them into wars, and then you would see the same people who used to embrace each other, fight each other.

Since the enemies had power and dominance by which they could separate people who were united for hundreds of years, suppress them and make them dissipate in spite of their own power and influence. So certainly they would not let Muslims, who had been suppressed for hundreds of years, meet and unite to form a powerful entity that would endanger their benefits and interests, even though these people were poor, underdeveloped and under great debts.

Suppose that we were united - what would we get from this poverty and underdevelopment? If we thought of driving the colonists away and cutting the hand of the thieves, we must be prepared with enough power and forces to repel the unjust and control the rioters. And how can we do that while we still buy the arms and weapons, which are not used except for killing Muslims and making citizens dread themselves?

If we advance one day, they will advance sixty years, and if we prepare one force against them, they will prepare seventy! If we want to face them in war, they will not trouble themselves much! They will incite our brothers in nationality or religion against us, and then one will kill another, while they will remain but delighted audiences clapping their hands.

The Gulf war is not far! Only some soldiers were killed from them, but hundreds of thousands of Muslims were buried alive. And the one, who used to threatened to burn Israel yesterday and many stupid Arabs believed him, came to burn his own people in the north and the south with the Napalm. Even the mosques and holy shrines were not safe from his evil mercenaries whom we saw coward and inactive towards disbelievers, but against the Muslims - they were ravenous beasts.[1]

---

[1] From the book *'The Secret File of the Gulf War'*, p.138-139. In a letter to the Iranian President Mr. Rafsanjani, the criminal Saddam praised peace and showed that he had given up his conditions...in few lines, this tyrant effaced the remembrance of hundreds of thousands of Iraqis killed in the eight-year-war which was the bloodiest since the Second World War!!! He adopted the slogan of "the way to Jerusalem passes through Tehran", and then he turned

The young Islamic Republic of Iran made every effort to unite the Muslims and offered every sacrifice in this way. It paid a very heavy price with the blood of its most loyal people. It resisted the west and the east and faced an international blockade (sanction). Its leader died while bemoaning the indifference of Muslims, as his grandfather the leader of the pious (Imam Ali (as)) had bemoaned before.

From the eternal sayings of Imam Khomeini (may Allah have mercy on him) is this one, "*If every Muslim spits once, the Muslims shall make Israel sink.*"

If Muslims are stingy with even one spit, so how is it expected that they will sacrifice their properties and lives? Therefore, many of them have friendly relations with Israel. So, do not look forward to unity, O you the inattentive!

Is it unknown to you that fifty thousand Palestinians wait every day for the mercy of Israel, and they hurry up every morning to work with meanness and disgrace to gain the daily bread for themselves and their families? If Israel closes its doors, these people shall die of hunger. So where are their Muslim brothers whom Allah has enriched with His favors to the extent that one emir of them receives

---

to occupy Kuwait and let his armies kill, rob and violate the honors of women, and finally set fire to the Kuwaiti oilfields. He issued a law to execute every one of his armies who refused to rob from Kuwait. After all that, yet he was called 'the Sword of the Arabs"!!!

It is worth mentioning that the Iraqi, the American and the third partner - the UN's information service refrained from announcing the true losses and damages caused by the allies in their bombing on Iraq. In fact, that which was bombed in Iraq was the public utilities, bridges, and hospitals. And now, the Iraqi people are suffering terrible famine that more than four millions people are likely to die and 75% of the newborn children are at risk of dying because of malnutrition and absence of medical care.

Moreover, the sanction shall not be annulled except after destroying the weapons of the regime which has been accumulated with the wealth and sweat of the Iraqi and Arab people and after offering the Iraqi people in sacrifice to Israel for its security and stability!!! (This book was published first in Arabic in 1995)

income that is too much more than the needs of those people who are obliged not to resist or fight Israel, as long as they feel that Israel is the benefactor and the cause of their livelihood.[1]

Peace be on Ali (as) who said:

Poverty is about to be atheism. If poverty were a man, I certainly would kill him.

It is true that there is powerfulness in unity, but it is supposed that there is power in every one of its elements. If all the elements of unity are weak and sick, then in their unity there shall be but more weakness and sickness. How is it possible for one, who is always busy thinking of the hunger of his stomach and the sickness of his body, to believe in unity?

About what shall I talk to you? Shall I talk to you about the children who cannot find any weapon except the stones to resist, although all the stones have been swept away? Perhaps, some of them look for a stone to place it on his abdomen to suppress hunger!

What makes one laugh and cry at the same time is that you see some drawlers try, with all their abilities, to convince us that the *Stone Revolution* has troubled and shaken Israel. In fact, this is a mere propaganda to justify the savage doings of Israel, that if one Israelite soldier is wounded by those stones, tens of innocent children shall be killed by machine guns and bombs.

So, where are the Arab countries that had united under the shade of the Arab Assembly since tens of years and promised of liberating Palestine?
Where are the Muslim countries that lead the Muslim World and claim to liberate Jerusalem?

Have you seen even one of these countries offer help, assistance, or arms to those children with stones (in Palestine) or the mujahidin who face the bombs and missiles of the enemy without having any other arms to reply with, except the stones? We have seen them in

---

[1] The media and journals have reported that after the decree of transferring the capital from Tel Aviv to Jerusalem, a high official from the Gulf countries visited the United States of America offering six milliard dollars for the luxury of the American people!

the Gulf War...we have seen our Arab Muslim brothers take out their hidden arms and spend millions from their wealth to overthrow the Iraqi government that in return threatened to do away with the Israelite government, agents and reactionaries!

However, the truth was that they were all plotting to do away with the Shiite Revolution. And actually, the Iraqi regime remained as it was, and so did Israel, the agents and the reactionaries, whereas the Shia were buried alive and the rest of them were displaced in the deserts and wild lands. Thousands of refugees are still living in camps under lowly conditions they face from the Saudis and insults from the Wahhabis.

I talk to you about the fate of Muslims in Afghanistan upon whom Allah had bestowed victory. They came out fighting with each other and enmity between their children and families, destroying their own houses with their own hands, after being instigated by foreign, unfaithful hands![1]

---

[1] I saw in a video cassette some horrible scenes of maiming and cutting of heads and burying the wounded in collective graves. I asked the owner of this cassette, "What for is all this brutal grudge and enmity?" He said, "These are innocent, peaceful old people, women, children...killed just because they are Shia."
These horrible crimes were committed by evil men under the leadership of Shah Mas'ud and Abd Rabb ar-Rasool the Wahhabi, who would be glad to see Satan but not a single Shia. He might even give a *fatwa* that the bloods and honors of the Shia were violable.
This attack was against a town called Afshar where about eleven thousand peaceful civilians were killed. Their women were raped and their properties were robbed. After killing the leader of the Afghani Unity Party, martyr Abdul Ali al-Mazari, there was another attack against innocent civilians where about thirteen thousands were killed, their women were raped and their properties robbed.
The Shia form one fifth (if not one third) of the population and have historical deep-rooted existence there. There is a holy shrine of one of the sons of the great martyr Zayd bin Ali (may Allah have mercy on him) in Jowzjan, now called Mazar Sharif.
The situations of the Shia (of Afghanistan) against the Umayyads, against the British colonists and lately their participation with their brothers in

I talk to you about the destiny of the Muslims in Yugoslavia where the powers of atheism had gathered together to remove them all from Eastern Europe. I talk to you about the Muslims in India, and about what I myself have seen. Their dignities were often violated and always to the extent that Alawid Muslim women were sold in the markets like animals.

I talk to you about the Muslims in Ethiopia, Somalia, Sudan, and all of Africa who die of hunger in thousands every day, whereas the dogs and cats in Europe enjoy all kinds of delicious food. The dignity and holiness of Muslims are violated, whereas many societies for defending and protecting animal rights are there and more are being founded.

Stop lying and deceit! Stop hypocrisy and misleading! If the people of one country are not in accordance with each other, then how can we ask the Muslims of different countries to unite?[1]

---

forcing the Red Army to leave Afghanistan, were and are so great that they cannot be ignored. However, instead of being grateful to them and acknowledging their creed, the others try to remove and do away with them and their beliefs!

[1] Imam al-Husayn (s) said addressing the followers of the Umayyads, "If you have no religion and you do not fear the Hereafter, then be free in your worldly life and have regard to your lineages if you are Arab as you claim!"

We have refused to take off the black dress of the reactionary religion that has taken us to underdevelopment and darkness! Let us keep pace with the ages of development and progress. The Iraqi regime said, "There is no place in this country except for development and socialism." Whenever religion was mentioned, it was described as reactionary and was detested. The Iraqi regime adopted the slogan of "One (united) Arab nation...", but it divided Iraq into pieces, and its army was divided. The then members of the government, the members of the president's family themselves, and now the president is surrounded not by the Republican Guards, but by those who are more loyal - Fedayeen of Saddam. This is an example of the Arab developed socialist leader who would suppress the reactionary religion and unite the Arab nation! He plotted and is still plotting against his own people and neighbors. (We have said before that this is from a book first published in Arabic in 1995 AD)

The sayings are too many, but the doings are too little!

One look at the history that we lived since the war of 1948 up until the Persian Gulf War would be enough. Victory was always with disbelievers. Every time the share of Muslims was defeat, loss, lowliness and disgrace. So take a lesson from the wrath of Allah, O people of understanding!

Recently, we said that we would not negotiate with Israel and that which was taken away by force, would not be taken back except by force. And today, we run after Israel and beg it to give back to us our lands that it had extorted from us. We entreat its close lovers to intercede for us!

Our hearts have become tired and bored, and our minds confused and submissive and now we believe neither in unity nor in the victory that shall come one day!

Can it be believed that the emirs of the Gulf, the kings and the rulers shall unite with the poor, the hungry and the destitute some day?

Yes, they unite in speech only! The testimony of "*there is no god but Allah and that Muhammad is the Messenger of Allah (s)*" is just a saying! Faith is just a saying, and even the prayer, zakat, fasting and the Hajj have all become sayings in sayings!

It is not difficult for an orator to say for example: "*our god is the same, our prophet is the same, our Book is the same, and our qiblah is the same; therefore, O Muslims, be united! Be united!*"

The aim of the Iraqi army in the war of 1967 A.D. was to overthrow the Jordanian regime. And in the year 1970, the Black September, the Palestinians thought that Saddam and his army tried to defend them against the massacre committed by King Husayn ibn Talal of Jordan, but they were massacred within the sight and hearing of all!

Yes, they gathered together to fight against their Muslim neighbor Iran, after they had been disciplined by the cudgel of the Shah! And after that came the scenario of the invasion of Kuwait to pave the way to coexist with the Zionists. As they took back Husni Mubarak to the Arab line, they shall take Saddam back to it as well, and whoever refuses shall be fought by them and with their new partner Israel, because in that there is the glory of the Arabs and their progress toward the eternal Arabic goals!!!

How easy it is to adopt a slogan saying "no Shiism, no Sunnism, but Islamic unity"!

However, it has disappeared from the minds of all these people to live the painful reality and face the naked truth with no cloak to mislead!

They have come to us in the last few years with a new opinion, as if it was unknown to their ancestors and to the infallible Imams! They said it should be prohibited to discuss the matters of history lest some of the Muslims be provoked. They went too far in that, until they said that there was no difference between the Shia and the Sunni except in the branches of religion exactly as there is difference between the Sunni sects themselves. They gave up the matter of imamate which to them is a fundamental that is separate from the fundamentals of religion.

As a result of this new situation, minds have become frozen and have stopped to search for the truth after their minds had been liberated claiming that they (those claiming Muslims) should be united in order to face the common enemy! These people have forgotten that our actual enemy is hidden inside our selves, living inside our houses, and being brought up by our eyes.

It is a wonder that when you talk to one of them about Marx and Lenin, he becomes proud and blooms and he considers you as a learned man. However, when you mention Imam Ali (as) and the infallible Imams of his progeny, he frowns and is depressed, and then accuses you of defaming the Orthodox Caliphs. Worse than that is that when you argue with him with clear evidences and proofs, then he pretends to adopt the slogan of the Islamic Unity and accuses you of trying to divide the Muslims.

After that, would we abuse those who call for the unity of beliefs according to the Book of Allah and the pure *Sunnah* of His messenger and then accuse them of trying to divide the Muslims?

In fact, some *ulama* hide the truth willingly and when they are asked, they do not answer fearing that they may be accused of striving against the Islamic unity.

I think that the scientific research to get to the sought truth is not a danger threatening the unity of Muslims, because it is not more than provoking some people's emotion - that shall disappear in the end when truth is arrived at.

The danger and the worst of dangers is to keep the mouths shut, tongues tied and prevent people from researching with frozen minds and keep them away from the truth under the pretense of unity! This is the very thing that the Baathist regime in Iraq did to separate between the Shia and the Sunni. The talk about Shiism was prohibited lest the Sunni would know the truth of the Shia.[1]

---

[1] Collective conversions to Shiism took place at the hands of some *ulama*. For example, Allama al-Qazwini could convert about thirty thousand people from the tribes of al-Jubour in Hillah (in Iraq). The same took place at the hands of other *ulama*. Some tribes of nomadic trends near Tikrit and Ramadi have a proverb saying, "May Allah afflict you with like of affliction of the tribe of Aal Alwan who gave up the religion of their fathers and became Shia!"

There were many meetings between the Shia and Sunni *ulama* during the struggle against the British colonialism, the communist expansion, and the Iraqi Baath's prevailing. Among those *ulama* was the Martyr Abdul Aziz al-Badri whom the tyrannical regime cut into pieces.

Thus, the Baathist regime in Iraq followed a hypocritical policy that his Masonic masters had trained him to. They exploited Saddam's ignorance, complexes, and nomadic nature that he had inherited from the village of al-Oujah (in Tikrit) which was terribly underdeveloped and nomadic, besides his vagrancy because of his uncle's bad and severe relation to his mother, besides his Jewish background and gypsy life that was with no moral bonds, lawful marriage, or pledges...so this nomad was worthier of not knowing the limits of Allah. He knew neither Sunnism nor Shiism. He was just to carry out what he had been ordered to do; therefore, he did not refrain from any crime or sin. He accused the Shia of treason for foreign countries, disbelief and of Persian origin. He accused me of his own guilt and ran away...and a suspicious one may expose himself!!!

Unfortunately, many Sunni people responded to him (Saddam), especially those who broke into houses, tortured, raped, and maimed innocent people with total rage to write with Saddam that "there would be no Shia after today". And due to their jurisprudence, it is not permissible to disobey the ruler and turn away from the group (congregation), and therefore they helped Saddam to do whatever he liked. Certainly, this is the continuity of the fatwa of the first (illegal) rulers of Muslims saying that it is not

It is the same thing like that which the first caliphs did when they prohibited people from writing down or mentioning the traditions of the Prophet (s). Therefore, the truth was hidden from most of Muslims who did not know about the Eid al-Ghadir and what happened on that Day, which made the Jews and Christians say to them, "If this (Qur'anic) verse was revealed about us, we would highly regard that day and take it as eid even if only two people remained from us:

This day I have perfected for you your religion and completed my favor on you. [Qur'an, 5:3]

The companions could not find an answer to that.

Some others have come to us relying on Imam Ali's saying:

I will submit as long as the affairs of Muslims are safe and when there is no oppression except against me only.[1]

These people have forgotten that it was Imam Ali (as) who revived the event of al-Ghadir after it had been buried and made to be forgotten. He made thirty companions from those who had attended the day of al-Ghadir, bear witness and he invoked Allah against those who denied it. Then, after him, his two sons (Imam al-Hasan (as) and al-Husayn (as)) revived it during the season of the Hajj before great masses of Muslims. In this concern, Imam Ali (as) said:

Do not be revilers or cursers, but you say that their doings were so and so, in order to be more effective in argument.[2]

We must take Imam Ali (as) as our example and not take only one of his sayings ("*I will submit...*") and leave the others and be not like children of Israel who said:

We believe in some and disbelieve in some... [Qur'an 4:150]

---

permissible to disobey a ruler even if he is unjust. Certainly, this is a clear rejection to the Prophet's tradition saying that "Whoever of you sees a wrongdoing let him repel it..."

[1] *Nahjul Balaghah* sermon 74.

[2] *Bihar al-Anwar* vol.32, p. 399

Perfection of the Religion

It is right that Imam Ali (as) was willingly patient for the sake of the welfare of Islam and Muslims, because he did exactly what he said. He fought the breakers of covenants (nakitheen - in the battle of al-Jamal), the unjust (qasiteen - who falsely sought arbitration in the battle of Siffin) and the renegades (mariqeen - in the battle of an-Nahrawan), until he straightened the pillars of religion, provided safety to all Muslims, and pardoned his enemies whenever the matter concerned the oppression against him only.

Those who argue against us by *Nahjul Balaghah*, must believe in everything in it, and not argue by what complies with their desires only. If there is praise to someone unknown mentioned in *Nahjul Balaghah*, they say: this is Imam Ali's speech about our master Umar al-Farouq. He praises and commends him!

Yet, if you say to them (that Imam Ali as) has said, "*By Allah, ibn Abi Quhafah (Abu Bakr) has dressed himself in it (assumed the caliphate) and he knew well that my position to it was like the position of the axis to the quern that flood flows down from and birds cannot ascend me in flight*", they say that this is the speech of ash-Shareef ar-Radhi[1] and not Ali's. Yes, they love Ali (as) and pray Allah to be pleased with him when he is sincere to the caliphs and does not disobey them.

These people forget that the self of Ali (as) is like the self of Muhammad (s) and the heart of Ali (as) is like the heart of Muhammad (s) from where Allah has kept away all impurity and purified with thorough purification. Ali (as) was a true copy of the Messenger of Allah (s) whom Allah had described as "*on exalted standards of character*" and that the hearts of the Ahlul Bayt (as) had no place for grudge or hatred.[2]

---

[1] He is the compiler of *Nahjul Balaghah*.

[2] And the same is said about us his Shia! If we say that Imam Ali (s) is the gate of the (Prophet's) city of knowledge. Their (the other than the Shia) arguers cries out loudly that this fact does not deny that this city has many gates. If we mention his great courage and that it was he who put the cornerstone of Islam, they say to us - do you want to invalidate all the history? How did the Muslims achieve all those conquests and victories and... and...etc?

For that, this was the Prophet (s) and that was the guardian - Muhammad (s) was the warner and Ali (as) was the guide. The first one fought for the revelation and the second one fought for the interpretation. For that, Allah chose him (Imam Ali as) for imamate by which He perfected the religion and completed the favor. As an honor to him, Allah crowned him with the imamate on the day of the Major Eid (of al-Ghadir).

Ali (as), with his patience and loyalty, did not overlook his right for even one day. You (Sunnis) have mentioned in your Sahihs that he did not pay homage (to the caliph) for six months during which he argued against them (the men of authority) with every proof and evidence, and he said to Umar one day:

Milk a milking that you shall have a half of it, and support him (Abu Bakr) today, so that he recompenses you tomorrow with caliphate...[1]

Muhammad is my brother and father-in-law...

This is if the argument is quiet, but if there is injustice and oppression against the Shia, they shall approve the setting of fire to Fatima's house, the murdering of Imam al-Husayn (s), the persecution of the Alawids, creating of al-Azhar University and Halab Sunnite, persecuting the seyyids from the progeny of the Prophet (as), the killing of the Iranian hajjis, fighting and trying to do away with the Shia and their *ulama* in Iraq like the descendants of the great religious authority Grand Ayatollah Sayyid Muhsin al-Hakeem and the great thinker Ayatollah Sayyid Muhammad Baqir as-Sadr (may Allah have mercy on him).

This is if they have not participated in the activities of the media or as soldiers in the different armies of the tyrant (Saddam), because, for them, it is not permissible to disobey the guardian of Muslim when he has not disobeyed Allah yet!!! How I wonder at this! I do not know how the color of disobedience would be for Yazid, al-Hajjaj, and Saddam!!!

Yes, we invite them to dialogues and discussions so that we do know the truth and its people, but they invite us today to keep silent. The invitation that they have accustomed us to is murdering and supporting the wrongdoers to defend the rulers whether good or bad they are!

---

[1] *al-Imamah wa al-Siyasah*, vol.1, p. 18, *Ansab al-Ashraf*, vol.1, p. 587

You also have narrated that he (Imam Ali (as)) took out his wife Fatima (sa) with him and they both frequented the meetings of the Ansar who apologized, saying to her:

O the beloved of the Messenger of Allah (s), if your husband and cousin preceded us, we would not prefer anyone to him at all.

Imam Ali (as) said in reply:

Would I leave the Messenger of Allah (s) without washing (ritually before the burial) and go out (to saqifah) disputing with the people for his succession (caliphate)?

Fatima (sa) said:

Abu Hasan only did what was his duty and they will be answerable for it before Allah for what they have done.[1]

Was it not Ali (as) who complained when burying his wife in the night by addressing the Messenger of Allah (s) saying:

Peace be on you O Messenger of Allah (s) and on your daughter who is coming to be your neighbor. She shall tell you about the rising of your Umma against me and the extorting of her right. So keep on asking her and know from her what happened?[2]

Did Ali (as) not refuse the caliphate when he was asked to follow the way of the two previous caliphs in rule? Does this show that he accepted and was pleased with what they did?

Did Ali (as) not refuse the caliphate when people forced him to assume it and did he not accept it when he made thirty men witness for him about (the reality of) the event of al-Ghadir and that the Messenger of Allah (s) had appointed him on that day as the caliph over all Muslims, until he said:

Whoever does not consider Ali as his guardian, is not a Muslim?[3]

Thus, Imam Ali (as) revived the Eid al-Ghadir after it was about to be buried forever. Nevertheless, most of Muslims do not know this

---

[1] *al-Imamah wa al-Siyasah*, vol.1, p. 19, *Sharh Nahjul Balaghah* Ibn Abi al-Hadid vol.6, p. 13.

[2] *Nahjul Balaghah* sermon 205.

[3] https://www.al-islam.org/ghadir/

and they cannot believe in those events, claiming that the courage of Imam Ali (as) would not let him keep silent before his right.

I say to these people that the courage of Imam Ali (as) was not greater than the courage of the Messenger of Allah (s) about whom Imam Ali (as) said:

When war became violent, we protected ourselves behind the back of the Messenger of Allah (s).

Nonetheless, the Messenger of Allah (s) kept silent and gave up his right when he accepted all the conditions of the polytheists for the welfare of Islam and Muslims, until one of his companions[1] accused him of being indifferent to the religion by saying to him:

Are you really the Messenger of Allah (s)?[2]

It was the same situation when some ignorant ones accused Imam al-Hasan (as) of degrading the believers when he concluded a truce with Mu'awiyah to spare the bloods of Muslims.

Thus, the Eid al-Ghadir is the borderline between the truth and falsehood. It stands between the perfecting of the religion and its comprehensiveness with the Book of Allah and the *Sunnah* of His Prophet (s) on one hand and its imperfection and being in need of the *ijtihad* of mujtahids on the other. It is between the completion of the favor and its belonging to the grateful on one hand and the wrath of Allah on the renouncers on the other hand. It is between the infallible imamate that Allah has made among His loyal, pure servants and the usurped caliphate that the *tulaqa'* (freed captives) and sinners had assumed.

When I remember the great martyr Sayyid Muhammad Baqir as-Sadr (may Allah have mercy on him), I do not and shall never hesitate even for one moment to announce the right of the Ahlul Bayt (as). One day, he (Martyr as-Sadr) said to his companions, "*When the letter of al-Tijani came to me from Tunisia, telling that some of our Shia brothers had celebrated the Eid al-Ghadir for the first time there, I cried and praised Allah that He had planted the seed of Shiism there.*"

---

[1] Umar al-Khattab

[2] *Musnad Ahmad* vol.4, p. 330. *Sahih al-Bukhari*, vol.3, p. 206.

The attendants understood then that the crying of Sayyid as-Sadr was because of his delight that some believers had been guided at his hand. However, with the passing of years, I have understood that his crying was for the great injustice against Imam Ali (as) and the pure progeny of the Prophet (s), because the injustice against them was an injustice against Islam and all Muslims. Sayyid as-Sadr had cried for most of the Muslims who had not heard about the Eid al-Ghadir and had not known about its great value and importance near Allah the Almighty.

After this brief discussion about the Eid al-Ghadir and its importance, I have to show my opinion as to the sought solution for the unity of Muslims. Anyhow, my opinion is not a personal one, but it is a following of the texts of the Qur'an and the Prophet's *Sunnah*, because after these two holy sources, my opinion and the opinions of all people shall be just deviation and supposition, and surely, supposition is nothing before the truth.

I think that the unity of Muslims shall not come true except when it is built on a firm basis, the basis of the same beliefs and the clinging to the firm rope of Allah, because the Prophet Muhammad (s) said:

If they disagree in the religion, they shall become the party of Iblis.

The signs of the unity were declared by the Messenger of Allah (s) when he said:

I have left among you the Two Weighty things which if you keep to, you shall never go astray after me at all; the Book of Allah and my household, my family. The all-comprehensive, the all acquainted (Gabriel) has told me that they will never separate until they will come to me at the Pond (in the Paradise).[1]

So whoever, whether knowingly or unknowingly, keeps to them is from the propagandists for the unity that the Messenger of Allah (s) had ordered and whoever turns his back to them is from the propagandists for separation and disagreement, which the Messenger

---

[1] More details of its sources please visit: https://www.al-islam.org/hadith-al-thaqalayn-a-study-of-its-tawatur

of Allah (s) had forbidden. If such a man claims that he is the leader of unity and uniting, his claim is certainly false, as long as he follows other than these Two Weighty things.

What one of scholars has said to me might reveal clearly the intentions of the Sunni propagandists of unity, whom no Muslim doubts about their love for the Ahlul Bayt (as). He said to me,"

I asked him, "What is our sign that you wait for?"

"We (the Sunni) cannot unite with you except by the appearance of your sign. He said, "Al-Mahdi whom you claim to be alive and hidden. When he comes to us, only then we can unite with you and know that you are truthful."

It is a painful conclusion, but it is inevitable, for this nation cannot unite except by his (Imam al-Mahdi) appearance. Even if we suppose that most of the Sunni shall return to the truth, there shall be some obdurate people there until the Last Day.[1]

---

[1] You may stand with the enemies of the grandfathers of al-Mahdi (as), of his followers, and supporters, supporting (the oppressors) and keeping silent before the injustice against them, or participating with their killers, or being a voice and echo for them, or a mere onlooker to be safe, imitating what you have inherited from the ancestors!

"(Abdullah) ibn Umar (Ibn al-Khattab) blamed Imam al-Husayn (as) for marching to Kufa and for his rising against Yazid ibn Mu'awiyah and separating from the group (congregation of Muslims)." Refer to *al-Bidayah wen-Nihayah fit-Tarikh*, vol. 8 p. 163. "And Ibn Umar secluded himself from the people of Medina when they renounced their pledge to Yazid ibn Mu'awiyah and ordered his children and family to keep on their allegiance to him (Yazid) and not to follow the people of Medina in renouncing him"......even though Yazid killed Imam al-Husayn ibn Ali (as), his children and companions, took his women as captives, and roamed with the heads of the martyrs on spears...destroyed the Kaaba, and violated Medina for three days by committing every kind of vices in it! *Ibid.* vol. 8 p. 218

As the Mufti of the Saudi royal palace (Ibn Baz) gives a fatwa that it is not permissible to eat from the meat of the sacrifices of the Shia, for they (the Shia) are polytheists and unfaithful and that it is not permissible to marry from them or marry women to them, we see him welcome the foreign armies in Hijaz. There are scenes where the American female soldiers use sunbaths

It is necessary at the end of this brief discussion to remind of the will of the leader of the *ummah* and founder of the Islamic Republic (Imam Khomeini may Allah have mercy on him) to close the way before pretenders. He prohibited disputing between the Shia and the Sunni for the sake of unity. He began his will[1] by the tradition of *ath-Thaqalayn* (two weighty things), and after explaining the tradition, he directly said,

"*We must say that what had been afflicted on the two trusts of the Prophet (s) by the tyrants afflicted the Muslim nation and in fact entire humanity in a way that the pen is not able to express. We have to mention at this point that the tradition of ath-Thaqalayn has been mentioned by so many narrators (mutawatir tradition) and it is well known among all Muslims. It has been mentioned in the main Sunni books of Hadith, such as the six Sahihs and other books in different wordings and in many places.*

This Prophet's tradition is an irrefutable argument over human beings especially the Muslims with their different creeds. All the Muslims, on whom the argument has been cast, have to undertake this responsibility. If the ignorant have an excuse, the scholars of the different sects have no excuse."

After Imam Khomeini had disclosed the stages of the plot against the Book of Allah and the Immaculate Progeny (s) and showed that the tyrants had made the Qur'an as a means to establish governments hostile to the Qur'an, although the call of the Messenger of Allah (s) "*I have left among you the Two Weighty Things*" was still resounding in their ears. They tried their best through different plots and tricks to keep away the true interpreters of the Qur'an and the real scholars of the Prophet's Hadith. He said,

---

freely (nude) and he considers their safety being secured by Islam, since they are in the land of Muslims, and he sees that peace with Israel is recommendable...with the full obedience to the rulers of Aal Sa'ud (Saudis)!

Then, why do we not wait for Imam al-Mahdi (as) under a good shade instead of this shade, so that Allah may hasten his reappearance to spread justice and remove injustice?

[1] For complete text of Imam Khomeini's last will, visit: https://www.al-islam.org/imam-khomeini-s-last-will-and-testament

"We are proud that we are followers of the creed that strives to release facts of the Holy Qur'an that all invite to the unity among all Muslims, and, in fact among all human beings.

We are proud that we are followers of the creed that forms foundation of the Messenger of Allah (s) by the command of Allah and the foundation of Ameerul Mu'minin Ali ibn Abi Talib (as) - loyal servant who was free from all ties and had been was ordered to liberate humanity from enslavement and all kinds of fetters.

We are proud that the book Nahjul Balaghah, which is, after the Qur'an, is the greatest course of material and moral life and the greatest book for liberation of human beings. Its moral and administrative teachings are the best way for deliverance from our infallible Imam.

We are proud of our infallible Imams right from the Imam Ali (as) to the Saviour of humanity - Imam al-Mahdi (thousands of blessings and peace on him) who by the power of Allah the All-Powerful is still alive and watchful of all affairs."

Then he said in the end of his will, *"I ask from the Muslim nations with all seriousness and all humility to take the infallible Imams as their examples and not to listen to any one who misleads, opposes the truth and the creed, and to know that any deviant step may form the beginning of the decline of the creed and the government of the Divine Justice.*

…from that, they have not to be indifferent at all to the Friday Prayer, congregational prayers, and the rituals of consolation of the immaculate Imams (as), especially the master of the wronged and martyred Imam al-Husayn (as).

…and to know that the teachings of the Imams (as) serve to liven up this great historical Islamic mission, and that the cursing against those, who were unjust toward the Ahlul Bayt (as) is all but a heroic, public cry in the face of the unjust rulers throughout history and forever. And you know that cursing the Umayyads (may Allah curse them) and the talking about their injustice - though they have become extinct and gone to the Hell - is but a cry in the face of all oppressors of the world.

It is necessary to mention openly in the consolation, eulogies, and elegies of the Ahlul Bayt (as) the disasters of the oppressors' oppression in every land and every time, including this very time. This is the age of the oppression by the United States of America, the Soviet Union and their followers among whom are the Aal Sa'ud (the rulers of the Saudi dynasty) also - the betrayers of the Divine Sanctum, may the curse of Allah, of His angels and of His messengers be on them. We must mention their injustice openly accompanied with invoking curse against them.

Let us all know that which lead to the unity of Muslims are these rituals that keep intact the identity of Muslims, especially that of Twelver Shia.

What I have to remind of is that my will does not concern the great Iranian people only, but my will is for all Muslim peoples and all wronged nations in the world with their different races and beliefs."

My brothers! this is the will of the leader of the *ummah*. It is clear in showing the necessity of openly mentioning the injustice of the unjust and cursing them. Thus the claim of those, who claimed that Imam Khomeini had prohibited that (unity), is a false claim without any proof at all.

In the end, I would like to say that all Muslims have to ride the Ship of Safety (of the infallible Imams (as)) if they seek the real unity. We see that the Prophet Noah (s) made, by the command of his Lord, a small ship which could not hold except a few believers, but the Prophet Muhammad (s) prepared, by the command of his Lord, a large ship which can hold the entire nation and all believers can ride on it. Certainly, the Ahlul Bayt (as) are not for the Shia only, but they are for all mankind.

May Allah make us all successful in doing all that which has welfare for all human beings and may He make us keep to the guardianship of Ameerul Mu'minin Imam Ali (as) and his infallible progeny. May Allah make you and us celebrate the Eid al-Ghadir again and again with glory and victory!

The last of our prayer is that praise be to Allah the Lord of the worlds, and blessing and peace be on the noblest of messengers our master Muhammad and on his pure progeny.

STRIVING TO REMAIN FIRM ON GUIDANCE

Allah the Almighty says:

And most surely I am most forgiving to him who repents and believes and does good, then continues to follow the true guidance. [Qur'an, 20:82]

This holy verse shows that repentance, faith, and good deeds are not enough for the forgiveness of Allah and His contentment cannot be acquired except by following the true guidance.

It has been mentioned that Imam as-Sadiq (as) said:

Surely Allah does not forgive, except one who repents, believes, does good and is guided through the guardianship of us, the Ahlul Bayt.[1]

By this, it is understood that guidance and being guided are two synonymous lines that each completes the other, but guidance is a divine favor that Allah endows His creatures with. Surely, His guidance has included all His servants with no exception. Allah says:

And the soul and Him Who made it perfect. Then, He inspired it to understand what is right and what is wrong. [Qur'an, 91:7-8]

Surely, We have shown him the way: he may be thankful or unthankful. [Qur'an, 76:3]

As for being guided, it is a personal effort that man exerts according to the general guidance to arrive after searching and trying to rely on his mental faculties, in distinguishing the truth from the untruth. And then chooses willingly the path of the truth after having been away from it. What explains this meaning is this saying of Allah:

---

[1] *Bihar al-Anwar* vol.27, p. 176, hadith no. 22

...therefore, give good news to My servants, who listen to the word, and then follow the best of it; they are those whom Allah has guided, and those it is who are the men of understanding. [Qur'an, 39:17-18]

The meaning of the verse is that a reasonable servant opens his ears for arguments and listens to all sayings and theories. He distinguishes the good from the bad, and then chooses to follow the truth and avoid the untruth. Such a servant returns to the original divine guidance willingly and so he deserves the praising of Allah to him that he is from the men of understanding.

The clearest example on the explanation of "guidance" and "being guided" is what has happened and is happening to the nation of Muhammad (s) whom Allah guided through the Prophet (s) and took them out of darkness into light and guided them to walk in His right path. He left them at the luminous destination after He had perfected to them their religion, completed His favor to them, and chosen for them Islam as a religion.[1]

---

[1] The love to the Ahlul Bayt (as) has been considered as the recompense for the fulfilling of the mission by the Messenger of Allah (s). Allah says:
'Say: I do not ask of you any reward for it but love for my near relatives. [Qur'an, 42:23]
This love is the gate and the way to the contentment of Allah the Almighty and without this love the house may only be entered from the rear (wrong side) as Allah says:
...and it is not righteousness that you enter the houses from their backs. [Qur'an, 2:189]
Imam Ali (as) is the gate of the Prophet's city of knowledge. The Prophet (s) often said, *"I am the city of knowledge and Ali is its gate"*. *"Ali is with the truth and the Qur'an. He has divorced this worldly life thrice..."*
Imam Ali (as) did never compete for authority, nor did he strive for power, wealth, pleasures, desires, or lusts, but his great soul struggled to build the religion and firm on its pillars. He said, *"By Allah, if the Arabs and foreigners gathered together against me, I would not run away."* His strike against Amr ibn Abd Wudd that equaled the worship of men and the jinn, his plucking out of the gate of Khaybar...etc. were just a drop in the sea of his achievements.

However, the nation separated, disagreed and divided after the Prophet (s) departed, into different groups, sects and creeds after it had been the best nation raised up for mankind.

The first reason behind this separation and disagreement belonged to the first companions who carried the banner of the Mission to deliver it to the next generations that followed. They disagreed and separated after the demise of their Prophet (s). They fought and killed each other. They considered each other as unbelievers and were free from each other.

The next generations followed them in that and made the problem more complicated. They widened the circle of disagreement with new thoughts and strange theories they attached to the religion of Allah. Therefore, sects and creeds came out and different groups disputed and fought each other. Muslims became confused in darkness that they did not know where to go and where the truth was, for every group claimed they had kept to the Qur'an and the *Sunnah*, every creed claimed that they followed the Prophet's line, and every party was pleased with what it had.

If we leave aside our emotions, give up blind following, turn our backs to fanaticism, look at things with the eye of insight and ask -

---

Allah the Almighty had supported His messenger (s) with Ali (as). Refer to *Tarikh Baghdad*, vol. 11 p. 173. The same is mentioned in *Zakha'ir al-Uqba* and *Kanzul Ummal*. We see him weep for a Jewish woman who had resorted to Islam when been wronged by some man. He said, "I was informed that a man from you broke into (the house of) a Muslim woman and another covenanted one whom he plundered her necklaces, jewels, and adornments and she could not defend herself except by sighing and seeking Allah's mercy." Refer to *Nahjul Balaghah*, by Subhi as-Salih, p. 69.

He often said, "It is my soul that I tame with piety." He said, "Ah, for the lack of provision (good deeds and means for the afterlife), long distance of the journey, and the loneliness of the way!" (*Nahjul Balaghah*, by Subhi as-Salih, p. 480).

The great man of letters George Jordac loved him too much and wrote on him the best of his works. One of the popes composed poetry on him. Ibn Abil Hadid loved and wrote on him. So did Muhammad Abdu, Subhi as-Salih, and the author of this book. Peace be on Ameerul Mo'minin, the lofitiest example for mujahidin!

where is the position of the Ahlul Bayt (as) among all these sects and creeds? This is especially so when we face the Prophet's traditions which order the nation to refer to the Ahlul Bayt (as) in all religious and worldly affairs to assure guidance and protection from deviation. These traditions are true and reliable in all sects of Muslims. One of these traditions is the tradition of *Thaqalayn* where the Prophet (s) said:

I have left among you the Two Weighty Things; the Book of Allah and my progeny, my family. If you keep to them, you shall never go astray after me at all. I recommend you to obey Allah through obeying my family.[1]

He repeated this three times.

One, who studies the Ahlul Bayt (as) and their position to the nation today, does not find but respect and reverence to them among all Muslims, but the will of the Messenger of Allah (s) was not limited to respect and reverence to the Ahlul Bayt (as). He ordered the nation to obey, follow and imitate them in everything. He said:

Do not precede them lest you perish, do not lag behind them lest you perish and do not teach them, because they are more knowledgeable than you.[2]

If it is so, we do not find today any group except one that does according to the will of the Messenger of Allah (s) and keeps to the line of the Ahlul Bayt (as) since the time of Imam Ali (as) until today. This group was called "*Shi'atu (followers of) Ali*" at the time of Imam Ali (as), and later on, everyone who followed Imam Ali (as) and the infallible Imams of the Ahlul Bayt (as), were called Shia (or Shiite).

If we look at the history and leaf through what historians have recorded, we find that the Ahlul Bayt (as) were wronged, kept away from the stage of the public life and were fought by the rulers and governments that ruled over Muslims during the first three centuries of Islam.

---

[1] *Hadith al-Thaqalayn–A Study of its Tawatur* at: https://www.al-islam.org/hadith-al-thaqalayn-a-study-of-its-tawatur

[2] *Al-Mu'jam al Kabir* vol.5, p. 186.

In fact, those rulers were successful in separating the nation from its real leadership, and keeping it away from the true path. However, they could not succeed in taking out the love and reverence for the Ahlul Bayt (as) from the hearts of Muslims. In spite of the abusing and cursing announced from above the minbars and the forcing of Muslims by all kinds of force, those rulers failed to extract the love of the Ahlul Bayt (as) from the hearts of the faithful.

Due to this, we justify the contradiction we find today in most of Muslims that they love the Ahlul Bayt (as) and acknowledge their superiority in virtues and knowledge, nevertheless they imitate other than them and refer to the rulings and legislations of imams who neither saw nor lived at the time of the Messenger of Allah (s), but they were born after the Great Sedition that distorted the religion, did away with the righteous leaving the Ahlul Bayt (as) and their followers discarded and isolated.

The infallible Imams of the Ahlul Bayt (as) remained unknown by most of Muslims whom if you ask about "the Ahlul Bayt", they shall say that they are the wives of the Prophet (s).

It is naturally clear that when the Prophet (s) ordered his nation to refer to his progeny, he did not mean his wives, but the twelve imams about whom he said:

After me there will be twelve caliphs; all of them will be from Quraysh.[1]

And it is well known for all scholars and researchers that the infallible Imams (as) tried their best and on every possible occasion to introduce themselves to people so that people might come back to them, but:

People are slaves to the world, and as long as they live favorable and comfortable lives, they are loyal to religious principles. However, at hard times, the times of trials, true religious people are scarce.[2]

Therefore, Imam as-Sadiq (as) said, when reciting this verse:

---

[1] *Sahih Muslim* vol.3 p. 1452.

[2] Saying of Imam Husayn (as): *Bihar al-Anwar* vol.78, p. 117.

And most surely I am most forgiving to him who repents and believes and does good and then continues to follow the right path. [Qur'an, 20:8]

and, then follows the right path of guardianship of we the Ahlul Bayt.

It may be understood from this holy verse too that it is not enough for the Muslims, who truly believe in Allah and His messenger to repent on their sins, do good deeds and give up bad deeds – in order to deserve the forgiveness of Allah the Almighty. They should be guided to the infallible Imams who are the successors of the Messenger of Allah (s) for they (the Imams) alone are the ones who can teach Muslims the real meanings of the Qur'an and the *Sunnah*. Thus, Muslims' faith, deeds and repentance would be according to what Allah had imposed on them with no misinterpretation or distortion.

Since misinterpretation took place in the Holy Qur'an and distortion in the Prophet's *Sunnah* and since every sect has relied upon a proof misinterpreted from the Qur'an and argued on basis of untrue traditions considered to be true by them, so disagreement, confusion and many doubts have surfaced.

Therefore, if a Muslim wants to know the truth, be protected from going astray, delivered on the Day of Resurrection and to win the Paradise and the contentment of Allah, he has to do nothing but to ride on the Ship of Deliverance and turn to the Ahlul Bayt (as), because they are the security for this *ummah* where Allah will not accept (the deeds of) a servant except when done in their way. No one shall enter (the Paradise) except from their gate. This is actually what the Prophet (s) asked the *ummah* to do due to the command of Allah the Almighty.

If we review the disagreement of the companions after the Prophet (s), we shall find that they disagreed for the sake of caliphate and authority over the *ummah* and every disagreement that came out after that was because of the caliphate. If unqualified people assume the rule and high posts, they certainly shall lead the nation to deviation because of their ignorance, selfishness and personal desires.

Today, as the Islamic Caliphate has gone to the unknown and there is nothing that may make it come back, would Muslims then return to their own reasons to observe the commands of their Prophet (s), follow the Book of their Lord and follow the progeny of their prophet in order to restore fraternity, concord and peace amongst themselves in order to make the *ummah* reunite and recover from its disagreement and separation? This is a cry from a pitiful, compassionate brother!

We have known from the previous discussion that guidance is a great blessing, which Allah has bestowed on His servants. And, we have known too that being guided to the guardianship of the Ahlul Bayt (as) and following them is a greater blessing that deserves the forgiveness of Allah the Almighty for His sinful servants. Then, how would *jihad* (strive) be for remaining fixed in this path?

Jihad in Islam is of two kinds; the *jihad* against enemy, which is called "the minor *jihad*", and the *jihad* against one's self (desires, fancies and lusts) which is called "the major *jihad*".

What concerns us in this subject is "the major *jihad*" which concern the soul and to treat it against perverse doctrinal diseases. One time, man is in *jihad* against himself and at another time in *jihad* against others. The *jihad* against oneself is accomplished by doing good deeds, being righteous, accompanying good people, offering worships and being truthful in dealing with people according to what the Ahlul Bayt (as) have determined by narrating from their grandfather (s) who had received it from Allah the Almighty.

As for the *jihad* against others, it is accomplished by the enjoining of good, forbidding from the wrong and inviting to the way of Allah through wisdom and good exhortation. Such kind of *jihad* can be accomplished through speaking at one time and through the pen another time. This kind of *jihad* is better and greater near Allah than the *jihad* by the sword. The Messenger of Allah (s) said:

The ink of scholars is better near Allah than the blood of martyrs.[1]

---

[1] *Kashf al Khafa* vol.2 p. 262.

What scholars write to show and support the truth and explain different affairs for people to be guided to the right path of Allah through irrefutable arguments and convincing proofs is better near Allah than the blood of martyrs, although the blood of martyrs is holy and highly sanctified in Islam. On the other side, we find that some people struggle to impose the religion by force and coercion, where Allah says:

There is no compulsion in religion; truly, the right way has become clearly distinct from error. [Qur'an, 2:256].

Therefore, scholars and thinkers must try their best to spread the true Islam,[1] to introduce the Imams of the Ahlul Bayt (as) and their

---

[1] From the situations that the *ulama* and jurisprudents face is the trial they are tried with, and here, the advantages of Major Jihad, the struggling against one's self, and suppressing it shall appear clearly!

Sheikh Murtadha al-Ansari was a religious authority and one of the *ulama* who had been educated in the school of the Ahlul Bayt (s). One night, one of his students saw in his sleep Iblis holding in his hands threads, ropes, and iron chains. When he asked him about that, Iblis replied, "These are traps by which I attract people to me. Last night, I tried all these tools against Sheikh al-Ansari, but I failed, and in the end, the thick iron chain was broken." When this student woke up, he hastened to the house of his teacher Sheikh al-Ansari and told him what he saw. After much insistence, the Sheikh said, "Last night, my wife was in parturition. My self enticed me to take from the monies of khums and zakat with me to hire a midwife, but I often and often resisted my self, and so on, until my wife gave birth to her child by herself. Then, I praised Allah too much."

On the other side, we see those who gave a fatwa on the killing of Imam al-Husayn ibn Ali (as) by saying, "Al-Husayn was killed by the sword of his grandfather (the Prophet Muhammad), because he rebelled against the imam of his time". This was the statement of Abu Bakr ibn al-Arabi al-Andalusi in his book *al-Awasim*, p. 232, verified by Muhyiddin al-Khateeb!

When Harun al-Rashid became the caliph, he was very fond of one of his father's bondmaids. He tried to sleep with her, but she said to him, "I am not fit for you, because your father has slept with me." However, he was very fond of her. He sent for his famous judge Abu Yousuf who was called as "the jurisprudent of the earth and its judge". The judge replied to the caliph, saying, "Violate the inviolability of your father and satisfy your lust, and

sciences, and spend from their monies and times. How many circles of disbelief, atheism and corruption are there which are financed with millions of dollars, whereas wealthy Muslims do not spend in the way of Allah except very scanty amounts!

We see that unbelievers come to Somalia under the pretense of saving its people from famine, whereas their brothers in religion are inadvertent to them.

We have seen the activities of the Christian Missionaries in the west and east of Africa, Egypt, Sudan, Indonesia and other Muslim countries. They offer to people over there, a little food and drugs that affect their hearts and they convert to Christianity after having been Muslims. Nonetheless, wealthy Muslims, whom Allah has endowed from His bounty and made as His deputies on earth to serve His people, are indifferent to everything. These wealthy people may go to the Hajj twenty times and spend much monies every year, whereas in their neighborhood there are many hungry, destitute sufferers who find no one to offer them a bite of food to satisfy their empty stomachs, or a piece of cloth to cover their naked bodies.

Did the Messenger of Allah (s) not say, "*The nearest of you to Allah is the most useful of you to His servants*"?[1]

Would Allah accept this deed (every-year-Hajj), which He has imposed on people as a one-time obligation throughout their lives? The Messenger of Allah (s) performed the Hajj one time in all his life because he might have wanted to make us realize that the wealthy people of this *ummah* may exaggerate in worships and ignore dealing with others (social communication and association), which is the basis of the Sharia. Therefore, the Prophet (s) often said:

Certainly, the religion is (human) dealing.

---

make it (the responsibility of sin) in my neck." Refer to *Tarikh al-Khulafa* by Jalaluddin Suyuti, p. 291.
Like al-Rashid, Abu Yousuf, and these stories there were many rulers, royal court preachers, drinking companions, officials…etc.
[1] *Bihar al Anwar* vol.77, p. 152, *hadith* no.110

So, how about the one who performs the Hajj many times while he is in debt to people, or that some of his relatives are poor whom he does not help or feel pity for?

If we add to that the wasting and prodigality of smoking among Muslims, then the punishment shall be severe near Allah on the Day of Punishment. If we look with a general view at what is spent on smoking by Muslims, we shall be surprised by the statistics. For example, the number of Muslims in the world today is more than one billion and if only one fifth of them smoke, then there shall be two hundred million smokers who spend two hundred million dollars a day, six billion dollars a month, and seventy-two billion dollars a year. Yes, Muslims spend at least seventy-two billion dollars a year to buy fatal diseases!

O Muslims fear Allah for your selves and properties! If these amount of only ten years are collected, they shall be 720 billion dollars, which shall suffice all poor Muslims in every spot of the earth:

And you deemed it trifle, while with Allah it is great. [Qur'an 24:15]

In the end, I would like to attract the attention of my Shia brothers, who follow the school of the Ahlul Bayt (as) towards the following points:

1. They have to argue with their Sunni brothers in the best manner and to avoid abusing and reviling which causes alienation. Imam Ali (as) said:

Do not be abusers or cursers, but you say: 'they did so and so', and this is more effective in argument.[1]

2. They have to avoid in their worships and dealings all the heresies that were not available at the time of the Prophet (s) or the time of the infallible imams (as) - such as beating oneself with injurious tools until bleeding in Ashura. It makes others keep away from embracing the creed of the Ahlul Bayt (as). Imam as-Sadiq (as) said:

---

[1] *Bihar al Anwar* vol.32, p. 399.

Be propagandists for us by your deeds not your sayings! Be a source of honor to us and not a source of disgrace for us![1]

3. They have to pay much attention in their lectures and discussions to scientific matters that have proofs and evidences in the reliable books of the Sunni themselves. They have to avoid weak traditions that provoke disputes and disagree with reason.

4. They have to try their best to be good, pious and righteous - as their infallible Imams (as) were. They have not to rely on the belief that Imam Ali (as) would intercede for his followers and adherents. Imam Ali (as) himself said:

Faith is not obtained by wishing or adorning, but faith is that which is fixed in the heart and proved by your sayings and doings.[2]

5. They have to take lessons from the lives of the infallible Imams (as) who have left incomparable treasures of knowledge and morals. For example, Nahjul Balaghah alone is a curative drug for all diseases. It is time for shaking off the ignorance and underdevelopment and take the nation to the high meanings of civilization and development. So, if the Imam of the Shia was the Gate to the City of knowledge, then his followers must be the first in all sciences.

6. The Shia have to unite and avoid all kinds of political partisanship and regional blocs. They have to strive to unite the religious authorities and obey them and thereafter, strive to unite all Muslims.

If the Shia followed these instructions, which I have taken from the Holy Qur'an, the Prophetic *Sunnah* and the school of the Ahlul Bayt (as) - security and peace shall prevail everywhere. If we changed the bad beliefs, ignorance and deviations inside ourselves, Allah will change our poverty and meanness into richness and glory, and make Imam al-Mahdi (as) reappear among us to fill the earth with justice and fairness after it has been filled with injustice and oppression.

---

[1] *Bihar al Anwar* vol.85, p. 136.

[2] *Bihar al Anwar* vol.69, p. 72.

THE SHIA ARE THE FOLLOWERS OF THE *SUNNAH*, BUT…

We have known from the previous discussions that the Twelver Shia are the true followers of the Prophet's *Sunnah*. This is a clear fact free from any doubt for whoever studies the teachings of Islam in all its beliefs, rulings and historical stages.

However, their enemies from "the Sunni", whose origin and goals we have known in the previous studies, defame the Shia. They criticize their beliefs and deeds, evoke suspicions against them, doubt their religion and sometimes fabricate false stories to defame and cause troubles and make others detest and despise them.

One of these fabrications is the claim that (a Shia believes that) Gabriel has betrayed the Trust and delivered the Mission to Muhammad instead of Ali. The second one is the unreal story of Abdullah ibn Saba' - the Jewish as the founder of Shiism. A third one is that the Shia have a special Qur'an called "*Mushaf Fatimah*"[1] other than the Qur'an available among all Muslims, or that the Shia prepare a horse every night at the door of the vault in Samarra' (in Iraq) waiting for al-Mahdi to ride that horse. They also claim that the Shia worship the graves and consider the Imams as gods, and they prostrate for stones. The worse of it is their claim that the Shia permit adultery and that they (more than one) sleep with the same woman in the same night. They fabricate many other lies against the Shia with not any bit of reality or evidence.

Anyhow, there are some objections that the Sunni put forth in our present time and make them as obstacles in the way of scientific research and then block the way to arrive at the sought truth. Such people when presenting such spurious arguments, which we shall discuss later on, have never read them in books or heard them from traditions. Yet, they swear that they have seen them with their own

---

[1] For details on *Mushaf Fatima* please visit: https://www.al-islam.org/mushaf-fatimah-abdullah-amini

eyes and have attended themselves. Therefore, this matter is too dangerous and serious and it may have a negative effect on the scholars and researchers who seek pure truth.

As we have promised readers that I will seek the truth and be neutral without any fanaticism towards any creed or sect, following the Prophet's tradition which says, *"Say the truth even if it is against you"*.[1] Also Allah the Almighty does not feel shy away from the truth. So, we must have a clear situation in this concern to be able say to the doers of good among the Shia that they have done well and to the wrong doers among them that they have done wrong and sinned. We do not fear in the blaming of any blamers, for we just seek the contentment of Allah the Almighty.

We must distinguish the fundamentals of Islam and that which is really in the sharia from traditions, habits and personal conclusions. And as we have been frank and daring in criticizing some companions of the Prophet (s) for the violations they had committed, we also have to criticize some Shia and not keep silent before their violations.

However, there is an important difference here. What the companions changed and invented became parts of the religion, which changed the rulings of Allah and His messenger, but what some of the Shia changed or invented did not change any divine rulings, nor did any one of them say it was obligatory; nevertheless, we must criticize it.

I shall discuss the most important points raised about these new invented things (heresies) through which some others criticize and try to falsify Shiism and ascribe to it different kinds of defects. Dear reader, you yourself may suffer from them and not find a satisfying answer that will assist you to face an opponent or convince yourself.

These new things in fact, are heresies fabricated against Shiism and Ahlul Bayt (as) who always refused and refuted every heresy whatever it was and whatever it adorned and called *"a good heresy"*. They, peace be upon them, have often and always declared that they did not say or do anything except according to the sayings and

---

[1] *Kanz al Ummal* vol.3, p. 359

doings of their grandfather the Messenger of Allah (s). Thus, everything that came out after the infallible Imams (as) are heresies - that harm and not benefit, alienate and not attract, complicate and not make it easy. The learned youth find in them a flaw in Shiism and may find it very difficult to justify or refute them.

We mention here, for example, some of those heresies, which the Sunni criticize the Shia for: the exaggeration in the rituals of consolation in Ashura where some people beat themselves with chains, daggers, and knives until they bleed, the disorder in offering the prayer and the indifference to other praying people, smoking in mosques and places of prayer, neglecting the Friday Prayer, and some other things that we shall mention later on which prevent many people from getting to the truth.

EVERY DAY IS ASHURA AND EVERY LAND IS KARBALA

If people would understand this meaning and observe it in every land they stay in and every day they live - the right of Islam for which Imam al-Husayn (as) was martyred, would be met!

If they did that, the face of Muslims in the world would change and they would be the masters instead of being slaves. However, a majority have understood it to be just to weep, wail, beat themselves with iron chains and knives - a dramatic performance which is repeated for a few hours of the year on the anniversary of Ashura and imitating some things like a parrot from the revolution of Imam al-Husayn (as). Then everything is to be forgotten thereafter. Most of the Sunnis criticize the Shia for such doings that are practiced on the day of Ashura which causes them to bleed.

Western and Arabic media in this age have spared no effort to show the Shia in Iran, during the season of Ashura, behaving as predatory beasts - knowing nothing but violence and admiring nothing better than to see bloods flowing from human beings. Though the Shia in India and Pakistan also practice this and much worse than that, the media - especially TVs, do not focus on them, rather they focus only on the Shia of Iran for a special purpose which is clear to everyone watching the events in the world and especially the affairs of Islam and Muslims.

The media do not show the Friday Prayer in Tehran where more than two millions gather to offer the prayer congregationally behind the President (as the imam of the prayer). The media do not show the wonderful reverence covering millions of Muslims while reciting the *du'a of Kumayl* on the nights of Friday when streets become fully crowded, avenues are closed and traffics stop. Here, you see men, women, old, young and children supplicating to their Lord humbly in the calmness of night and asking for forgiveness in the dawn.

These media are only concerned in showing the rituals of Ashura - focusing on the beating of heads with knives and chains and the bloody scenes involving a few persons!

It is true that what some of the Shia do during these rituals is not from religion at all, even if *mujtahids* give fatwas to say that there are great rewards in such deeds. These doings are but habits, traditions and emotions that overcome some people and make them behave unusually and little by little these habits become part of the folklore inherited by one generation from another in blind imitation and without sense. In fact, some ordinary people feel that the shedding of blood by beating oneself is a deed that brings man closer to Allah and that whoever does not do that does not love Imam al-Husayn (as).

When I ponder with myself and in spite of my being Shia, after knowing satisfactorily that Shiism is the true creed - I am not satisfied with those ugly scenes that alienate souls and sound minds, especially when someone unclothes himself and beats himself with an iron tool in crazy movements shouting out too loudly: Husayn, Husayn!

The odd thing in this matter that makes you doubt it is that you see those very persons, who behave unusually and whom you think that the sorrow for Imam al-Husayn (as) has affected terribly, a little after the end of the rituals, jest, laugh and eat sweets as if everything ends with the end of the rituals. The oddest of all this is that most of these people are not religious or pious. Therefore, I have permitted myself to criticize them directly many times and say to them that what they did was just folklore and blind imitation.[1]

---

[1] These doings are doings of ignorant and underdeveloped people; they are a way of expressing their love and allegiance to Imam al-Husayn (s) as they think. Once, one of them said to a religious authority that he had served food for al-Abbas (s) and all the time he did not take off his shoes. The alim (scholar) asked him how he performed wudhu' and prayers then, but he paid no attention, thinking that he would get his reward from al-Abbas (s).
On the other side, we find the circles of dhikr (remembrance) near the Sunni with their different methods like Qadiriyyah, Naqshabandiyyah, and others, as shows for nothing but to be close to the chief of the creed (method). These

May Allah have mercy on the martyr Muhammad Baqir as-Sadr who helped me much in this calamity when I asked him before my converting a Shia. He said to me, "*The beating of bodies and shedding of blood that you see is from the practices of ordinary and ignorant people. No one of the ulama ever practices it. In fact, they always prevent and prohibit it.*"

I hate heresies and fight them wherever and with whomsoever they are. We must make the Shia aware to be able to give up heresies and make the Sunni understand that these practices cannot be obstacles preventing them from knowing the truth and following the Ahlul Bayt (as). They do not have to observe the practices of ordinary and ignorant Shia which are unfounded in true Shiism.

Anyhow, we have to imitate our great example the Messenger of Allah (s). When his uncle and protector Abu Talib died, he felt great sorrow for him. He felt this when his most beloved wife Khadijah died. And then he suffered the terrible loss of his uncle Hamza who was martyred and maimed and his body was found torn into pieces with no liver which had been taken out and chewed by Hind, the wife of Abu Sofyan. He felt great sorrow in all these instances, but he just wept out of his affection for them. He wept for his son Ibrahim, for his grandson al-Husayn (as) when Gabriel told him that he would be murdered, and wept for his brother and cousin Ali (as) when he

---

shows are done by inserting nails in the head and eyes, and daggers and swords in the body with tambourines and smokes and shaking the heads and bodies in harmony with the melodies. Some of them rotate for continuous hours.

We knew some of them well that so-and-so drank intoxicants, so-and-so did not offer prayers, so-and-so was impious... did not refrain from abusing Allah and His messenger...committed adultery or sodomy...etc. However, those persons were invited by the chief (Sheikh) to attend the circles. They did not leave except when blood came out of their bodies, and then the Sheikh cried out: "Get out! Either you have not washed after janaba (sexual intercourse), or you have come here while having drunk wine...!"

I say that these things are recent heresies, which the colonists have emphasized on and fed for certain purposes. They are about to vanish among the Shia; so would they be so among our Sunni brothers?

foreknew that the most wretched of people would dye his (Imam Ali as) beard with the blood of his head.

The Prophet Muhammad (s) often wept and he ordered Muslims to feign crying if they could not cry. He sought the protection of Allah from the eye that did not shed tears. Nevertheless, he prohibited Muslims from being excessive in expression of their sorrow, beating their faces or tearing their clothes. Then, what is this about beating one's head or body with iron tools until one bleeds?

Our first imam after the Prophet Muhammad (s) - Ali ibn Abi Talib (as) did not do anything like that when his brother and cousin the Messenger of Allah (s) died. After a short time of six months, his wife Fatima (sa) left to join her father in the better world. Imam Ali (as) felt great pain and sorrow, but he did never do anything unusual as what ordinary people do nowadays.

Imam al-Hasan (as) and Imam al-Husayn (as) did nothing of that when they lost their merciful grandfather Muhammad (s), and their kind, loving mother Fatima (sa), nor when their father Imam Ali (as), who was the best of all human beings after the Prophet Muhammad, was killed by the cursed ibn Muljam in the mihrab.

Imam as-Sajjad (as) as well, did nothing unusual when he saw scenes that had never happened anywhere else at all. He saw with his own eyes the massacre of Karbala when his father, uncles, brothers, cousins and companions were murdered and after this terrible event also he faced great difficulties and suffering that even mountains would not be able bear.

History did not record that any of the infallible Imams (as) did something of that or ordered their followers to do it. The only thing they did was that they liked to hear from some poets' elegies about the Ahlul Bayt (as) where they wept and felt sorrow and ordered people to weep and be sad for the Ahlul Bayt (as). In fact, this is a recommended thing if not obligatory.

I myself, attended many occasions of Ashura in many countries and did not find anyone of the *ulama* doing that at all. Scholars and learned people of the Shia avoid that and try to refute and forbid it.

We, after having become Shia, do not imitate ordinary people of the Shia in all what they do without researching and being certain of its truth. We celebrate the anniversary of Ashura by reciting the *maqtal* (the story of Imam al-Husayn's martyrdom) and the tragedies that the Ahlul Bayt (as) faced. We weep and feel sad for that. The point is that the heart should respond and weep with the eyes. Thereafter all of man's entity should submit to the remembrance of Allah the Almighty and to the truth that He has revealed. The hearts should promise their Lord to follow the path of Imam al-Husayn (as) which is the same path as of the Messenger of Allah (s) and all the Ahlul Bayt (peace be on all of them).

Ashura - with its condolence, sorrows, weeping, observing of remembrance and taking lessons from its situations and heroes, remains pure for the loyal Shia who abide by the true *Sunnah* of the Prophet (s) and the instructions of the infallible imams (as). On the other hand, the acts and practices of ordinary Shia remain liable to criticism and fabrication by those who fish in troubled waters to distort the beliefs of the Shia and separate them from the Ahlul Bayt (as) and then consider them as disbelievers.

Praise be to Allah Who has made us from the discerning Shia who has been guided to the truth through study and research and not from imitating the Shia.

Thus, readers have to be exemplar in abiding with the true Prophet's *Sunnah* transmitted by the infallible Imams (as).[1]

---

[1] It is well known that many *ulama* like Sayyid Muhsin al-Amin and nowadays Ayatollah Sayyid Ali Khamenei, Ayatollah Sayyid Muhammad Husayn Fadhlullah, and many others have given a fatwa that these practices (beating oneself with iron tools) are not permissible. Those, who say they are permissible, mean some things else. That one of the scholars said, "The swords that the Shia unsheathed in the face of oppressors are used today to strike their heads with" - is so that the British gave some swords to the processions of the Shia on Ashura!

These traditions came from the nations of Asia and India where there were groups practicing such rituals in their celebrations. When they gathered in Karbala, every group (procession) showed its way in expressing emotions. It is worth mentioning that different colonies lived in Karbala and kept on imitating their ancestors that made others admire what they practiced. Therefore, these things became as a part of the rituals of Ashura…

In addition to that, some people, who love Imam al-Husayn (s), think that the issue of Imam al-Husayn (s) shall die out if there is no shedding of blood...etc.

The pressures against the Shia in the past, during the Ottoman reign, and then during the oppressive rule of the Iraqi tyrannical regime that prevented military men, placemen, and state officials from going to Karbala on Ashura and punish (if not hang) them if they went there, made people emotionally practice these traditions.

Nowadays, these practices have become limited because of wide comprehension and the fatwas of the religious authorities. In the Islamic Republic of Iran, these practices have abated 98%. So have they in Iraq, Lebanon, and in different percentages in India, Pakistan, and other places according to the milieu surrounding them. In fact, these practices are practiced by the ignorant among ordinary people who think that the cause of Imam al-Husayn (s) to them is greater than the fatwas of so-and-so of *ulama*!!!

THE SHIA AND THE PRAYER

Some young Sunnis criticize the Shia about what they call as "the confusion in prayer and lack of submission".

In the congregational prayers, some of the Shia do not care for the rows and it does not impact them that there are always gaps left between the praying men. It is often noticed that the first row is not yet complete whereas there are great numbers of people offering the prayer behind the imam in the other rows without caring for the order of the first row.

It is also noticed among the Shia that some people come in and go out of the mosque during the prayer, passing between the praying ones. They often pass between a praying person and the place of his prostration in the direction of the qibla, which annuls the prayer according to the beliefs of the Sunni.

It is true that the prayer of the Sunni is more orderly than the Shia's. When you offer the prayer with the Sunni brothers, you see the imam, before beginning the prayer, turn towards the people coming to offer the prayer behind him and asks them to straighten out and form the rows saying to them, *"Be orderly (in your lines), may Allah have mercy on you! Impact your rows and do not leave gaps for Satan, because the impacting of rows is from (the conditions of) the prayer."* Therefore, you see the praying ones press together until their shoulders and bodies stick together and see that they compete to fill the gaps.[1]

---

[1] These things are true and real, but we see that the Sunni mosques are built very big and adorned with ornamentations and decorations and great monies from inside and outside their countries are spent on them, besides that their *ulama* too much breach and emphasize on these matters. However, we find that the Sunni do not care much for the matter of purity and impurity. We find this in their creeds and especially the Hanbali School.
Earlier I thought that wearing gold by Sunni men was permissible, because many of their men did that, but it appeared that all their creeds prohibited it. They invite to pray behind every good and bad man (as the imam in the

When the prayer is being offered, they do not permit anyone to pass in front of a praying one, even if the prayer is a recommended and not an obligatory one. They believe that according to some traditions narrated in their *sihah* (books of Hadith), that the prayer is annulled when someone passes in front of a praying one. In some of their traditions, it is said that the one, who passes in front of a praying one, is a devil who must be repelled and pushed away.

As for the Shia, they do not care for such things during their prayers. I offered prayers behind many Shia imams[1] most of whom were from the known religious authorities and in many countries, but I did not see anyone of them turn to the people, who had come to offer the prayer behind him, before the beginning of the prayer to ask them to regulate their lines or fill the gaps between them. I also saw no one, whether an imam or one who led the praying ones, prevent others from passing in front of a praying one.

I am convinced that the school of the Ahlul Bayt (as) does not say that the prayer becomes null when someone passes in front of a praying one. This is in accordance with neither reason nor traditions, because the things that annul the prayer are limited and known to the

---

prayer). You may find in the row of prayers a disbelieving, secular ruler and his mercenaries, and this is a very doing of Satan!

As for the Shia, they see that mosques are Allah's...and they are shelters for all Muslims, and that the building of a mosque is something spontaneous, simple, and with no constrictions. The Shia pay very much attention for mosques to be purified. Mosques for the Shia have many strict rulings that must be observed and they are often breached by the Shia *ulama*. Anyhow, this problem can be solved through a lecture or by hanging a poster on the wall.

Are we not invited to (make it easy and not difficult and not to make others alienate the religion)? How often I find Sunni youth, who do not go to mosques, for either they have been shocked and driven away or because of those difficult rituals! We the Shia, think that the important thing is the coming of people to mosques first, and then to educate about it and not to shout at people just because they pass in front of us. Let us deal with others through the Islamic morals and manners and not through disgusting nomadic fanaticism.

[1] "Imam" here refers to the one leading others in offering a prayer.

Shia and the Sunni, and certainly, the passing in front of a praying one is not one of them.

Al-Bukhari himself mentions in his *Sahih* that once it was mentioned to Aa'isha that a dog, a donkey and woman (when passing before a praying one) would annul the prayer. She denied that and said, "*You have compared us (women) to dogs and donkeys! By Allah, I saw the Messenger of Allah (s) offer the prayer while I was on the bed between him and the qibla...*"[1]

This is a strong proof and a convincing argument showing that the prayer is not annulled by the passing of man or animal between the praying person and the (direction of) *qibla* even to the Sunni.[2]

---

[1] *Sahih al-Bukhari* vol. 1 p. 137.

[2] This matter is like that of building a mosque or offering the prayers where there is a grave. The matter is based on the rule of "the preventing of excuses" for fear that it may be regarded as worshipping the one in the grave. Certainly, we have not found until now even one Muslim who worshipped a grave in the last 1416 years (the book in Arabic was published in 1416 A.H.).

According to precautionary basis, some of the Sunni destroyed the graves of their saints or separated them with high fences. They and especially the Wahhabis criticized impudently the Shia for making graves inside the mosques. Once, one of my friends was in Hijaz. Some Sunni people from different Muslim countries gathered around him asking, "Why do you make the graves of your imams as mosques?!"

Importantly, since the passing in front of a praying one does not annul the prayer for the two sects (the Shia and the Sunni) and since they depend on Hadith, so this is refuted and they (the Wahhabis) have no right to impose it on any Muslim. In fact, they harm and accuse other Muslims of different accusations because of silly rulings.

This reminds me of an event where someone was committing an impermissible thing inside a mosque. He saw someone else spit on the ground of the mosque. He got up and beat him why he spat on the ground. The other one resisted and beat him up saying to him, "Is your committing of sin worse or my spitting on the ground?"

Would that they cared for purity – they will not prostrate on permissible things, refrain from wearing gold (by men), wearing foreign leather clothes (coming from non-Muslim countries), standing before Allah (during

However, not everything permissible is worthy of recommendation or praise. If a Muslim is careful not to pass over the necks of praying people lest he treads on them while in prostration to Allah, it is a recommended, praiseworthy moral act that Islam prefers and civic sense acknowledges. It shows reverence and respect to the prayer and the one who is praying to his Lord, solemnly supplicating in a very high spiritual state. So is it not acceptable from anyone to interrupt a praying person's submissiveness and state of spirituality?

Do you not see that the Messenger of Allah (s) has prohibited to sit in the public ways where there is embarrassment for passers and especially women who feel shy and embarrassed to walk through a way where there are men sitting in?

Since we talk about and seek the truth in all our studies, and since we know that Allah does not feel shy of the truth, we say that the Shia should benefit from their Sunni brothers in this morality that gives praying ones sanctity and holiness as long as they are standing, bowing or prostrating before the Lord of the worlds.

Once, I said this to some imams of the Shia and they confessed their shortcoming in this regard, but one of them objected to me saying that these matters were superficial and the advantage lay in the essence. I replied, "These matters are not superficial, but they are systematic. These bring gravity and reverence and make others respect us. Surely, our religion is a religion of a system that loves orderliness and hates confusion. Allah says:

Attend constantly to prayers and to the middle prayer and stand up truly obedient to Allah. [Qur'an, 2:238]

Surely Allah loves those who fight in His way in ranks as if they were a firm and compact wall. [Qur'an, 61:4]

The Surah in which this verse is, has been called 'the *surah of as-Saff* or rank', since rank or order is very important near Allah.

Perhaps, the problem of the Shia concerning the congregational prayer where some lack of seriousness and indifference is found is

---

prayers) while their stomachs are filled with impermissible meat (of unlawfully slaughtered animals)…etc?.

because throughout the history they have faced severe conditions. It was very difficult for them to offer congregational prayers behind Sunni imams who changed the rulings of prayer and used to abuse Imam Ali (as) and the Ahlul Bayt (as) in their prayers. On the other hand, they avoided offering the prayer in a special congregation, because this meant that they would be accused of being "*rawafidh*, rejecters" and this would lead to doing away with them.

Therefore, they often offered congregational prayers with the Sunni out of *taqiyya*[1], then immediately left the place after the end of the prayer. Most of them might offer the prayer again when they would be in their houses.

We may conclude from this too that the dissenters of the Ahlul Bayt (as) have called themselves "*the people of the Sunnah and congregation*" because the majority of Muslims followed them and offered the prayer in their congregation, whereas the Shia offered their prayers behind their own imam, and thus they were minority, like a white spot in a black dress, after their appearing as a special sect.

After their having appeared as a special Islamic school adhering to the jurisprudence of the Ahlul Bayt (as), the Shia limited themselves to strictly pray behind a just, knowledgeable, abstinent imam in accordance with the religious texts in this regard on one hand and as a reaction to the Sunni, who were permitted to pray behind any good or corrupted man on the other hand.

This has also affected the congregational prayer of the Shia - so you see that when one of them comes into a mosque and does not know the imam of the congregational prayer, he offers the prayer individually in one of the mosque's corners. It is because he does not know the imam, so he does not trust him (as to be a just person or not).

On the other side, the Sunni are wasteful in this concern in that they permit the prayer behind anyone whether good or bad, pious or impious, abstinent or corrupted. We have talked before about Abdullah ibn Umar who offered prayers behind Yazid ibn

---

[1] Precautionary concealing of one's real belief.

Mu'awiyah, Hajjaj ibn Yousuf Thaqafi and Najdah al-Khariji, and all of these three were openly corrupted and dissolute.

The same thing can be said about the Shia that some of them do not consider it permissible to offer prayer behind anyone except when he is known to the praying person himself, as a just and pious person. Some of the Shia are not satisfied to see tens of Muslims offer prayer behind so-and-so imam except when they themselves become certain of his justice and piety. Only then they would offer their prayer behind him.

All this is because of precaution in the religion and care to offer their prayer in the best way possible, so that Allah may accept it. It is as if the Shia think that their prayer shall not be accepted if it is offered behind an imam not known to them. It is as if Allah has ordered them to inquire very about the affairs of religion in an accurate manner[1] and as if they always think of this verse:

...and you deemed it an easy matter while with Allah it is grievous. [Qur'an 24:15]

I believe that Islam is the religion of nature, and nature is the most moderate of affairs. Allah the Almighty says:

And thus We have made you a moderate (just) nation.

---

[1] Since the Shia were exiled from the stage of the Muslims' life, their fatwas are very strict and precautionary. For example, you see that they are very careful and strict to the precedents of the prayer such as purity, ghusl, and wudhu' to a degree that you cannot see any of their mosques empty of men who are scrupulous about purity, recitation or the number of rak'as of the prayer. Some stipulate conditions for the imam of congregational prayer as if they are conditions of a high religious authority.
However, most of the recent *ulama*, including Ayatollah Sayyid Muhammad Husayn Fadhlullah who criticize in his lectures this excessive strictness, consider the matter easy with no complications. This fact results from care, precaution, and perfection of deeds. But as for those who say "even though"...in any how the wudhu' is performed, to offer the prayer led by a pious or impious person, to be indifferent to impurities that stain one's body and clothes...to say 'everything is alright' and 'everything is permissible'...it is a very serious matter that requires much pondering!

[Qur'an, 2:143]

The Messenger of Allah (s) says:

The best of affairs is the moderate one. There should be neither excess nor waste.

So the Sunni's belief which is much indifferent, to a degree that it permits the offering of the prayer behind every good or bad person is excessive. And, the Shia's belief is also excessive to a degree in that they do not permit the prayer except behind the just imam who is unique of his kind. It is wasteful of the opportunity to pray in congregation.

The true Islam stops in the middle between the two, in this concern. It does not agree with those who say it is permissible to follow a corrupt or the other side which stipulates for justice (honesty) of an imam who does not commit corruption openly. This is enough for others to offer the prayer behind him.

The Prophet (s) often recommended his companions and all Muslims by saying:

Make it easy and do not make it difficult. Give good news and do not alienate others from the religion.

Do not complicate it for yourself, lest Allah makes it more complicated for you, as He did for the children of Israel.

Since we are talking about excess here, it may be useful to mention what some Muslims do in excess. You may see some who when performing the *wudhu'*, move from this side to that side under the lamp while turning their hands and arms up and down to see if there is a needle-eye-spot untouched by water – in which case they repeat the *wudhu'*- again just because of doubt (although for the Shia, doubt does not annul certainty).

You see this also when they come to prayer and begin reciting the sura of al-Fatiha. Their tongues begin to stutter and they are unable to pronounce the words, and then they repeat "*walladh dhalleen*" four or five times, and this happens to them in every rak'at.

Once, I attended the congregational prayer with one of them, and then I regretted my praying behind him, because that prayer became boring in the way he offered it. Later on, I spoke to him frankly and mentioned to him before a group of other friends, the saying of an American man who had become Muslim and written a book. He had said in it, *"Praise be to Allah Who has made me know Islam before I knew Muslims."* I added, *"If I had known this kind of Shia initially, I would have become alienated from them and not bothered myself with all the research."*

Certainly, Islam is the religion of ease, simplicity and leniency. I do not mean by this being indifferent to the rulings of the Sharia - God forbid! I myself disapprove of the schools that interpret the religion of Allah according to their own opinions. However, when you see that all excess and exaggeration that is from the human beings themselves, your soul may be alienated from the religion.[1]

You recite these sayings of Allah:

...and has not laid upon you any hardship in religion. [Qur'an, 22:78]

Allah desires ease for you, and He does not desire for you difficulty. [Qur'an, 2:185]

---

[1] The Shia say that the imam (the leader of prayers) is to offer (as) the prayer of the weakest of the praying ones that means to pay attention to the old, weak, or sick persons.

Nevertheless, some people, and because of precaution often seek perfection in worships, wudhu', and purity, especially when they read that their infallible imams (as) did not perform wudhu' except with pure water, did not wear except permissible (well procured) clothes, and even did not carry a sword belt if it was from leather that was unknown whether or not the animal was legally slaughtered, and that when they stood before Allah, they would shake and change color...

Therefore, our jurisprudents see that such people are sick with scruple, and they often blame them for this. A scholar, who wants to do so (being excessive or scrupulous), is not to lead congregation or give a fatwa in these matters.

Our thought is the same about Sufis, Salafites (puritans) and others who have violated the right path. Whoever wants to practice such things has to practice them inside his house and away from people, because such things are from Satan, whereas our religion is a religion of ease and a civilized way of life for all humankind.

When you see the sayings and doings of such people who make the religion of Allah a nightmare with all hardships that an ordinary man cannot bear - it makes you doubt and suspect everything. It then paves the way for Satan to enter your heart.

The most dangerous disease is when a Muslim becomes so obsessive that he does not know how many rak'ats he offers, or he has offered them all or not, or when he has offered the prayer. Satan plays with him in every worship and ritual. This may exceed so much as to hinder the worship in their dealings and relations with people. Then one's life becomes unbearable hell, from which may Allah protect you and us.

THE SHIA AND THE FRIDAY PRAYER

The important matter which the Sunni raise and criticize the Shia for on all occasions, is the matter of neglecting and not offering the Friday Prayer. Some of them are so excessive in their view that they consider the Shia as disbelievers for not offering the Friday Prayer, relying on a Prophet's tradition that says:

"*Whoever gives up the Friday (prayer) three times does turn his back to Islam.*"

They also narrate another tradition that the Prophet (s) when once was asked about someone who gave up the Friday Prayer, he said:

"*He shall be in the Fire.*"[1]

Regarding the truth, we say that the Shia disagree among themselves on the legality of the Friday Prayer during the age of the Occultation of Imam al-Mahdi (as). The Shia jurisprudents are of two opinions; some say it is obligatory at all times, and others say it is not obligatory unless all its conditions are available and one of its conditions is that it must be offered under the rule of a just ruler.

Before I turned a Shia, I truly say that I too much approved of Sheikh al-Khalisi who offered the Friday Prayer in the Mosque of Imam al-Kadhim (as) in Baghdad. Sometimes I traveled from Najaf or Karbala to participate in the Friday Prayer there. At that time, I wondered at the courage of Sheikh Mahdi al-Khalisi[2] who did not

---

[1] *Al-Muwatta* vol.1, p. 111.

[2] It is worth mentioning that once Sheikh Muhammad al-Khalisi, the father of Sheikh Mahdi al-Khalisi, went to the religious authority Sayyid al-Khoei in Najaf, talking with him about the matter of the Friday Prayer, relying on this Qur'anic verse:

O you who believe! when the call is made for prayer on Friday, then hasten to the remembrance of Allah... [Qu'ran 62:9]

Sayyid al-Khoei pondered for a while and then said to him, "Who is the caller?" Sheikh Muhammad al-Khalisi could not answer and he went back to Baghdad, keeping on offering the Friday Prayer there.

care for the criticism of some ulama who did not think that the Friday Prayer was obligatory. He believed it was obligatory and he offered it in the best way. I noticed at that time (in 1968 AD) the masses of people who gathered in his mosque, showing him great reverence and respect.[1]

I also wondered at those who criticized him for offering the Friday Prayer. I said to myself, "How do these people defame an alim (scholar) who, due to his ijtihad, offers the prayer that Allah the Almighty has ordered it to be offered when He has said:

O you who believe! when the call is made for prayer on Friday, then hasten to the remembrance of Allah... [Qur'an 62:9]

I repeated this saying before some of those people, defending Sheikh al-Khalisi and seeking for him different excuses and proofs. However, some of them revealed what was inside their hearts. They said to me that Sheikh al-Khalisi did not recite in the *azan* - "*the third witness*". I asked what "the third witness" was, and they said that it was, "*I bear witness that Ali is the friend (wali) of Allah*".

I spent that night asking myself if that is reason enough to criticize and defame that man. I researched much in the books, and I read the books of his (Sheikh Mahdi al-Khalisi) father, but I did not find anything except true knowledge, piety and concern for the unity

---

It has been mentioned that Abu Hanifa too thought that it should not be offered except when available under a just ruler. Be it known that it is now offered in the Islamic Republic of Iran that calls for offering it in the other countries and in Syria. Sayyid Fadhlullah calls for it in Lebanon. In fact, it is offered in Lebanon now.

In any case what kind of Friday Prayer is that which is offered under the authority of an oppressive ruler - when the Friday Sermon is dictated under his supervision, or when the imams of mosques are appointed according to his desire and mood from among those who praise and glorify the regime and its policies?!!

[1] In past and present times, many of the great *ulama* considered Friday prayers as obligatory. For example, Ayatullah Araki established Friday prayers 50 years ago in Qom.

of Muslims. This (concern about the unity of Muslims), some people considered to be flattery of the Sunni.

However and despite the fact that some people tried to make me dislike and keep myself away from him, whenever I visited al-Kadhimiyyah (in Baghdad where Imam al-Khadim (as) is buried), I offered the Friday Prayer behind Sheikh al-Khalisi and listened to his sermons, from which I benefited much. Whenever I sat with him and listened to his talks, I liked him more. Still I remained reserved, justifying that the Shia knew him more than I did.

On the other hand, I remained confused between the two *ijtihads* (deductions) of which one said that the Friday Prayer was obligatory and the other said it was not.

I said that I could not understand that, except when I would reach the required degree of *ijtihad*. However, after the victory of the Islamic Revolution in Iran and the establishment of the Islamic Republic there, the Friday Prayer was offered since the first Friday after the victory. And since then, the Islamic Republic has spared no effort for the sake of the unity of Muslims. Then, I knew the value of Sheikh al-Khalisi and became certain of his loyalty and the truth in his mission. I remain until today with desire to see him, so that Allah may make me meet him from a near distance as a happy occasion and Allah is powerful over everything.

Anyhow, the Shia are until now on two thoughts; some offer the Friday Prayer, and the others do not, waiting for the reappearance of Imam al-Mahdi (may Allah hasten his reappearance).

I wish from the depth of my heart that the Friday Prayer is offered in every village and town of the Muslim countries, for it evokes great reward and has many benefits that only Allah the Glorified knows about.

In many lectures, I invited the Muslim colonies in the different countries which I visited, to offer the Friday Prayer, taking the Islamic Republic of Iran and its leader as their example and trying to bring their hearts close to each other and make Muslims - Sunni and Shia - love each other as a single united nation.

We pray to Allah, the Powerful to help us thank and worship Him well, as is His due and to reconcile our hearts with each other to be true brothers by His Grace, He is Hearing, Responding to the prayer.

SMOKING IN THE PLACES OF PRAYER

How often is it that the Sunni criticize the Shia for smoking in the mosques and say that it is an abominable doing from the deeds of the Satan?

We can say that smoking is a common phenomenon among the Shia. When you come into their mosques for the first time, you are shocked by that.[1]

I remember that when I traveled to Holy Najaf for the first time, I was shocked by this phenomenon. I found it odd and so I asked some of their (the Shia) *ulama* about it. They gave answers which have not convinced me until now. Some of them say that smoking is neither impermissible nor disapproved because there is no (legal) text concerning it either from the Prophet (s) or from the infallible Imams (as) and that analogy is not permissible to them. Some others say that they do not smoke in the mosques, but only in *Husayniyyahs*[2] which are not from mosques.

As for the first answer, a Muslim cannot accept that everything about which no religious text have been mentioned, is permissible, because the texts are either general including all prohibited vices like this saying of Allah:

Say: My Lord has only prohibited indecencies, those of them that are apparent as well as those that are concealed. [Qur'an, 7:33]

Or special, in which something is mentioned by name, like these sayings of Allah:

...And go not nigh to adultery. [Qur'an, 17:32]

---

[1] To be the truth, we should say that this custom cannot be seen in the mosques in Iran.
[2] Holy places like mosques but do not have the same rulings and conditions of mosques.

..And do not kill any one whom Allah has forbidden, except for a just cause. [Qur'an, 17:33]

O you who believe! do not devour usury. [Qur'an, 3:130]

Or, the sayings of the Prophet (s):

He, who cheats us, is not from us.[1]

Whoever fabricates lies against me (as if I have said), let him take his seat in the Fire.[2]

Cigarettes were not available at the time of the Prophet (s) and the times of the infallible Imams (as). Therefore, it is not possible to have a religious text about smoking from Allah, His messenger or the infallible Imams. It is the same as with regard to many impermissible things available nowadays that are included by the general texts, such as lottery, horseracing and modern games that cause many profits with no effort.

Smoking can be included by this saying of Allah the Almighty:

... and do not squander wastefully. Surely, the squanderers are the fellows of the devils and the devil is ever ungrateful to his Lord. [Qur'an, 17:26-27]

The Messenger of Allah (s) said:

Squandering is to spend even one dirham on what does not benefit you.

Is there squandering worse than to spend one's money on things that are harmful to his health and dangerous to his life?

Smoking is also included by this saying of the Messenger of Allah (s):

There should be no harm (against oneself) and no harming (against others) in Islam.[3]

---

[1] *Sahih Muslim* vol.1, p. 99

[2] *Sahih al-Bukhari* vol.1, p. 38

[3] *Sunan Ibn Maja* vol.2, p. 48

Is there any harm worse than cancer, which has been proven by medicine and sciences of today to affect smokers and do away with their lives? Smoking is proven to cause dyspnea and that the nicotine in cigarettes causes addiction, which a smoker can hardly get rid of.

Sociologists in the developed countries knew the dangers of smoking; therefore, smoking was prohibited in the public halls, state centers, airplanes, trains and other means of transport. Lastly, the British government forbade smoking in the metro and the same was done by the French government.

Modern medicine has proved that a smoker, in addition to harming himself, harms others who sit with him in a place or in a vehicle during a journey. Therefore, smokers are forbidden to smoke inside public places and are forced to go out to smoke in the open air if they want to smoke, as a kind of regard for others' feelings and safety.

This is actually what the Prophet Muhammad (s) meant when he said:

There should be no harm (to oneself) and no harming (against others).

In fact, in this saying there is a prohibition for smokers not to smoke even if they are alone, because a Muslim is prohibited from harming himself, as he is prohibited from harming others.

Do you not see that Islam has prohibited suicide? Islam considers suicide as one of the major sins. A Muslim is not free to harm even his own body, because his body is a possession of Allah and a Muslim has no right to do anything to his body except that which pleases Allah the Glorificd.

Nowadays, we hear that the developed countries prohibit drivers from having alcohol while driving their vehicle, because it may cause a fatal accident. In the same way as they prohibit smokers from smoking in public places because they may harm others, we see them apply the rule of "no harm to others" and they neglect the rule of "no harm to oneself" in accordance with the law of FREEDOM which considers man to be free to do to unto himself whatever he likes, as long as he keeps the condition that he does not harm others.

Islam does not acknowledge this absolute freedom and does not permit man to do anything to himself except what Allah has permitted within the limits that the Sharia has determined for him. Therefore, Allah has said:

...and cast not yourselves to perdition with your own hands. [Qur'an, 2: 195]

And, the Prophet (s) said, "*There should be no harm to oneself and no harm to others.*"

If we supposedly agree with Muslim smokers, who say that there is no any text which prohibits smoking, then we do not agree with them on allowing smoking inside the mosques and other places of prayer, worship and meeting of Muslims. Therefore, smokers must attend these places as non-smokers.

Here comes the problem of their second answer when saying that smoking is not practiced in mosques but in *Husayniyyahs*. To define a *Husayniyyah* for those who do not know it, we say that a *Husayniyyah* is a building built by the Shia and entailed for Imam Husayn (as) where ceremonies of anniversaries of births and deaths of the infallible Imams (as) are held besides the anniversary of Ashura and the Eid al-Ghadir. Other ceremonies of different occasions are also held in the *Husayniyyah*. These *Husayniyyahs* are often furnished with precious carpets and most of them have a mihrab of prayer.

If one of the Shia says that it is permissible to smoke inside a *Husayniyyah* because it is not a mosque, we say that this is a confession that smoking is not permissible in mosques first of all. Secondly, every place in which a prayer is offered is "a mosque". When we attend on any occasion in a *Husayniyyah*, we find the meeting full of remembrance of Allah and people praying to Him to send blessings on the Prophet Muhammad and his progeny (peace be on them all), surrounded by the angels who pray Allah to forgive the believers. So, is it nice to pollute such meetings with bad smells that harm people besides the angels?

I myself find it odd from the religious authorities of the Shia who prohibit the playing with chess, but do not prohibit smoking, though there is a great difference between the harms of each of them. And I find it odd too that one of the grand authorities prohibits his followers by *ijtihad*, from smoking tobacco as a way of resisting the British companies that promote it, but does not prohibit it again, by *ijtihad* too, to keep his followers safe from the fatal diseases and the squandering that Allah detests much!!

I often criticized this state and discussed these matters with some of *ulama*, but I did not find any one who had enough courage to prohibit smoking,[1] neither among the Shia nor among the Sunni.

---

[1] From the *ulama*, who have given a fatwa on prohibiting smoking, is Ayatollah Sayyid Muhammad Husayn Fadhlullah, relying on this Qur'anic verse that prohibits wine:
They ask you about intoxicants and games of chance. Say: in both of them there is a great sin and means of profit for men, and their sin is greater than their profit. [Qu'ran 2:219]
It is understood that everything, whose sin (and harm) is more than its benefit, is impermissible, and according to this rule, smoking is impermissible too. Justifying it in this way, Ayatollah Sayyid Fadhlullah has given a fatwa of "obligatory precaution", because there are many believers and *ulama* who have been addicted to smoking, and it may be difficult for them, or they may suffer physical harm if they give up smoking.
As for mosques and those who frequent them, it may be considered by a new Muslim, who has recently embraced Islam, in the west as a kind of binding to his freedom; this is beside the bad treatment that a smoker may face there. Perhaps out of ignorance, a smoker may be invited negatively not to smoke there.
It has been mentioned that once Imam Hasan and Imam Husayn (peace be on them) saw an old man perform the wudhu' incorrectly. They did not scold him, but kindly said to him, "O old man, would you please watch us both and say which of us performs the wudhu' correctly?" When they finished their wudhu', the old man said, "By Allah, the wudhu' of both of you is better and more correct than mine." By this way, the old man corrected his wudhu'. Would that we learn from the Ahlul Bayt (s) the morals and etiquette of inviting others to do something!
In a very polite manner, we can invite the youth, who have been attracted by the places of gambling, impermissible amusement, and ill-educating cinemas, and who think that they enjoy their freedoms, to follow the right path. In the same way and through wisdom and goodly exhortation, we can

Martyr Muhammad Baqir as-Sadr (may Allah have mercy on him) never did smoke at all. When once I asked him about smoking, he said, "I do not smoke and I advise every Muslim not to smoke." However, I did not hear from him the prohibition of smoking openly.

It is said that some *ulama* have prohibited smoking for the ones who have never smoked and they want now to smoke and considered it unapproved for smokers themselves. Some *ulama* consider it impermissible, but they do not dare to announce openly for fear that they may be accused of following analogy.

I want to say that the religious authorities have to give an open, clear opinion about smoking without fearing the blame from any quarter. They have to prohibit it even by their own *ijtihad*, as long as it causes harms to smokers themselves and to others, besides the squandering and waste that it results in.

Have we not agreed from the beginning that when a *mujtahid* is right in his *fatwa*, he shall get two rewards, and if he is mistaken, he shall get one reward on condition that there is no religious text from Allah or His messenger on that matter concerned?

Let us suppose that there is no clear text on smoking and that it is not included by this saying of Allah:

...and do not squander wastefully.. [Qur'an, 17:26]

nor the saying of the Prophet (s), "*There should be no harm (against oneself) and no harming (against others)*", then the way is open before the *ulama* and religious authorities to follow their *ijtihad* and prohibit smoking because of the harms and fatal diseases it causes. When the *ulama* and religious authorities choose to keep silent just because people accept it - it is a really big problem.

Or, they may fear the reaction of smokers and so they do not give a *fatwa* for the sake of being disapproved. Someone from them has tried his best to convince me that smoking has many benefits and to disapprove this is really a dangerous thing having a dangerous effect!

---

invite our Sunni brothers who wear gold, or who do not care for impurities to correct their behaviors.

It encouraged a Muslim youth who knew this man, to keep on smoking.

At the same time we find that charitable societies and social organizations in the atheist countries sparing no effort against smoking and smokers, and preventing even its advertisement. They ask the manufacturers of cigarettes to write on the packets of cigarettes the word "SUICIDE" to encourage people to keep away from it. Yet we find in the Islamic religious societies widely embarking on it and encouraging others towards it. We even find women carrying packets of cigarettes with them to places of worship and religious meetings.

When a child opens his eye to see his mother and father smoke, he is likely to imitate them before he tries to follow the religious authority. When such a child becomes a youth with love of smoking and intoxicated with cigarettes, it will be very difficult to convince him to give the habit up, particularly when he becomes an adult and he is used to seeing his father smoke in places of worship.

If Muslims know how much monies they lose because of smoking and that it has been a plot against them, they will be thunderstruck!

For example and in a simple mathematical operation, we can see the danger of the situation. In the world today, there are one milliard Muslims. If we suppose that only a fifth of them smoke, we shall find two hundred millions smokers. And if we suppose that every smoker spends one dollar a day, which is the least price of an ordinary packet of cigarettes - and we do not talk about those who smoke two or three packets a day nor those who spend two or three dollars on the expensive brand of cigarettes - we shall find that two hundred million (200,000,000) dollars are spent by Muslims on smoking every day, and seventy-three million (73,000,000,000) dollars every year. Thus, Muslims squander seventy-three million dollars on smoking every year to buy fatal diseases.

If we add to that the amount which Muslims spend on the treatment from the diseases caused by smoking itself, like cancer, infection of lungs, angina pectoris, dental caries, pyorrhea, and others - the amount spent is unimaginable, something that mind cannot believe easily.

If Muslims spare these amounts for ten years, they shall have a paradise on the earth. There shall be no poor amongst them. They shall not need to beg the atheists, and they shall definitely do away with poverty, diseases and underdevelopment. They can with such monies, buy modern technology and develop in all fields.

After this brief discussion, we want to say that Muslims have to prohibit themselves from everything that harms and does not benefit them. Even if there is no clear text on that, surely their religion encourages and orders them to keep away from everything harmful and not of use to them. Allah says in the Qur'an:

...and (Allah) makes lawful to them the good things and makes unlawful to them impure things. [Qur'an, 7:157]

The Messenger of Allah (s) forbade his companions from eating garlic on Fridays, lest the people in the mosque would be hurt by its bad smell, though garlic is permissible and it has many medical benefits. Certainly, the smell of garlic cannot be compared to the smoke of cigarettes that spreads everywhere, pollutes the space and bothers others too much. Nevertheless, the Prophet (s) forbade the eating of garlic on Fridays (for those who would mix with people) according to the rule of "no harming to others". Those, who eat garlic, get advantages from it, but it is not liked for them to eat it when they want to mix with others especially during the Friday Prayer, lest others be hurt by its bad smell.

Moreover, only the bad smell of garlic may hurt others. It causes neither diseases nor infections, unlike it is not with smoking. Yet, the Prophet (s) forbade it. After this example, is there any lesson in that for men of understanding?!

Mujtahids prohibit the playing with cards and chess, even if they are used for amusement and not gambling and they prohibit amusing singing, music and other things for which there is no any clear text about neither in the Book of Allah nor in the *Sunnah* of the Prophet. Could they not then prohibit something that clearly causes harm and diseases for Muslims?

But, if some Shia insists on permitting smoking and not prohibiting it, then let them observe the feelings of non-smokers and observe the sanctity of the places of worships, as their Sunni brothers do inside their mosques. Would you try that individually?

If you come into a mosque of the Sunni while having a lit cigarette in your hand, you shall be prevented and denied, and may be hurt by some of them.

I can swear that Allah and His messenger hate smoking, because reason, sound nature, and logic hate it.

This bad habit made many of the Sunni, who visited the countries of the Shia, be alienated and go back to their countries, criticizing the Shia, though they did not know anything about Shiism other than those bad habits. Therefore, I always remind of Imam as-Sadiq's saying to his followers:

Be propagandists for us by your deeds and not your sayings. Be a cause of honor to us and not a cause of disgrace for us.[1]

How many doings one may see and alienate and then become displeased so that afterwards he does not accept any invitation, even if it is true! What is said about some of the Shia in this concern can be said about some of the Sunni.

In the end, I say that reform is necessarily required, and returning to the truth is a virtue. Let one not be deceived by saying: Can that which has been corrupted throughout too many centuries be repaired?

Yes, it can be. If there is loyalty, and causes are available, the nation shall be recovered from this chronic disease, even if it takes a long time, by the power of Allah the Almighty.

---

[1] *Bihar al Anwar* vol.85, p. 136

I BEAR WITNESS THAT ALI IS THE FRIEND OF ALLAH

There remain some other criticisms that do not deserve defaming or causing fear. These things, which are criticized unfairly by the Sunni are mentioned among the Shia in the past and present, as recommended and a cause of blessing, such as adding to the *azan*[1] and *iqamah*[2] the saying - "I bear witness that Ali is the friend (*wali*) of Allah".

All the Shia have agreed that this is not a basic part of the *azan* or the *iqamah* and that it was available in the *azan* at the time of the

---

[1] The *azan* in Islam is a means of announcing to people about the time of prayer. It has no certain, inviolable text as the texts of the Holy Qur'an, which cannot accept a decrease or increase even for one letter.
As for *azan*, the books of the Sunni sometimes mention that the *azan* was not available and that Abdullah ibn Zayd al-Ansari heard it in sleep and told it to the Prophet (s) who acknowledged and confirmed it. Perhaps, this is what made the Caliph Umar, when he was sleeping and the muezzin awaked him saying, "Prayer is better than sleep", approved the statement and ordered to add it to the *azan*.
Bilal al-Habashi, the Prophet's muezzin, pronounced [sh] as [s] and he said "ass-hadu" instead of "ash-hadu". When some Muslims criticized this, the Prophet (s) said, "The [s] of Bilal is [sh] near Allah."
Once, when I was in Sham (Syria), I passed by the Umayyad Mosque at the time of the Isha' Prayer and I heard a collective *azan* recited in tones like oration. So, why all these reactions when Ameerul Mo'minin Ali ibn Abi Talib is mentioned?!
Let us say it is a good heresy or bad heresy (as the Sunni believe), then what for are all these reactions? However, they (the Sunni) are excessive in this concern. They have fixed "prayer is better than sleep" and considered it a part from the *azan*, but we (the Shia) do not say it is a part from the *azan*, but only recommended. *Azan* is a means that announces the prescribed time of prayer. As long as it is within the required limits that have no excess and do not harm Islam and Muslims, there shall be no serious problem.
[2] *Iqamah* is a recommended (not obligatory) part before the prayer. It has the same wordings of the *azan*, but with a little difference.

Prophet (s). They have agreed that considering it a basic part of the *azan* or the *iqamah* invalidates both. This is the belief of the *ulama* and religious authorities of the Shia.

As long as the truth is our goal, the sayings of Allah and His messenger are our sayings and their contentment is our aim and intention. And as long as we face criticism from some of our (Sunni) brothers, so we have to approve of others what we approve from ourselves and find ugly in ourselves what we find ugly of others.

We have criticized Umar ibn al-Khattab in our previous studies for adding "*prayer is better than sleep*" to the *azan* and omitting "*come on to the best of deeds*" from it, and said that it was impermissible because it was a heresy that was not available at the time of the Prophet (s). We were not convinced by their saying that "*prayer is better than sleep*" was mentioned only in the *azan* of the Fajr (dawn) Prayer and their justifying that at dawn, man would be in the best moments of his sleep and rest; therefore, "*prayer is better than sleep*" would be used to encourage him to give up his rest and get ready for prayer.

It was nice speech, justifying and defending the matter, but we denied it, because the clear texts would not submit to personal opinions and desires. We said, "*Whatever the Messenger of Allah (s) (s) did not do is heresy.*"

On this basis, we say to the Shia the same statement and argue against them with the same argument. There should be no difference between these and those.

Therefore, we confess that "*I bear witness that Ali is the friend (wali) of Allah*" is extra in the *azan*, because the Messenger of Allah (s) did not say or order it, nor did the infallible Imams (as) do it. If they really did it, we would find some proofs for it. If they did it, then it would not be permissible for the ulama of the Shia and their religious authorities to consider the *azan* and *iqamah* as null when this statement is mentioned as an actual part of them (the *azan* and the *iqamah*) as we have said before.

Fairness and justice require us to say the word of the truth and not to deny the Sunni for something while we ourselves do the like. Allah says:

What! do you enjoin men to be good and neglect your own souls while you read the Book; have you then no sense? [Qur'an, 2:44]

Once, one of the Shia said to me, "O my brother, do not mix between "prayer is better than sleep" and "I bear witness that Ali is the friend (*wali*) of Allah"!

I said, "Why? Prayer is really better than sleep, and Ali is really the saint of Allah, but they are parts added later on and the Messenger of Allah (s) did not do that."

He said, "But the guardianship of Imam Ali (as) has been revealed in the Qur'an, and you yourself have acknowledged that in your book 'Then I was Guided'."

I said, "So, the Messenger of Allah (s) was to be blamed, for he did not make that in the *azan*!!!"

Not everything that has been revealed in the Qur'an is to be added to the *azan* or *iqamah* and my acknowledgment that it has been revealed in the Qur'an does not make it necessary to be added to the *azan* or *iqamah*.

Is it right for one to recite for example, in the azan, "I bear witness that there is no God but Allah, bear witness that Adam is the choice of Allah, bear witness that Noah is the prophet of Allah, bear witness that Abraham is the friend of Allah, bear witness that Moses is the spoken to by Allah, bear witness that Jesus is the Holy Spirit of Allah, and I bear witness that Muhammad is the beloved one of Allah"? All these facts are true and they have come in the Qur'an.

However, we cannot recite that in the *azan*, because the Messenger of Allah (s) has taught us to recite in the azan only the two witnesses "I bear witness that there is no god but Allah, and I bear witness that Muhammad is the Messenger of Allah (s)". We must abide by the saying of Allah:

...and, whatever the Messenger gives you, accept it and from whatever he forbids you, keep back. [Qur'an, 59:7]

It is true that some of the Shia *ulama* do not mention "I bear witness that Ali is the friend (*wali*) of Allah" in the *azan* or the *iqamah*. I offered prayers with some of them and did not hear them say so. That they might mention it in their hearts, is something else. However, there are some Shia who doubt the loyalty and faith of whoever does not mention this in the *azan* or the *iqamah*."

My opponent, praise be to Allah, was convinced. Still he said to me that he could not give it up, because his tongue had been used to it since his childhood.

I say this and I am certain that some of the Shia will not approve of it, because man by his nature, is an enemy to what he ignores and the satisfaction of all people is an unreachable goal.[1]

As I have said before in this book, I do not flatter anyone nor do I seek his satisfaction (with me) however high a position he has. I only seek the satisfaction of my conscience through the satisfaction of Allah, His messenger (s) and the infallible Imams (as) - who are my Imams and masters, at the head of whom is Imam Ali (as).

In the depth of my soul, I am certain that Imam Ali (as) would be pleased with those, who try to guide people to the right path more than he would be with some of his Shia and lovers, who bear witness in every *azan* and *iqamah* that he is the saint of Allah, but they do not do anything to guide people towards this guardianship (of Imam Ali) or to prove the truth to them (people). In fact, they make people alienated and unknowingly keep them from reaching the truth.

Would Imam Ali (as) be pleased when we bear witness of his guardianship and sainthood while we hold it as a big obstacle before those who search for the truth? Certainly not!

---

[1] Heresy, as we have said before, is a thing, which is not from religion. It is fixed and added to religion. "Prayer is better than sleep" was added and considered as a part of the very *azan*, but as for recommended things mentioned before or even through the *azan*, such as "Say: praise be to Allah Who has not taken a wife nor a child" or "blessing and peace be on you O Messenger of Allah (s)" besides "I bear witness that Ali is the saint of Allah, or is the commander of the believers" are mentioned as recommended. According to general evidence the little statements of ordinary people (neither Allah nor the Prophet) do not annul the *azan*, on condition that these things are not considered as parts of the *azan* or the *iqamah*.

I often argued with obstinate people in the best manner, but I found in them a psychological obstacle that prevented them from keeping on with the argument in order to get to the truth. I tried to destroy that obstacle daring with a certain heart to keep on researching and getting to the sought goal. Then, I found that the obstinate ones advanced little by little with me and broke the psychological obstacles. Most of the time and about eighty percent of them acknowledged the truth and were guided to the guardianship of Ameerul Mu'minin Imam Ali (as) and the guardianship of the infallible Imams (as) after him.

Once, I was in Poona and Jabalpur in India. I met there with a big group of Sudanese students. In an evening gathering, I felt loyalty and true intention to know the truth in them. Most of them objected to the beliefs of the Shia concerning the matter of infallibility[1] that

---

[1] Why do they (the Sunni) deny the infallibility of the Ahlul Bayt (s), whereas they themselves believe in the infallibility of all the nation as to the matter of consensus, or the infallibility of all the Prophet's companions, and of the men of authority? Al-Fakhr ar-Razi says in his Tafsir, "...and it has been proved that all those, whom Allah has ordered to obey, must be infallible, and thus, it has been definitely proved that "the men of authority" mentioned in this verse must be infallible.

Then we say: that the infallible ones are either entire nation or some of the nation... those infallible ones meant by Allah's saying 'men in authority' must be the men in power from the imams (rulers), and this makes it necessary that the consensus of the nation is evident." The interpretation of the Surah of an-Nisa', verse 59, p. 144 in ar-Razi'a Tafsir

It is not unknown that those men in power were themselves who gave Mu'awiyah ibn Abi Sufyan the authority (and considered him a legal Wali) and his son Yazid the drunkard and the killer of Imam Husayn son of Imam Ali (s) and (killer of) seventeen men from the Ahlul Bayt (s)...and the results were all Mu'awiyah and his son's crimes and vices, the rule of al-Waleed and other criminals from the Umayyad dynasty, and then the allegiance to the Abbasids among whom were Abul Abbas as-Saffah (slaughterer), Abu Ja'far al-Mansur (the tyrant), and others. As for those in power who were pious, they were either exiled, or forced to be neuter, though keeping silent at that time would be a heavy burden.

Then, why do they find the infallibility of the Ahlul Bayt (s) odd and unacceptable, whereas their infallibility has been confirmed by many

they (the Shia) proved for their imams. They also objected to the witness that "*Imam Ali is the friend (wali) of Allah*" recited in the *azan*. They said that the Shia were excessive and extravagant in their love to the imams.

I said to them, "O my brothers in Islam, I do not try to impose on you the concept of "infallibility" and do not consider it the goal leading to the truth, although I myself believe in it, but I shall avoid it completely to prove to you that the Holy Qur'an and the Prophet's *Sunnah* impose on every Muslim to be a Shia following the Messenger of Allah (s) and his immaculate progeny (peace be on them).

You are not required to prove and believe in this infallibility in order to get to the sought goal, which is the adherence to the saints of Allah and His messenger (s) and to be free from the enemies of Allah and His messenger (s). You are as well, not required to bear witness to Imam Ali's guardianship and sainthood in the *azan* and not required to believe in all what the Shia narrate about Ali and his progeny that you consider as excessive and extravagance.

Imam Ali (as) is much greater than the need prove for him a virtue that is considered as one of miracles and say that Allah the Almighty has returned the sun to him because he missed the afternoon Prayer, or the earth was shrunk for him to travel from Medina to Mada'in in order to ritually wash Salman al-Farsi (after his death) and come back on the same day, which was a distance of some month's travel at that time. These narrations are about miracles of the Unknown. A Muslim is free to believe or not to believe in them, for these shall neither increase nor decrease his faith.

However, we are required to believe that Imam Ali (as) was the successor of the Prophet (s) and the best of all people after him and that the Prophet (s) had appointed him as his successor over the nation after his death.

Qur'anic verses, Prophetic traditions? On many occasions and situations, the Prophet (s) proved this virtue for them and they were preferred to the whole nation after the Prophet (s).

We have to prove that Ameerul Mu'minin Ali (as) was the gate of the city of the Prophet's knowledge and there was no one more knowledgeable than him at all in the entire nation. We have to prove that he was most courageous of all companions and the most loyal of all of them in wars and during difficulties. It was by his sword and courage that Islam became strong and firm. We have to prove that he was the first to believe in Islam, he was the most loyal in all the battles, and that he sacrificed everything to preserve Islam after the Prophet (s) therefore, following him is obligatory on every Muslim.

We have to prove that he was the only one who spared no effort to enliven the Book of Allah and the *Sunnah* of the Prophet when they were about to be buried. We have to prove that he was the most ascetic to the worldly life among all human beings and the nearest to Allah in all his behaviors and actions. We have to prove that he was the most just and fair of all people at all, and most pious to Allah, and that he fought the *nakithin* - breakers of covenant - in the battle of al-Jamal-the camel, the *qasitin* - the unjust - in the battle of Siffin and the *mariqin* - renegades - in the battle of an-Nahrawan to preserve Islam and Muslims.

We have to prove that Muhammad (s) was the first and Ali (as) was the second, and they were the best of Allah's creation at all.

Yes! We have to prove all that from the Qur'an, the true Prophetic *Sunnah* and the true history and show clear evidences and convincing arguments that are irrefutable.

But, if we repeat that Allah had created Muhammad and Ali one hundred thousand years before He created Adam, and that all the prophets and messengers prayed to Allah the Almighty by the right of Muhammad, Ali, Fatima, al-Hasan, and al-Husayn, or that it has been written on the leg of the Throne that "*Ali is the friend (wali) of Allah*", it is something else and it neither benefits nor take us to the sought goal.

We cannot convince others with these things, for which we do not have any scientific proof. If we insist on proving the miracles, the infallibility, or the guardianship of Ali (as) - each side will insist on his own situation and be fanatic as the Sunni who narrate on Abu Bakr and Umar more than what the Shia narrate on Imam Ali (as) and his progeny. In this case, time shall be wasted in unfruitful disputes, and the Sunni shall accuse the Shia of being extravagant in praise of their Imams, and then the Shia shall accuse the Sunni of being extravagant in praise of the three caliphs especially and to the companions in general. Thus the dispute shall remain unfruitful.

O brothers, today, we are required to show clear arguments and scientific proofs. I do not argue with you except by reasonable and traditional proofs that have been proved by history, reality and what all Muslims - Sunni and Shia - have agreed on. I pray Allah to guide us all to the truth."

After we had spent that night until the dawn in scientific argumentation and logical discussion, most of them turned to the truth and longingly read the book '*Then I was Guided*'. Two days later, they came to say farewell to me before my travel while thanking Allah for guiding them to His Right Path and wishing to know the beliefs of the Twelver Shia and to read their books.

One of them came alone with me and I think he was the emir (leader) of the group as they called him, and said after thanking me and offering compliments, "I met with the Shia in Egypt, Sudan, and in India here, but no one of them could convince me like what you did."

I said, "The book '*Then I was Guided*' convinced many researchers and this is a favor of Allah to me, so I often praise and thank Him."

He said, "I did not yet read your book, because I am busy with examinations, and I do not read any book except when I am tranquil."

I said, "Then, how were you convinced when you did not read the book?"

He said, "On that night when you began your talking by putting aside the "infallibility", "Ali is the friend (*wali*) of Allah", and many other concepts that the Shia adopt, I admired your talks, because you talked to people with what they understood. If you kept to those concepts, the arguments would be unfruitful and that night's discussion would be in vain. However, you knew the truth and could guide us to it. If you give a lecture in Sudan before the university students, you will make them all turn Shia by this way and method."

I thanked him for his kind feelings and asked him to read the book *(Then I was Guided)* and send me his notes on it. We embraced each other, while our hearts were beating with the love and loyalty to the Ahlul Bayt (as).

EPILOGUE TO THE PREVIOUS CHAPTERS

These were the most important objections and criticisms that the Sunni often raise against the Twelver Shia. They deserve to be studied impartially by every researcher and scholar who seeks the truth in everything and does not have fear on the way of Allah about being blamed and states the truth, however bitter it is.

Today the learned youth of our Muslim nation no longer believe in superstitions, false fables, and rumors that the media broadcast here and there against the Shia to show them as groups of extremism and terrorism, or "*the insane of Allah*" as they call them.

I have already discussed some mistakes practiced by ordinary Shia, though these (mistakes) are not from the religion or from the necessities that may make impermissible things permissible. They do not cause but harms and disagreements among Muslims.

I have confirmed in my previous works and studies that I have published among Muslims through clear evidences, that the Twelver Shia are the most right of all the Muslim sects with respect to the beliefs and laws of the religion, and that the Shiite sect is the saved one from among all the Muslim sects by the will of Allah. This is not for anything, but because they are truly adherent to the Two Weighty Things (the Book of Allah and the Immaculate Prophet's Progeny).

Nevertheless, this cannot prevent me from criticizing the Shia when I find errors or slips in the conduct of some of them, for I believe that "there is nothing other than the truth, except that it is untruth".

Sometimes, a good doing may turn to be a bad doing if it exceeds the usual. For example, once when I was invited for an Islamic conference in the United States of America, some Muslims invited me to their houses to be their guest as a kind of honor and respect. I accepted their invitations unwillingly. Many others were invited me in my honor. Foods and refreshments were unimaginable in excellence and sometimes they cost thousands of dollars.

On the following day, or even the same day, I was invited by others and the same things happened, as if they competed with each other. The same invitees attended with me. I would not be excessive in saying that the kinds of western and eastern foods served were more than ten in each meal. Whatever guests ate - half of that food would be leftover without doubt, to be thrown into the rubbish bin.[1]

This habit has become a necessity for them. Whatever is said about the Arabic generosity and the honoring of guest, and whatever some people argue by means of this verse:

---

[1] Yes! This has changed to be a habit and tradition. People pride and compete with each other and the victim is the guest who compliments to satisfy the host. Otherwise, the guest even if he is a scholar or a thinker and attracts their attention to the offensiveness of this practice, might not be invited anymore. So how about ordinary people?!

In this way, detestable social classes appear which look down on the poor and prevent them from attending such invitations. (The rich are invited and the poor are kept away). Its undesirable outcome is division of people into different classes. Such invitations affect the mentality of the guest (when he is a scholar or thinker) that he acknowledges their conducts, or they pervert his thinking of caring for the right affairs of Muslims to their own world and life.

Unfortunately, an example is one of the wealthy people in Iraq who was in such a reckless state that he did not know how to spend his wealth, so that whatever he did to it, it would not run out because of abundance. Saddam exiled him out of Iraq and confiscated all his wealth and properties. In the place of immigration, I heard a wealthy man saying, "I cannot be convinced the Iraqi people suffer famine, except when they become like Indians who die in the streets and then, the municipality personnel carry their corpses altogether."

Surely, a Muslim cannot be a true Muslim except when he follows the true Islam, imitates its high examples, and apply it in the true way. A true Muslim must be a true faithful away from vanities, wastefulness, dissipation, and worldly desires; otherwise, life shall be beastly.

Say: Who has prohibited the embellishment of Allah which He has brought forth for His servants and the good provisions... [Qur'an, 7:32]

I shall not be satisfied and I will criticize that and try my best to convince people of other than this.

Those, who take their evidence from the Qur'an on the permitting of good provisions, forget or overlook this saying of Allah

...and eat and drink and be not extravagant; surely He does not love the extravagant, [Qur'an, 7:31]

Or, this saying of the Prophet (s):

We are a people who do not eat, except when we feel hungry, and when we eat, we do not become fully satiated (do not eat much).

Where are we from the education of Imam Ali (as) who has accustomed himself to eating dry barley and who sealed his bag lest al-Hasan or al-Husayn (peace be on them) wet his dry piece of bread with oil?

Do Muslims not feel shy today before their Lord that they sleep in silk beds with stomachs full of all kinds of foods, whereas their Iraqi Shia brothers die of hunger in the Saudi camps, not finding the simple means of living?

I thank those who invited and honored me, but my duty requires me to remind them of what is better, for reminding benefits of the faithful. It is my duty to encourage them to do good for the sake of Allah, in the way of Allah and not for fame and hypocrisy. Many wealthy Muslims, who live the life of kings, become very stingy when they are asked to help the poor and the needy, whereas they spend millions of dollars recklessly on their lusts and desires.

The fact that makes you wonder too is that most of these wealthy people had escaped with their faith from the oppression of unjust rulers and emigrated to the United States of America or England while they had no money in their pockets. Then Allah made them rich and they possessed buildings, shops and millions of dollars. Thereafter, they behaved like Th'alaba who came to the Prophet (s) complaining of his poverty and asking the Prophet (s) to pray Allah for him to be rich as he wanted to help the poor and the needy.

The Prophet (s) prayed Allah for him, and he became too wealthy. When the Prophet (s) asked him to pay the zakat, he refused to pay anything. Then, Allah revealed this verse about him:

And there are those of them who made a covenant with Allah: if He gives us out of His grace, we will certainly give alms and we will certainly be of the good. But when He gave them out of His grace, they became niggardly of it and they turned away, averse. [Qur'an, 9:75-76]

Certainly, there are wealthy people who spend their monies charitably in the night and the day, openly and secretly, looking forward to the mercy and contentment of their Lord. However, these people are few in comparison to the majority who run after fame and refuse any charitable doing.

You may see wealthy Muslims, whom Allah has given too much to be trustees on it and to give from their wealth a share to the beggars and the destitute. They perform the major Hajj every year and the minor Hajj two or three times a year - and I am not being excessive when I say that some of them have performed the Hajj twenty times and the minor Hajj more than forty times. They show their pride of that openly before people.

Such people from among the Shia are too many. They do not know the actual amount of their wealth. They spend their times in the best hotels, eat the most expensive meals, and travel in the first class airplanes. After that, they go to visit the holy shrines of the infallible imams (as). When you see how they eat and what they throw in their rubbish bins, you say with no hesitation that they are too far away from the Islamic ethics and human morals.

It is true that the Hajj is recommended after performing the first obligatory one, but do these people not understand that Allah, first of all orders them to help His poor people, the needy, orphans and the oppressed? Has Allah the Almighty not said to them in His Book:

It is not righteousness that you turn your faces towards the East and the West, but righteousness is this that one should believe in Allah and the last day and the angels and the Book and the prophets, and give away wealth out of love for Him to the near of kin and the orphans and the needy and the wayfarer and the beggars and for (the emancipation of) the captives...? [Qur'an, 2: 177]

O Muslims, righteousness is not to go every year to perform the Hajj or to visit the holy shrines of saints...yes, the Hajj is obligatory and recommended and so is the *ziyara*, but to be a habit every year while your brothers are dying of hunger - this is something that does not please Allah at all.[1]

Did the Messenger of Allah (s) not say

The nearest of you to Allah is most helpful among you to His people.[2]

Did he not say

Who sleeps his night satiated while his neighbor is hungry is out of the covenant of Islam.[3]

Did your first Imam, Ali ibn Abi Talib, whom you pride on and follow, not say?

Surely, every led one has a leader (imam) whom he follows, and from the light of whose knowledge he seeks light. Surely, your Imam (Ali) has been satisfied from all his life with his two coarse garments, and from his food with his two loaves...by Allah, I have never hoarded from your world gold, nor have I saved from its booties anything...

....and if I wanted, I could follow the way to the pure honey, the kernels of this wheat, and the textiles of this silk - but how far for my fancy to overcome me, or my greed to lead me to choose between foods, that there may be in Hijaz or Yamama one who cannot even

---

[1] The responsibility of changing the conducts of these people is on the *ulama* and preachers that they may repent and return to the true path of Islam and the Ahlul Bayt (s).

[2] *Bihar al Anwar* vol.77. p. 152

[3] *Bihar al Anwar* vol.75. p. 362

wish for a loaf of bread and one who has never been satisfied with food? Or, can I sleep my night satiated, while around me there are hungry stomachs and very thirsty lives!

...I was not created to be busy with good foods and pleasures like a tied animal, whose concern is only its fodder, or a released one whose business is seeking in rubbish...

O worldly life, be away from me! Your halter is on your wither (free to do whatever it likes). I have sneaked away from your claws and escaped from your traps, and avoided going into your slips.

Where are the generations, whom you incited with your plays? Where are the nations, whom you fascinated with your adornments? Here they are captives in the graves and hidden in the tombs...Be away from me! By Allah, I do not submit to you so that you degrade me, and do not be mild for you, so that you drive me (as you like)...

Blessed is a soul that offered its obligation for its Lord and was patient in distress, gave up its sleeping in the night until slumber overcame it, took the ground as its bed and its hand as a pillow, from among people whose fear of the Hereafter made their eyes sleepless, and whose bodies kept away from their beds, and whose lips always murmured with the remembrance of their Lord, and whose sins were dispelled by their long asking for forgiveness:

...those are Allah's party; surely the party of Allah are the successful ones. [Qur'an, 58:22]

This speech[1] is addressed to every Shia who takes Ali (as) as his imam after the Prophet (s).

As we have confirmed in our previous studies that the Shia are the true Muslims who have kept to the Book and the Prophet's progeny after the Prophet (s). We must obey the commands of the Book and the immaculate progeny (as). They order us to glorify and sanctify the rites of Allah, because it is from true piety.

---

[1] *Nahjul Balagha* letter 45. From the letter of Imam Ali (s) to his governor on Basra, Uthman ibn Hunayf al-Ansari, when he (Imam Ali) was informed that Uthman was invited to a banquet and he accepted and went to it. *Nahjul Balaghah* - commentary by Muhammad Abduh, p. 558.

Observing the rites of Allah includes observing of congregational prayers inside and outside the mosques, the keeping to prayers in the best way and keep the mosque sanctified, clean and unpolluted with cigarettes smoke. Rather, mosques must be refreshed with good scents and perfumes. Certainly, all these are the rites to be observed for Allah.[1]

How better it is for us to be ascetic towards many pleasures of this life, not to squander our monies in what does not benefit us, and not to be excessive in food and amusement while our faithful brothers are dying of hunger! How better it is for us to think of serving the servants of Allah and save them from deviation instead of performing the Hajj forty times and the minor Hajj eighty times!

If these monies are spent on publishing and sending books as gifts to the Muslim countries that do not know anything about the Ahlul Bayt (as) nor do they hear anything about the Shia except the fabrications. They shall be effective means to make millions of

---

[1] It is noted in general that a praying person usually stands to offer prayers with the clothes he usually wears, not caring whether they are tidy and clean or not. The important thing is that they must be ritually pure. People think that there is no problem for this with Allah! But, if one of them wants to meet someone, he puts on the best of his clothes, especially if that someone is an important personality. Thus, is person whom one meets in life more important than Allah? One does not perceive or think of this!

Let each one of us think of this matter - when one of us is inside his house wearing night clothes, he does not let others (visitors) see him in that clothes, because this is as a kind of insult to them. Should he offer the prayer in these clothes so easily? We have to be aware of Whom we are standing before to offer our prayer. We have to put in mind that Allah the Almighty is always with us wherever we are and behave on this basis,

...and He is with you wherever you are... [Qur'an, 57:4]

We stand before Him all the time and especially in the prayer. Therefore, we have to put on the best of our clothes, using perfume, in order to appear in an acceptable state to Him. After preparing our appearances, we have to purify our inwards to be real travelers toward Allah the Glorified. It is not bad to pay attention to the recommended things as to the prayer's clothes and etiquettes especially for women who may put on white clothes and...be in the best shape that makes us actually feel that Allah is with us.

deviated people, who seek the truth, turn to the right path and the reward of this near Allah shall be greater than the reward of a recommended Hajj that one goes to offer, wishing that Allah may forgive his sins of the last year. The Prophet (s) said:

The ink of scholars is holier near Allah than the blood of martyrs.

Fear Allah by maintaining kinship, because it is better near Allah than all prayers and fasting.

How it is better for us to think of the future of Muslims in the world who face a plot of annihilation in every place on the earth!

After all this and through my personal experiment of twenty-five years the most of which was arguments and disputes with learned and unlearned Sunni, I knew that overlooking some beliefs that are not from the essence of Islam is the only way to get to the sought goal.

How many obstinate opponents, who never preferred anyone at all to Abu Bakr and Umar, began after turning Shia to wish that Imam Ali (as) had fought and relieved Muslims from them? And, how many protestant deniers, who denied the concept of "infallibility" and considered it as being excessive from the Shia, believed in it after having turned Shia, more than the Shia themselves?!

All that would lead to enmity and grudge if I insisted on the concept of "infallibility" or "I bear witness that Ali is the friend (wali) of Allah" in the *azan* or that "Ali is the best of all human beings and whoever denies that is a disbeliever".

I am sure that Muslims shall be near to each other and would be united if both the Shia and the Sunni tried to overlook some of their beliefs that are not from the fundamentals of the religion. If the Sunni gave up their belief that all of the Prophet's companions are totally fair, just and honest, (and certainly this belief has nothing to do with the religion), they would relieve their Shia brothers from their continuous efforts to prove the opposite.

And if the Shia overlook "I bear witness that Ali is the friend (wali) of Allah" which was not a part from the *azan* or the *iqamah* at the time of the Messenger of Allah (s), they would relieve their

Sunni brothers, who criticize and accuse them of being extravagant and excessive, from toiling for that.

Do Muslims, Shia and Sunni, not take a lesson from what the Messenger of Allah (s) did on the day of Truce of al-Hudaybiyyah? He gave up many things and did not oppose the polytheists in anything? He did so because he knew that resisting them and not giving up some of his conditions would be an obstacle in the way of guidance and the getting to the truth.

They said to him, "*We do not acknowledge that you are the Messenger of Allah (s). You are Muhammad son of Abdullah.*"

He said, "*Yes, I am Muhammad son of Abdullah. O Ali, do not write down 'Muhammad the Messenger of Allah (s)'.*"

If one of the Shia says, "*How do we give up 'Ali is the friend (wali) of Allah' which is right and the truth and we remember that the Prophet (s) said that 'whoever keeps silent before the truth is a dumb devil'?*" We respond that, just as Muhammad son of Abdullah (s) gave up his attribute as the Messenger of Allah (s) before the polytheists in order to not cause an obstacle between him and them and to invite them towards guidance when he actually was the Messenger of Allah (s) whether the polytheists accepted or denied that.

And Allah is sufficient as a witness. [Qur'an, 58:22]

In the same way - "*Ali is the friend (wali) of Allah*" is also right and true, whether people bear witness to that or not. Their witness does not add anything to his value, nor does their denial decrease anything from his virtues."[1]

---

[1] We have confirmed before that no one of the Shiite *ulama* say that "I bear witness that Ali is the saint of Allah" is a basic part of the *azan* or the *iqamah*, and whoever calls it as a "good heresy" is totally mistaken. It is but a witness that Imam Ali (s) is the saint of Allah and the commander of the believers, and a witness of the injustice he suffered and the suppression of history against him, though he was the establisher of the cornerstone of Islam after the Prophet (s) with his knowledge and jihad. It is like the qualities of Talut mentioned in the Holy Qur'an when the Israelites asked

Alli is the Friend of Allah 185

from their prophet to send for them a king so that they would fight under his leadership.

And their prophet said to them: Surely Allah has raised Talut to be a king over you. They said: How can he hold kingship over us while we have a greater right to kingship than he does, and he has not been granted an abundance of wealth? He said: Surely Allah has chosen him in preference to you, and He has increased him abundantly in knowledge and physique, and Allah grants His kingdom to whom He pleases, and Allah is Ample giving, Knowing. [Qur'an, 2:247]

This is besides many other instances that this and that has witnessed of (and the virtue is that which opponents witness of). So why do we not actually take a strict situation against heresies like the omitting of "Come on to the best of deeds" from the *azan* by Umar ibn al-Khattab? It is related to Akrimah that he said, "Once, I said to ibn Abbas, 'Would you tell me why "come on to the best of deeds" was omitted from the *azan*?" He said, 'Umar wanted people not to rely on prayer and give up jihad; therefore, he omitted that from the *azan*." Refer to *Sunan al-Bayhaqi*, vol. 1 p. 524-525, *as-Sira al-Halabiyyah*, vol. 2 p. 105, *Sa'd as-Sa'oud*, p. 100, *Mizan al-I'tidal* by ath-Thahabi, vol. 1 p. 139, *Lisan al-Mizan*, vol. 1 p. 261, *Nayl al-Awtar* by al-Shawkani, vol. 2 p. 32, *Kanul Ummal*, printed in the margins of *Musnad Ahmad*, vol. 3 p. 276, *Kanul Ummal*, vol. 4 p. 266, *ar-Rawdh an-Nadhir*, vol. 2 p. 42.

On the other side, Umar added to the *azan* of the Fajr (dawn) Prayer "the prayer is better than sleep". This shows that Muslims do not wonder at this omission and the addition, because the Sunni do not believe that the *azan* and the *iqamah* have been legislated by Allah through His revelation to the Prophet (s), or that the Prophet (s) has done it like the other rites and rulings that he received from Allah the Almighty!!! They narrate that the *azan* was a dream which one of the companion saw in his sleep after the Prophet (s) had been confused (as they say) either to call people for the prayer by the bell or by beating two pieces of wood against each other...Refer to *Sunan Abu Dawud*, vol. 1 p. 335, *as-Sira al-Halabiyyah*, vol. 2 p. 93, *Sahih at-Tirmizi*, vol. 1 p. 359, *al-Muwatta'*, vol. 1 and its explanation by *az-Zarqani*, vol. 1 p. 120-125, *Sunan al-Bayhaqi*, vol. 1 p. 390, *Sira of Ibn Hisham*, vol. 2 p. 154, *al-Bidaya wal-Nihaya*, vol. 3 p. 232, *al-Mawahib al-Laduniyyah*, vol. 1 p. 17, *Muntakhab Kanul Ummal*, printed in the margins of *Musnad Ahmad*, vol. 3 p. 273, *Tabyeen al-Haqa'iq* by az-Zuray'ee, vol. 1 p. 9, *ar-Rawdh al-Anaf*, vol. 2 p. 285, *Hayat as-Sahaba* (the lives of the companions), vol. 3 p. 131, *Kanul Ummal*, vol. 4 p. 263, *Sunan ad-Darqutni*, vol. 1 p. 241, and others.

The result of Muhammad's concession in the al-Hudaybiyya Truce was so great that no one of the companions had ever imagined. It was a great victory after one year when groups after groups embraced Islam willingly and without effort or fighting.

If you both (the Sunni and the Shia) take the Messenger of Allah (s) as your example and you claim that you do according to the Book of Allah and the *Sunnah* of His messenger, then follow his (the Prophet) deeds, O you men of understanding!

Allah the Almighty says:

Thus, the *azan*, for you (the Sunni), has not been legislated by Allah, and you omit from and add to it, and even if you add to the *azan* of the Noon Prayer the statement of "the prayer is better than lunch" it shall be given legality by you and you shall approve it as you have approved some things else, whereas you deny those who have consensually agreed that the *azan* and the iqamah in their actual chapters had been revealed to the Prophet (s) by Gabriel (s).

Yes, we all have to deny everything that contradicts the real *azan*. Once, Muslims heard the muezzin saying in the *azan*: "They say that Muhammad is the Messenger of Allah (s)". They were astonished and they denied that. They went to the imam of the mosque objecting to him. He said to them, "I found no one to announce the *azan* in the mosque; therefore, I hired a Jewish man to announce it, and he does not believe in the prophethood of Muhammad (s)."

As for the mention of Imam Ali and the Ahlul Bayt (peace be on them all), we do not say that it is a part of the *azan*, nor do we add it instead of another basic part. We do not omit from or add fixed part to the *azan*, which was revealed to the Prophet (s) by Gabriel in his sleep. We believe that the revelation to the Prophet (s) in his sleep is like the revelation to him in his wake state.

However, they (the Sunni) chanted the *azan* in tones and recited it in groups like anthems. They omitted and added, since they believe that it (the *azan*) has not been divinely legislated, but a vision of one of the companions.

The Shia unanimously say that the *azan* was a revelation from Allah, and therefore, they believe that any omission or addition to it is not permissible; otherwise, it is considered a man's legislation against Allah's legislation, and this is impermissible among the Shia. This is not that case in saying "I bear witness that Ali is the saint of Allah", because this is mentioned as generally recommended and to show our adherence to the saint of Allah.

If you obey Allah and His Messenger, He will not diminish aught of your deeds; surely Allah is Forgiving, Merciful.
[Qur'an, 49:14]

THE SHIA AND THE SUNNI REFUTE THE WAHHABIS

As for the criticism, revilement, exaggeration and the accusation of disbelief that the Wahhabis raise against the Shia because they take the Prophet (s) and his progeny - the infallible Imams (as) - as means of intercession between them and Allah and they visit the shrines of these Imams and consider them as a source of blessing; this accusation is something new that neither the Shia nor the Sunni knew before.Muslims, since the time of the Prophet (s) until now, have kept and are keeping on visiting and seeking blessings from holy places and celebrating it in all the lands of Muslims. No one denied that, except for the Wahhabis who came up with their new doctrine in the fourteenth century of hijra.

It was very natural for the Wahhabis to contradict all Muslims in order to appear as reformers and as people of monotheism on the one hand and on the other hand, to justify their aversion and objection of Muslims to their heresies.[1]

---

[1] The tombs of the imams and saints are still visited in all the lands of Muslims. In fact, new tombs were found during excavations that made even secular and atheist governments to keep them safe with no damage. An example is what happened to the regime in Iraq, when the government with its different machinery and equipment failed to remove those tombs after the happening of many miracles that forced the government to give up the project or change its place. The same thing took place in Lebanon and other places in the Muslim countries in the world. In fact, when people see the miracle, they ascribe the tomb to a prophet, a saint, or a descendant of the Ahlul Bayt (as), until a group of scientist come and prove who the identity of the person is in the tomb.

We have never heard in any place that people worshipped the tomb. They honor those who have been buried in those tombs, because they are our role models and means to Allah, and honoring them is from the rites of Allah.

Indeed, Muslims have never been tried as they have been tried by the Wahhabis in this century.[1] It is so because of the following reasons:

Firstly, their mission is false, but they have dressed it in the garment of the truth. They prohibit the beseeching Allah by the means of the Prophet (s) and his progeny and punish for it, claiming that it is a kind of polytheism where Allah says:

Call not upon any one with Allah. [Qur'an, 72:18]

---

[1] Wahhabism is ascribed to Muhammad ibn 'Abdul Wahhab...ibn Wahhab at-Tamimi. He was born in 1111 A.H and died in 1207 A.H. In his early life, he studied at the hands of many 'ulama of Mecca and Medina who were experts in deviation and misleading. His father often dispraised and warned people against him, and so did his brother Sulayman ibn Abdul Wahhab, who denied him and wrote a book refuting him.

He was fond of reading about false claimants of prophethood such as Musaylama the Liar, Sajah, al-Aswad al-Ansi, Tulayha al-Asadi, and others...! Refer to *"The Emirs of the Inviolable Country"* by Sheikh Ahmad ibn Zayni Dahlan, and *"Kashful Irtiyab fi Ittibah' Muhammad ibn 'Abdul Wahhab"* by Sayyid Muhsin al-Amin al-Aamili.

Thus, he grew up deviant, doubtful, and spiteful. He was just like Kemal Ataturk and many rulers of the Muslim countries who claim that they are Muslims; however, they are directed by Freemasonry and nursed by the world intelligence agencies.

Muhammad ibn 'Abdul Wahhab was fed by the British agent in Iraq. Mr. Hanfer has mentioned this in his autobiography. He prepared and assisted him to achieve his ambition in prevailing over Hijaz. He and his likes are worse than their ancestors such as the Kharijites because the Kharijites had risen out of ambiguity. On the other hand these people are mercenaries working for the welfare of the enemies of Islam.

It is natural that his misleading mission did not incite any except the ignorant nomads, as it was with Musaylama - the Liar and his group opposite to the true mission of the Prophet (s) and his progeny and followers. Therefore, his mission of deviance did not spread through conviction, but through treason, deceit, invasion, oppression, suspicious treaties and breaking of covenants in order to get to his satanic desires.

And this is like the mission of the Kharijites who accused Imam Ali (as) of disbelief and said to him, "*The judgment is not yours, Ali, but to Allah.*" He said:

This sentence is true but it is interpreted wrongly.[1]

It means that the saying of the Kharijites "the judgment is but to Allah" was a word of truth, but the Kharijites intended falsehood by it when they said, "the judgment is not yours, O Ali." It is certain that the judgment is for Allah alone and not for any human being, but Allah the Almighty made His judgment appear at the hand of His messenger who did not speak out of desire, and then at the hands of the Prophet's successors whom the Prophet (s) defined and appointed to judge among people with the truth that he had legislated to them.

Surely, the legislative authority is Allah's alone and does not belong to anyone else and the executive authority is to people alternating with one another. This is something natural that all reasonable people understand. Then, how was it unknown by the Prophet's companions to say, "The judgment is not yours, O Ali"?

Imam Ali (as) reveals to us that they knew the truth, but they wanted the untruth by raising this doubt.

Allah the Almighty says in His Book:

If you judge, judge between them with equity. [Qur'an, 5:42]

Surely, Allah commands you to give over trusts to their owners and that when you judge between people you judge with justice.... [Qur'an, 4:58]

Surely, We have revealed the Book to you with the truth that you may judge between people by means of that which Allah has taught you...[Qur'an, 4:105]

O Dawud! Surely, We have made you a ruler in the land; so judge between men with justice. [Qur'an, 38:26]

And that you should judge between them by what Allah has revealed, and do not follow their desires. [Qur'an, 5:49]

---

[1] *Nahjul Balaghah* saying no. 198

But no! by your Lord! they do not believe (in reality) until they make you a judge of that which has become a matter of disagreement among them, and then do not find any straightness in their hearts as to what you have decided and they submit with entire submission. [Qur'an, 4:65]

Surely We revealed the Torah in which was guidance and light; with it the prophets ...judged. [Qur'an, 5:44]

After this and through these Qur'anic verses, it becomes clear to us that the mission of the Kharijites was of truth but they did not want it except through untruth and to raise sedition among naive people, who did not know the actual objective of the Sharia.

The same can be said about the mission of the Wahhabis. It is a mission of truth, but they do not want it except through untruth with which they deceive simple people, who do not know the actual objectives of the Sharia. They claim that they alone are the true monotheists and the others are polytheists because they call upon human beings with Allah.

It is true when they say, "Allah has said:

The mosques are Allah's; therefore, call not upon any one with Allah. [Qur'an, 72:18]

Say: I only call upon my Lord, and I do not associate any one with Him. [Qur'an, 72: 20]

But they intend the untruth when they prohibit the supplicating to Allah with intercession of the Prophet and his immaculate progeny (peace be on them) and deceive people, claiming that this is a kind of polytheism.

It is clear that there is a difference between those who believe that there are partners to Allah who benefit and harm, where they make a god for everything - the god of goodness, the god of evil, the god of peace, the god of war, the god of love...etc., and those who believe that Allah is One and only with no partner, and that no one can repel His decree, and that He has given them the right to call upon Him through the means of His prophets and saints.

This is the difference between the two beliefs - polytheism and the supplicating through intercession. This is the similarity between the Kharijites and the Wahhabis. The Kharijites said, "There is no judgment but Allah's" and the Wahhabis said, "There is no supplication except directly to Allah." The Kharijites said, "The judgment is not yours, O Ali", and the Wahhabis said, "The means is not yours, O Muhammad!"

In the two sayings there is untruth dressed up with truth. The judgment is to Allah alone, but He has legislated for it for His people to judge among themselves with truth and justice. The means to pray as well is to Allah alone, but He has determined it for His people to take His prophets and saints as a means to Him. This is clear in the Islamic religion and all the previous religions too, since all the divine religions are from one source. The religion near Allah is Islam.[1]

---

[1] The origin of the suspicion of Wahhabis in their judgment that all Muslims are polytheists and that their blood and properties are to be violated - as they actually did in Mecca, Medina, Iraq and other places of the Muslim lands - is because they (Wahhabis) claim that those Muslims worship graves when honoring, kissing and circumambulating them besides building the domes and minarets over them and some things like that!
In fact, there are many Prophetic traditions narrated by the Shia and the Sunni about seeking the intercession of the Prophet (s) and other than the Prophet (s) in this worldly life and for worldly or afterlife needs.
Abdullah Ibn Abbas narrated that the Prophet (s) said, *"If any Muslim dies and forty men who associate nothing with Allah stand over his prayer (they offer prayer over him), Allah will accept them as intercessors for him."* Refer to *Sahih Muslim*, vol.2, p. 654. Part on Funerals. For online version and more *hadithes*, visit: https://sunnah.com/muslim/11
Sayyid Muhsin al-Amin (may Allah have mercy on him) comments (mockingly) on this tradition, saying, "The forty men must be from the nomads of Najd (Wahhabis) so that their intercession would be accepted!" (Najd now is Saudi Arabia). In *Sahih Muslim, Ibid.,* it has been mentioned from Aa'isha that the Prophet (s) said, *"If a company of Muslims numbering one hundred pray over a dead person, all of them interceding for him, their intercession for him will be accepted."* visit: https://sunnah.com/muslim/11
According to the thought of the Wahhabis, this must be a kind of polytheism, because, as they claim, it contradicts this saying of Allah –

All the Qur'anic verses that the Wahhabis rely on in concluding their proofs do not have any sense of prohibiting the supplication to Allah through His loyal, righteous people. In fact, all these verses have been revealed to refute the polytheists from men and the jinn, who fabricated lies against Allah and worshipped many gods, thinking that those would bring them closer to Allah.

...so invoke not any one along with Allah. [Qur'an 72:18]
We seek the protection of Allah from this great fabrication against His Holy Prophet (s)! There are many Prophet's traditions about intercession, and *ulama* say that there is no difference between a dead and alive person.
As-Samhudi Al-Shafi'i, the alim of Medina, says in his book *Wafa al-Wafa bi-Akhbar al-Mustafa*, vol. 2 p. 419, quoting al-Hakim that Umar ibn al-Khattab narrated that the Prophet (s) said, "When Adam committed the sin, he said, 'O my Lord, I ask You by the right of Muhammad that You but forgive me.' Allah said, 'O Adam, how do you know Muhammad while I have not created him yet?' Adam said, "O my Lord, when You created me and inspired in me from Your Spirit, I raised my head and saw on the posts of the Throne written "There is no god but Allah, and Muhammad is the Messenger of Allah (s)...' Allah the Almighty said, 'O Adam, you are right. Surely, he is the most beloved of all creation to Me. Since you asked Me by his right, I forgive you. Were it not for Muhammad, I would not create you." He mentioned that this tradition was mentioned by at-Tabarani, and by al-Bayhaqi through true chain of narrators in his book *Dala'il an-Nubuwwah*.
In other traditions, it is mentioned that Adam and Noah supplicated to Allah by means of the Five of the Aba (Muhammad, Ali, Fatima, al-Hasan, and al-Husayn, peace be on them all).
About this matter, Imam Malik asked al-Mansur, "Why do you turn away from him (the Prophet) while he is your means and the means of your father Adam to Allah the Almighty?"
As-Samiri al-Hanbali, al-Kirmani al-Hanafi, and the Shafiite *ulama* believe in the supplication by the means of the Prophet (s) and believe in his intercession after his death. Imam Al-Shafi'i supplicated to Allah by means of the Ahlul Bayt (s) after their death. He supplicated to Allah by the means of Imam Abu Hanifa, and he approved the supplication of the people of Morocco by the means of Imam Malik after his death. Ahmed ibn Hanbal supplicated to Allah by the means of Al-Shafi'i and so on. These are the *ulama* and jurisprudents of Islam, then, who are the rude nomads?!

The saying of the Wahhabis is not applied to the Nation of Muhammad (s) that is called "the nation of monotheism" and "the nation of faith", for this nation is free from polytheism. All Muslims recite day and night, the *surah* of monotheism and faith:

Say: He is Allah, the One. Allah is He on Whom all depend. He begets not, nor was He begotten. And none is like Him. [Qur'an 30:1-4]

The Prophet (s) referred to this fact by saying:

I, by Allah, do not fear for you that you become polytheists after me, but I fear for you that you may compete with each other for worldly pleasures.[1]

This is irrefutable evidence that the Muslim nation is free from polytheism, and it is a clear evidence that the nation would compete for the worldly pleasures and authority. The nation would apostatize and judge with other than that which had been revealed and that would lead to oppression, lack of faith, and atheism but would not lead to polytheism at all.

Allah the Almighty has fixed this fact in His Book when saying in the Surah al-Ma'idah:

Whoever did not judge by what Allah revealed, those are they that are the unbelievers. ...and whoever did not judge by what Allah revealed, those are they that are the unjust. ...and whoever did not judge by what Allah revealed, those are they that are the transgressors. [Qur'an, 5:44-45, 47]

This is actually what has been happening in the Muslim nation after the death of the Prophet (s) until today. They inserted in the Sharia what was not from it; many positive rulings were added from personal opinion. Thus they changed the rules of Allah. However, Allah does not say that they are polytheists, but He says that they are unbelievers, unjust and transgressors.

All of us know well that the presidents and kings of the Arab and Muslim countries may rule with what is unlike the Book of Allah

---

[1] *Sahih al-Bukhari*, vol. 7 p. 207.

yet, we do not call them polytheists because they believe in Allah alone with no partner to Him and bear witness that Muhammad is His slave and messenger. In fact, we do not consider even the Jews and the Christians, who believe in the Torah and the Gospel, as polytheists when they believe in the oneness of Allah and do not ascribe to Him a child.

Allah the Almighty says:

How do they make you a judge and they have the Torah wherein is Allah's judgment? Yet they turn back after that, and these are not the believers. [Qur'an, 5:43]

And,

And the followers of the Gospel should have judged by what Allah revealed in it; and whoever did not judge by what Allah revealed, those are they that are the transgressors. [Qur'an, 5:47]

Thus, the matter has become clear with no need for more details.

Secondly, the Wahhabis have occupied the most sacred places for all Muslims of all colors, races and countries. The Holy Mecca has the Inviolable House of Allah to which Muslims from everywhere come to perform one of the pillars of Islam - the Hajj - every year, and they are very eager and full of incomparable longing to circumambulate the Kaaba, to stop at the *Inviolable Mish'ar*,[1] run between the *Safa* and the *Marwa*, and stop at *Arafa*.

All these places live inside the consciousness of every Muslim who wishes to visit them even once throughout his life... and Medina where there is the Holy Mosque of the Prophet (s) and his holy tomb inside it. Besides there are other monuments that all Muslims sanctify - the mihrab of the Prophet (s), his minbar, the pure yard (rawdhah), the tombs of Abu Bakr and Umar, the Baqee' Graveyard that includes the tombs of the Prophet's companions and wives, the holy tombs of the Ahlul Bayt (as) and the worth visiting places that are highly regarded by Muslims, like Uhud Mountain, the Martyrs Graveyard, the Two *Qiblas* Mosque and *Qabaa'* Mosque.

---

[1] A place where one of the rituals of the hajj is performed.

The Wahhabis trade on these rituals to the top, materially and morally. They propagate their new doctrine with all means through gifting or terrorizing, especially during the season of the Hajj when millions of Muslims gather together. They hold conferences and meetings, and their agents spare no effort in propagating Wahhabism by direct contact with different sects, groups and individuals. Add to that all kinds of the media, which are very effective on the Hajjis who give up arguments and disputes during the rituals of the Hajj and retire to worship Allah alone.

Thirdly, the vast wealth coming from petroleum, the mines of gold, and the continuous economic activities refreshed by the masses of pilgrims during the seasons of the Hajj, the minor Hajj and the rest of the year, have helped Wahhabism to spread everywhere in the world.

The Wahhabis spend great monies on the imams of mosques, who are incited by monies in all places in the world. They have built in every Arab and Muslim capital a mosque or several mosques working day and night to spread this new doctrine. They have established schools, colleges, and universities graduating missionaries to propagate Wahhabism throughout the world, sparing no effort in turning people to this new creed.

They have established many press and foundations of publication and distribution and financed more than one hundred daily, weekly, and monthly magazines and newspapers. They spend millions of dollars on mercenary writes to write for them what they like in assisting their beliefs and considering the others as unbelievers. They publish millions of copies of the Holy Qur'an and some books that assist their creed and distribute them freely as gifts everywhere.

After the Gulf War and because people hated them, they began distributing milk and dates among the visitors in Ramadan, and then gifting them at airport with big bottles of *Zamzam* water written on them "A gift from the servant of *Haramayn* – the two sanctums", whereas before, they prevented pilgrims from taking *Zamzam* water with them onto airplanes.

Fourthly, the international relations the Wahhabis have through their firm relation with the United States of America, which has direct and indirect influence on the Arab and Muslim countries, and in fact on the entire world after the decline of the Soviet Union

It is known to everyone that the welfare of the United States of America is assured and guarded in the east and the Gulf States by the Wahhabis especially after the fall of the Shah and the coming of the Islamic Republic in Iran - that threatened to attack all the American interests in the region.

It is known too to everyone of understanding that the Wahhabis are as much the right eye of the United State of America, as Israel is its left eye; however it (the United States) takes everything from the Wahhabis and gives everything to Israel.

It takes from the Wahhabis, because it spends great efforts in defending them and guarding their Royal throne (of the Saudi family) and has made its Intelligence Agency ready to reserve the Wahhabi regime and do away with all its opponents. It gives to Israel to assure the votes that are controlled by the Jewish Lobby inside the United States and Europe.

This is another subject that requires an individual book to be written about it, but what concerns us in this study is that the Wahhabis through their relation with the United States of America have come to be feared in the Arab and Muslim countries and all over the world. While mosques are closed after the prayers in some Arab and Muslim countries for fear that some groups may use them as centers for propagation of their beliefs and thoughts, we find that the mosques of the Wahhabis are open all the time for their propagandists to give lectures on what they like for spreading their thoughts.

Wahhabism has acquired this legality because of the great gifts, helps, and loans given to those countries. Therefore, those poor countries submit to the conditions of the Wahhabis in permitting them to spread their creed, and preventing the books and magazines that reveal their plots.

This has happened even in France, the strong modern country that claims it defends freedoms, human rights, and freedom of speech. It is France itself that defended Salman Rushdi and adopted his book, but at the same time, it prevented the book "*the History of Aal*

Sa'ud' which reveals the reality of Wahhabism. The French government collected the copies of this book from libraries, because the Saudi Kingdom saved France from the economic collapse in 1984.

Then, Saudi Arabia gave to France seven hundred million dollars, and it has been said to be much more than that. After that, hundreds of mosques were built in Paris only to propagate Wahhabism there, whereas the Ahlul Bayt Center (a Shiite foundation) was closed under the pretense that it had adopted excess and terrorism. The French police began pursuing everyone following the line of the Ahlul Bayt (as), while Wahhabism and its followers flourished there.

Add to that the league of the Islamic world that has been established by the Kingdom of Saudi Arabia. It includes the Arab and Muslim presidents and kings who have been under the Saudi influence.

This is just a small insight, but what is plotted behind the scenes is known by Allah alone. Therefore, I often say that Muslims have never seen a calamity worse than Wahhabism

KHARIJITES' DOUBT IN THE PAST AND WAHHABIS' IN THE PRESENT ARE THE SAME

The Kharijites, in the past raised the doubt of "the judgment is Allah's alone" and the Wahhabis in the present raise the doubt of "servitude is to Allah alone". There is no place for criticizing their mere calls when there is no context. But if the mission is coupled with a political doubt or a certain benefit in contradicting the beliefs of others, then it is a false mission dressed in the garment of truth.

As for the mission of the Kharijites, it was buried on the first day, because Imam Ali (as) disclosed it and revealed its false reality when he said, "It is a word of truth by which untruth is intended." Rather, Imam Ali (as) fought the Kharijites with no leniency according to the will of his brother and cousin the Messenger of Allah (s) and he did away with them and with their mission forever.

As for Wahhabism, it became strong and widespread with the assistance of the British firstly and the support of the United State of America and the West secondly. This was for a certain purpose that analyzers and learned people of the Muslim nations knew well. The United States of America especially and the West in general, fights Islam and considers it the only danger that threatens their beliefs and welfares.[1]

---

[1] They call Islam as "the great danger coming from the east". Since the time of colonialism until now, the plundering of Muslim countries has been continuous by England, France, Italy, the United States of America and others... After that, came out new serpents calling themselves with new names - mandate, defending or guardianship. All that was not enough and it appeared that it was the stage of incubation. After that, came the international organizations to assure the welfares of the great countries:
League of Nations, established in 1919 after the First World War
The United Nations, established in 1945 after the Second World War
North Atlantic Treaty Organization (NATO), established in 1949...and many others...even the Treaty of Baghdad...and finally the time is for the

We saw how they allied with each other in fighting the Islamic Republic of Iran and tried and are still trying, to do away with it as much as they possibly can by all means. Some of their presidents openly announced that they had supplied their agent Saddam with all fatal weapons and all experiences to do away with the Islamic Republic. When they failed here and the Iraqi opposition became strong inside and outside Iraq, they feared that their experience with Imam Khomeini might be repeated in Iraq, where the Shia are more than two thirds of population. They feared that the revolution in Iraq might unite with the revolution of Iran.

Then, they played their filthy trick by occupying Kuwait and declaring war not against Saddam, as they claimed, but against the Iraqi people, where the Shia are more than seventy percent of population. And this is actually what happened - Kuwait was rebuilt better than before and the regime of Saddam became stronger than before, but the oppressed Iraqi people who were terribly destroyed, began selling their furniture and clothes to get a piece of bread.

By doing so, the Wahhabis obtained victory over all the Shia in the world. In fact, the plot was to degrade the Shia and drive them to the camps in Saudi Arabia to meet there all kinds of insults, torture and killing.

Allah says:

The Jews will not be pleased with you, nor the Christians until you follow their religion. [Qur'an, 2:120]

Today, we see the Jews and the Christians (the United States of America and western countries) show cordiality to the Wahhabis. Or, are they pleased with them, because they themselves flatter and show them cordiality? At the same time, they are also full of grudge against the Shia in Lebanon, Iraq, and Iran and even in France.

American policy to be defined after it showed you the Statue of Liberty, but the liberty that must be in compliance with the American style that has become a play in the hands of the international Zionism! We see today the competition between many Arab governments to win the Israelite content, as if they have mistakenly interpreted this verse:
...and for that let the aspirers aspire. [Qur'an, 83:26]

They used all kinds of the media to defame and accuse the Shia of terrorism, fanaticism, and puritanism.[1] The media, financed by the Wahhabis, was successful in dividing the Shia, making some of them disagree with others, doubting their beliefs, and concentrating on some negative practices that some of ignorant Shia follow in Ashura. They openly criticized the great religious authorities, suspected their justice and honesty and accused them of leaving the wealth of Muslim for their children to spend it recklessly. The media was successful in buying the consciences of some prominent Shia personalities to raise the banner of deviation for misleading.

In fact, there was no time more dangerous to the Shia than this time. The true Shia must think of the affairs deeply, because they are threatened by many enemies. Anyhow, their patience and faith bring good news of optimism. Allah the Almighty says:

Obey Allah and His Messenger and do not quarrel for then you will be weak in hearts and your power will depart, and be patient; surely Allah is with the patient. [Qur'an, 8:46]

As we have said that the doubt of the Kharijites was based on the saying that "the judgment is Allah's alone", the doubt of the Wahhabis was based on the saying that "servitude is to Allah alone". Despite the fact that two sayings are alike, the saying of the Wahhabis is more effective than the saying of the Kharijites who focused on the rule (judgment).

Before Imam Ali (as), the rule was assumed by Abu Bakr, Umar and Uthman who all ruled as they liked and gave judgments that contradicted the clear texts of the Qur'an and the *Sunnah* of the Prophet (s), but no one objected to them. At least, history did not mention to us any objection that was worth mentioning.

People were used to the rules of the caliphs and they accepted them as continuity to the rules of Allah, misinterpreting the actual rulings as they liked. Therefore, this saying (of the Kharijites) did not

---

[1] Of course, they do not mean by puritanism the keeping to the fundamentals of religion, for this is a virtue, but they mean by it the middle ages of oppression and darkness, which means underdevelopment, ignorance and being opinionated.

find any influence in the selves of the majority of Muslims who adopted the doctrine of the Saqifah which showed that people were free to choose their ruler and they did not believe in the choice of Allah.

They relied on the Qur'anic verses in deriving their evidences that the obedience to the ruler, who is a human being, was obligatory; these verses confirmed the doctrine of the Saqifa and were called "the verses of consultation" like this verse:

O you who believe! Obey Allah and obey the Messenger and those in authority from among you," [Qur'an, 4:59]

The prophet's traditions which they relied upon in concluding that the obedience to the ruler was obligatory, were too many as well.

Therefore, the doctrine of the Kharijites was sentenced to death by the majority of Muslims even if Imam Ali (as) did not refute, because it was strange to them and to their concept of the rule. Thus it would not receive any acceptance especially from those who were greedy to rule and take authority from the Umayyads and the Abbasids, and how many they were!

But as for the doubt of the Wahhabis, it depends on the saying that "servitude is to Allah only", and surely there is no Muslim who does not believe in this obligation, when Muslims always recite this verse:

They were not enjoined anything except that they should serve Allah, being sincere to Him in obedience, upright, and keep up prayer and pay the poor-rate, and that is the right religion. [Qur'an, 98:5]

The Wahhabis made use of the behaviors of some ignorant Muslims during the age of decline when there were many juggleries, jugglers and quacks being fed by colonialists. The Wahhabis took such kind of people as a clear argument to accuse Muslims of disbelief and polytheism. And then went on to permit their killing in bloody wars and continual assault of peaceful places that were overcome by force and oppression.

If we ponder on their argument they rely on, which is this saying of Allah,

"And that the mosques are Allah's, therefore call not upon any one with Allah," [Qur'an, 72:18]

we shall find that it is like the saying of the Kharijites that "rulership (judgment) is Allah's alone" where Allah says:

There is none to be a guardian for them besides Him, and He does not make any one His associate in His Judgment. [Qur'an, 18:26]

Even though this verse shows that Allah does not let anyone participate in His judgment, many other verses give the right of judgment to man. We have mentioned some of them and said that there was no contradiction or difference between them, but the meaning is that the legislative judgment is to Allah alone and not anyone else, even if it is a prophet or messenger. Allah has declared this in His saying:

If he had fabricated against Us some of the sayings, We would certainly have seized him by the right hand. Then We would certainly have cut off his aorta. And not one of you could have withheld Us from him. [Qur'an, 69:44-47]

As for the executive judgment, Allah has made it for His prophets, messengers, the caliphs from His saints and the imams whom He chooses. By this interpretation, the meanings of the verses become right.

It is the same about the verse that prohibits man from calling upon anyone with Allah as there are many verses that give man a right to supplicate to Allah by means of His prophets, messengers, and saints. There is no contradiction between the verses; the first verse talks about deity and servitude and that deity is Allah's alone. The other verses declare that Allah has given the right of intercession and being a means to His prophets and saints.

To explain this matter, which is ambiguous to the Wahhabis and to some Muslims who have been influenced by the Wahhabis, it is useful to mention a debate between one of the Wahhabi *ulama* and me. Because of its uses, I shall mention it as it was.

In the year 1983, I was preparing a thesis on the rights of woman in Islam. During my reading in some magazines, I was surprised by the fact that the Muslim woman in Comoros is the custodian of man. She builds and furnishes her house. Then, when getting married, she brings her husband to her own house, and if she divorces him, she drives him out of her house. She works in the market, and the role of her husband is fishing in the sea, working in the field, and fetching goods to her in the market. She herself sells and buys. Thus, women in Comoros are custodians of men. How wonderful it is!

I traveled to this place after a difficult journey. I knew that France had given independence to three of the islands of the country and kept one until now. Comoros, as a new country, had joined the League of Arab States, which offered their help. Among those help was the educational delegation from Tunisia and other countries that was sent to Comoros to teach the Arabic language to the students of religious studies, most of whom were Arab from Yemeni origins called *Hadharimah* (related to Hadhramaut). Among them, there were *sayyids* from the pure progeny of the Prophet (s) who spoke Arabic besides French and the local language.

At the airport, I met with one of the Tunisian teachers whom I had known twenty years ago from a meeting in my youth. He recognized me and I recognized him. He invited me to his house where his wife and children had traveled to Tunisia and he was alone at home. I accepted his invitation and remained with him in his house.

During my residence there, I became acquainted with the *Mufti* of the Republic and the Judge of judges. I talked with them on many subjects. They trusted and loved me when they knew that I was from the followers of the Ahlul Bayt (as). They complained to me about the bad treatment and hatred they were facing from the Wahhabi *ulama* who had begun coming into the country successively in greater numbers with monies and books.

The Wahhabi *ulama* were successful in attracting many youths to their line of thought through money because these youths were living below the poverty level. Thereafter, those youths began blaming and disrespecting their fathers while before they had highly regarded and kissed their hands and heads and stood up when they passed by. They had inherited these morals generation after generation. The Prophet (s) has said:

He is not from us (not a Muslim) who is not kind to our little children, does not regard our old people and does not observe the right of our scholars.[1]

He[2] said to me, "However, when the Wahhabi *ulama* - the *ulama* of evil - came to us, their intention was not but to do away with these good morals and habits that we had been brought up with. A man from us, even though he is married and has some children, kisses the head and hands of his father and seeks his satisfaction and supplicates for him. But now, our children resist, criticize, and accuse us of polytheism, claiming that kissing of hands and the bowing before someone is a prostration for other than Allah and it is mere polytheism. There is a distance and resentment between fathers and children since the first day when these people came to our country. There is no power save in Allah!"

One day, the *Mufti* of the Republic invited me to accompany him to inaugurate a new mosque built in Moroni Island. I went with him in addition to the Judge of Judges, whose name was Abdul Qadir al-Gilani. When we arrived in the mosque, it was full of guests and ordinary people. The *Mufti* introduced me to the attendants and asked me to make a speech on that occasion. I responded and thanked him for that honor.

I made a speech, in which I emphasized on the love to the Ahlul Bayt (as) and their great position to Allah and to the Messenger of Allah (s), who had ordered Muslims to love and observe them and declared that loving them would be from faith and hating them would be from hypocrisy. I talked in details about their virtues and the great favors they offered to Islam and Muslims. At the end of my speech, I talked about their vast knowledge and sciences that filled

---

[1] *Musnad Ahmad* vol.2, p. 207. *Al Mujam al Kabir* vol.11, p. 449.

[2] The author means either the mufti or the judge.

the world and benefited the Muslim scholars everywhere on the earth and I said that if the Ahlul Bayt (as) were not available, people would not know these features of their religion.

The *Mufti* asked one of the *ulama* there and made him stand beside me to translate what I said. At the end of my speech, people came kissing and greeting me and praying Allah to have mercy on my parents.

This scene made one of the Wahhabi *ulama* angry, whom I recognized by his long beard and Saudi uniform. He came, shook hands with me, and said, "Fear Allah O Sheikh! All of us love the Ahlul Bayt, but you were too excessive in loving and honoring them."

I said, "I pray Allah to make me die on that."

He said, "You are my guest inshallah."

I said evadingly, "I am guest of the Mufti of the Republic."

He said, "Tomorrow then!"

I said, "Tomorrow, I am guest of the Tunisian teachers."

He said, "All of them are my friends, and we shall meet there."

DISCUSSION WITH ONE OF THE WAHHABI ULAMA

My friend, the Tunisian teacher, told me that his Saudi friend would come the next day to debate with me for a scholarly discussion. He told me that he had invited a group of teachers to participate in the argument so that everyone might make use of it. He told me that he had served lunch for the invitees. He said to me, "Today is the weekend holiday and we have enough time. How much we are eager to such meetings! We want you to be victorious; so do not disappoint us, because this Saudi man often talks and talks alone without giving us a chance to talk."

At the appointed time, the teachers came and with them was the Wahhabi scholar. We were nine - seven invitees, the host and me. After the meal, we began our argument whose subject was "*Tawassul* (supplicating to Allah by means of a prophet or a saint) and the intercession between a servant and his God"

I said that I believed in *tawassul* to Allah by means of His prophets, messengers and righteous saints. I said that man's supplication might be repelled because of his many sins and business with the pleasures of this life and then he might seek the intercession of the beloveds and saints of Allah.

The Wahhabi scholar said, "This is polytheism and Allah does not forgive the association of anyone to him."

I said, "What is your evidence that this is a kind of polytheism?"

He said, "Allah says -

'And that the mosques are Allah's, therefore call not upon any one with Allah.' [Qur'an, 72:18]

This is a clear verse that prohibits the supplication to anyone other than Allah. Whoever calls upon other than Allah makes a partner to Him that benefits and harms, whereas the benefiting and harming one is Allah alone."

One of the attendants approved his speech and wanted to support him, but the host stopped him, saying, "Take it easy! I have invited you not for dispute and competition, but I have invited you to listen to these two scholars. As for this Tunisian man, I have known him since long ago, but I was surprised when I discovered recently that he is a Shia, following the Ahlul Bayt (as), and this is our Saudi friend that all of you know and know his beliefs. We have just to listen to them both and see their arguments and evidences, until they have finished their debate. After that, it is our time to participate in the discussion, and every one can give his opinion if he wants."

We thanked him for his kindness and polite way, and we kept on with our arguments.

I said, "I agree with you that Allah the Almighty is alone the Benefactor, the One who can harm, and not one of Muslims disagrees with you on this, but our disagreement is on *tawassul*. The one, who supplicates to Allah by means of the Messenger of Allah (s) for example, knows well that Muhammad (s) neither benefits nor harms, but his (Muhammad) supplication is accepted and responded to by Allah. If Muhammad (s) asks Allah, saying, 'O my Lord, have mercy on this servant, forgive that servant, or enrich this one', surely Allah will respond to him.

The true Prophetic traditions narrated in this context are too many. For example, one day one of the companions who was blind, came to the Prophet (s) and asked him to pray Allah for his sight to be restored to him. The Prophet (s) ordered him to perform *wudhu'* and offer a two-*rak'a* prayer for Allah, and then to say, 'O Allah, I beseech You by means of your beloved Muhammad that You restore my sight.' After doing so, his sight was recovered.[1]

One day, Tha'laba, who was a destitute companion, came to the Prophet (s) and asked him to pray to Allah for him to become wealthy, because he liked to be benevolent to help the poor and give charities. The Prophet (s) prayed Allah for him, and he became so wealthy that his livestock were uncountable, but then, he stopped

---

[1] *Tarikh al Kabir*, vol.6, p. 209, hadith no 2192

coming to the mosque to offer prayer, and he did not give zakat...and this story is famous to most of people.[1]

One day, the Prophet described to his companions the bliss of Paradise, and what Allah had prepared to its inhabitants there. Ukasha asked the Prophet (s), 'O Messenger of Allah (s), pray Allah for me to make me one of them (the inhabitants of Paradise)'!

The Prophet (s) said, 'O Allah, make him one of them!' Another one got up and said to the Prophet (s), 'And to me, O Messenger of Allah (s)!' The Prophet (s) said, 'Ukasha has preceded you to that.'[2]

In these three traditions, there is clear evidence that the Messenger of Allah (s) made himself the means between Allah and His servants."

The Wahhabi interrupted me, saying, "I argue by the Holy Qur'an and he argues by weak traditions that neither fatten nor avail against hunger."

I said, "Allah says in the Holy Qur'an,

O you who believe! Be careful of (your duty to) Allah and seek means to Him. [Qur'an, 5:35]

He said, "The 'means' refers to a good deed."

I said, "The verses, concerning good deeds, are many and clear. Allah says:

And convey good news to those who believe and do good deeds, [Qur'an, 2:25]

But, in this verse He says - '*Seek means to Him*' - and in another verse, He says,

'Those whom they call upon, themselves seek the means to their Lord.'[Qur'an, 17:57]

These two verses indicate that the seeking of a means in supplicating to Allah has to be with piety and good deeds. Do you not see that Allah says:

---

[1] *Al-Isabah fi Tamyiz al-Sahabah* vol.1, p. 198
[2] *Musnad Ahmad* vol.1, p. 454

'O you who believe, be careful of (your duty to) Allah' -

in that He mentions faith and piety before the seeking of a means?"

He said, "Most of scholars interpret "means" as good deed."

I said, "Keep us away from interpretation and the sayings of scholars! What then if I prove 'intercession' by the Qur'an itself?"

He said, "This is impossible, except if it is in another Qur'an that we do not know!"

I said, "I know what you mean, may Allah forgive you! But I will prove that from the Qur'an that all of us know. Allah says,

They said: O our father, ask forgiveness of our faults for us, surely we were sinners. He said: I will ask for you forgiveness from my Lord; surely, He is the Forgiving, the Merciful [Qur'an, 12:97-98]

Why did our lord Jacob, the prophet of Allah, not say to his children: you yourselves ask Allah for forgiveness and do not make me intercessor between your Creator and you? He did accept that intercession and said: I shall ask my Lord to forgive you. Thus, he made himself a means to Allah for his children."

The Wahhabi felt it difficult to repel these verses that could not be doubted or misinterpreted. He said, "What do we do with Jacob who was from the children of Israel and whose religion was abrogated by the religion of Islam?"

I said, "I will give you evidence from Islam, from the religion of Muhammad the Prophet of Islam (s)."

He said, "We are listening."

I said,

'In the name of Allah, the Beneficent, the Merciful...and had they, when they were unjust to themselves, come to you and asked forgiveness of Allah and the Messenger had (also) asked forgiveness for them, they would have found Allah Oft-returning (to mercy), Merciful', [Qur'an, 4:64]

Why did Allah order them to come to the Prophet (s) to ask for Allah's forgiveness near him, and then the Prophet (s) would ask Allah to forgive them? This is clear evidence that the Prophet (s) was their means to Allah and that Allah would not forgive them except by him (the Prophet*).*"

The attendants said, "This is clear evidence that cannot be refuted."

The Wahhabi, feeling defeated said, "Yes, this was right when the Prophet was alive, but the man had died fourteen centuries ago."

I said with astonishment, "How do you say about the Messenger of Allah (s) 'the man had died'? The Messenger of Allah (s) is alive and not dead."

He laughed mockingly at my saying, and said, "The Holy Qur'an said to him,

'Surely you shall die and they (too) shall surely die,.' [Qur'an, 39:30]

I said, "And the Qur'an itself says,

'Reckon not those who are killed in Allah's way as dead; nay, they are alive (and) are provided sustenance from their Lord,' [Qur'an, 3:169]

And,

'Do not speak of those who are slain in Allah's way as dead; nay, (they are) alive, but you do not perceive.' [Qur'an, 2:154]

He said, "These verses talk about martyrs who were killed in the way of Allah, and they have nothing to do with Muhammad."

I said, "Glory be to Allah, and there is no power save in Allah! You demote the Prophet Muhammad (s) who is the most beloved to Allah, lower than the rank of a martyr! As if you want to say: Ahmad ibn Hanbal had died a martyr and he is alive near his God, but the Messenger of Allah (s) is dead like any other dead one."

He said, "This is what the Holy Qur'an says."

I said, "Praise be to Allah Who has uncovered to us your nature and made us know your reality by your own tongues. You have tried your best to wipe out the signs of the Prophet (s) to a degree that you tried to remove his tomb, as you had removed the house in which he was born."

At this moment, the host intervened, saying to me, "Let us not go out of the circle of the Qur'an and the *Sunnah*. We have agreed on this."

I apologized and then said, "What is important is that our friend has acknowledged 'intercession' during the Prophet's life and denied it after his death."

The attendants all said it was so, and they asked him again, "Did you agree that 'intercession' was permissible during the Prophet's life?"

He replied, "It was permissible during his life, but it is not permissible now after his death."

I said, "Praise be to Allah! For the first time, the Wahhabis acknowledge '*tawassul*', and this is a great victory. Please, allow me to add that *tawassul* was permissible even after the Prophet's death."

The Wahhabi said, "By Allah, it is not permissible. It is from polytheism."

I said, "Take it easy! Do not be hasty and swear that you may regret it after that."

He said, "Give evidence from the Qur'an!"

I said, "This is not possible, because the Revelation stopped by the death of the Prophet (s). We have to rely on the books of Hadith."

He said, "We do not accept any tradition, except that it is true. What the Shia narrate is of no value to us."

I said, "Do you trust in the Sahih al-Bukhari which is the most reliable book to you after the Book of Allah?"

He said astonishedly, "Does al-Bukhari say that *tawassul* is permissible?!"

I said, "Yes, he says that, but unfortunately, you do not read what there is in your Sahihs, and despite that, you resist out of fanaticism to your opinions.

Al-Bukhari has mentioned in his Sahih that Umar ibn al-Khattab asked Allah for rain by means of al-Abbas ibn Abdul Muttalib when there was famine. He often said, 'O Allah, we beseeched You by means of our prophet, and You sent down to us rains, and now we beseech You by means of the uncle of our prophet. So send down rain to us!' Al-Bukahri says, 'And they had rains'."[1]

Then I said to him, "It is Umar ibn al-Khattab, who is to you the greatest of companions, and you have no doubt in his loyalty, strong faith, and good beliefs. You say that if there would be a prophet after Muhammad, he would be Umar ibn al-Khattab. Now, you are between two things with no third; either you acknowledge that *tawassul* is from the essence of Islam and that the saying of Umar 'O Allah, we beseeched You by means of our Prophet, and You sent rains down to us, and now we beseech You by means of the uncle of our Prophet. So send rain down to us!'- is an acknowledgment of *tawassul* during the Prophet's life and after his death, or you say that Umar ibn al-Khattab was a polytheist because he made al-Abbas as his means to Allah. It is well known that al-Abbas was neither a prophet, nor an imam and not even from the Ahlul Bayt (as) from whom Allah has kept away uncleanness and purified with thorough purification.

Besides, al-Bukhari, who is the master of traditionists to you, has mentioned this tradition acknowledging its reliability and adding, 'and they had rains', which means that Allah responded to them. Thus, al-Bukhari and the narrators from the Prophet's companions, who narrated this tradition, are all polytheists in your view!!!"

He said, "If it is proved that this tradition is true, it shall be an argument against you."

I said, "How is it an argument against me?"

He said, "Because our master Umar did not supplicate to Allah by means of the Prophet because he was dead and he supplicated by means of al-Abbas because he was alive."

I said, "The doings and sayings of Umar are not evidence and have no value to me. I just mentioned this narration to prove the

---

[1] *Sahih al-Bukhari*, vol. 4 p. 209, Chap. The virtues of Ja'far ibn Abi Talib.

subject of our discussion, which is the denial of *tawassul* by you and all your *ulama* and that you consider it as polytheism.

I am astonished why Umar did not supplicate to Allah, during the absence of rains, by means of Ali ibn Abi Talib (as), who was to Muhammad (s) as was Aaron to Moses. No one of Muslims ever said that al-Abbas was better than Ali (as). However, this is another subject that does not concern us in this debate. I just say that you now acknowledge *tawassul* by means of living people and this is a great victory to me. I thank Allah Who has made our argument prevailing, and your argument vain. Since it is so, now I will use *tawassul* in your presence."

I got up from my seat, turned toward the *qibla*, and said, "O Allah, we call upon You and supplicate to You by means of Your righteous servant Imam Khomeini."

Suddenly, the Wahhabi leapt and shouted with denial, "I seek Allah's protection! I seek Allah's protection!" He left hastily.[1]

The attendants looked at each other, saying, "How strange he is! How often he criticized and refuted us! We thought that he was full of knowledge, but it has become clear that he is emptier than the heart of Moses' mother!"

One of them said, "We are Allah's and to Him we shall return! O Allah, I turn to You in repentance." He turned to us and said, "How much I was influenced by his sayings. Until today, I believed as he believed - that *tawassul* is a kind of polytheism. If I was not with you today, I would remain misled. Thanks to Allah, and to you."

And say: *The truth has come and the falsehood has vanished; surely falsehood is a vanishing (thing).* [Qur'an, 17:81]

---

[1] The Lebanese al-Bilad Magazine mentioned in a report on Bosnia, "We have met with a teacher of Arabic Language and Holy Qur'an in one of the mosques of the city, and he expressed his worry about the actions of some Muslim countries. The teacher Janiti said that a Tunisian volunteer, whose name was Ahmed, asked him to give a lecture on Wahhabisim, and when he refused to do that, he threatened to kill him and said that whoever did not embrace Wahhabism would be in Fire." Refer to al-Bilad Magazine, vol. 191, p.35.

WAHHABISM REFUTED BY THE PROPHET (s)

There is no doubt that the Holy Qur'an has acknowledged intercession and *tawassul* between Allah and His people, and not prohibited that nor prevented His messenger from it. Rather, the Qur'an has made it permissible and recommended it.

The Qur'an has made the Prophet's deeds, sayings, and approving of others' deeds an example for us to follow in our lives, when saying:

Certainly you have in the Messenger of Allah (s) an excellent exemplar. [Qur'an, 33:21]

On this basis, we will take the Prophet's doings and sayings as our evidence. We shall not derive our evidence from the books of the Shia nor from any of the books of the Sunni, for that shall be uncountable. We shall be satisfied with what al-Bukhari has mentioned in his Sahih alone, so that the answer to the Wahhabis shall be by the knockout that they may not argue with it, if they are fair. Otherwise, their obstinacy and blind fanaticism shall expose them to all Muslims.

After we have proved the permissibility of *tawassul* from the Qur'an and the Prophetic *Sunnah*, we discuss what to the Wahhabis is more defamed and more deniable than *tawassul*; it is the asking the blessing of and wiping one's body against holy shrines and sacred places.

The Wahhabis have reached an extent that they beat the Hajjis for doing so and accuse them of polytheism.

THE COMPANIONS SEEK THE BLESSING OF THE PROPHET'S HAIR

It is worth mentioning to say that the deeds of the Prophet's companions are an argument against the Wahhabis, because they believe that all the companions are totally just and honest. They claim that they follow them. They call themselves as Salafis meaning that they follow the "pious ancients" and that all the companions were pious and righteous in their view.

Al-Bukhari has mentioned in his Sahih that Malik ibn Ismaeel narrated from Israel ibn Aasim from Ibn Sirin who said, "*Once, I said to Ubaydah, 'We have some of the Prophet's hair. We have got it from Anas or the family of Anas.' He said, 'If I have one hair from him, it shall be more beloved to me than the world and all that is there in it'.*"[1]

Al-Bukhari also mentioned a tradition narrated by Muhammad ibn Abd ur Raheem from Sa'eed ibn Sulayman from Etad from ibn Sirin that Anas said, "*When the Messenger of Allah (s) had his hair cut, Abu Talha was the first one to take from his (the Prophet's cut) hair.*"[2]

Since Anas ibn Malik, the famous companion, kept the Prophet's hair and gave from it to his relatives and friends, and since a companion said, "*If I have one hair from him, it shall be more beloved to me than the world and all that is there in it*", (I swear) by my life, this is the clearest evidence that the companions sought blessing in the belongings of the Prophet (s) and everything related to him. And, by my life, this refutes the Wahhabis who beat the Hajjis who seek blessing in the Prophet's belongings.

In my book '*Then I was Guided*', I have mentioned the nice story of the Shia scholars who offered a copy of the Holy Qur'an wrapped

---

[1] *Sahih al-Bukhari*, vol. 1 p. 54.

[2] *Ibid.*

in leather as gift to the Saudi king at that time. The king kissed the Qur'an and put it on his forehead as a kind of honoring. The Shia Scholar said to the king, "Why did you kiss the leather and honor it?"

The king said, "When I kissed the leather, I intended to kiss what was there inside the leather, which is the Holy Qur'an."

The Shia scholar said, "And so do we! When we kiss the window of the Prophet's room (inside which he has been buried), we know that it is iron, which neither benefits nor harms, but we mean what is beyond the iron, and it is the Messenger of Allah (s)."

COMPANIONS AND CALIPHS SEEK BLESSINGS IN THE PROPHET'S BELONGINGS AFTER HIS DEATH

Through my research on this subject, I have found more than twenty traditions in the six Sahihs (the Sunni books of Hadith) showing that the companions in general and the caliphs especially, sought blessing from the Prophet's belongings. However, as I have promised, I shall only mention one or two traditions from al-Bukhari who seems to be strict in such traditions.

Al-Bukhari has mentioned in his Sahih in a chapter *"On what was narrated about the Prophet's armor, stick, sword, drinking-vessel, ring and what the caliphs used of that after him... and from his hair, shoes, and vessels by which his companions and others sought blessing after his death."*[1]

Al-Bukhari has mentioned in his Sahih that az-Zubayr said, *"On the Day (the battle) of Badr, I met Ubaydah ibn Sa'eed ibn al-Aas (in fighting), who was heavily armed and nothing was seen of him except his eyes, and who was surnamed as Abu Thatil Karsh. He said, 'I am Abu Thatil Karsh.' I attacked him with my iron-tipped stick. I hit him in his eye and he died."* Hisham said, *"I was told that az-Zubayr said, 'I put my leg against him and stretched myself and with effort I could take spout (the stick) - where its ends were bent."*

Urwa said, *"The Messenger of Allah (s) asked him (az-Zubayr) to give it to him, and he gave it to him. When the Messenger of Allah (s) was taken away in death, he (az-Zubayr) took it back. Then, Abu Bakr asked for it, and he gave it to him. When Abu Bakr died, Umar asked for it, and he gave it to him. When Umar died, he took it back, and then Uthman asked for it, and he gave it to him. When Uthman was killed, it became in the possession of Ali's family, and then*

---

[1] *Sahih al-Bukhari*, vol. 4 p. 100. Chapter 'The Prophet's call for Islam and Prophethood.'

Abdullah ibn az-Zubayr asked for it, and it was with him until he was killed."[1]

AN IMPORTANT POINT

We notice from this tradition that the Messenger of Allah (s) himself sought blessing in that stick, which az-Zubayr had and with which he had fought heroes in the wars. With this stick, he fought Ubaydah ibn Sa'eed ibn al-Aas who was heavily armed and armored that only his eyes were seen. Despite that, az-Zubayr struck him with this stick in his eye and killed him, and then he took it out with difficulty. It was really a wonderful stick, and it might be from the kind of stick that Moses had, with which he had split the sea for the Children of Israel.

Allah says:

Then We revealed to Moses: Strike the sea with your staff. So it had cloven asunder, and each part was like a huge mound. [Qur'an, 26:63]

And when Moses prayed for drink for his people, We said: Strike the rock with your staff So there gushed from it twelve springs. [Qur'an, 2:60]

It is no wonder then that the Messenger of Allah (s) asked az-Zubayr to give him that iron-tipped stick to seek the blessing in it, or it could be to teach people that seeking blessing is permissible in Islam. This possibility is too strong, especially when we know that all the caliphs after the Prophet (s) had asked for this stick, which moved from one to another until finally it came to Abdullah ibn az-Zubayer, for it was his father's heritage.

We find in the Holy Qur'an many references to seeking blessing in things that were related to prophets and messengers. It has been said in the Qur'an:

---

[1] *Sahih al-Bukhari*, vol. 5 p. 14. Chapter 'The presence of angels in the battle of Badr' from the book al-Maghazi (raids).

The Caliphs Sought Blessings

He said: What was then your case, O Samiri? He said: I perceived what they perceive not, so I seized a handful from the footsteps of the messenger, and then threw it in. Thus, my soul commended to me. [Qur'an, 20:95-96]

Perhaps Samiri perceived what the rest of companions, did not perceive when he seized a handful from the earth that the Prophet had stepped on, or which might have achieved some miracles. So he thought that Moses was a great magician and the miracles he showed to people were just magic that whoever had means to do it, could do.

Therefore, he threw the handful of earth and his soul incited him to take the Children of Israel back to worship the calf. The story confirms what we have said that he showed some charismata and miracles to the Israelites until they were deceived and they followed him.

We find other references in the Holy Qur'an to the seeking of blessing and cure by the belongings of the prophets. Allah says in the Surah Yousuf:

Take this my shirt and cast it on my father's face, he will (again) be able to see, and come to me with all your families. And when the caravan had departed, their father said: Most surely I perceive the scent of Yousuf, unless you pronounce me to be weak in judgment. They said: By Allah, you are most surely in your old error. So when the bearer of good news came, he cast it on his face, so forthwith he regained his sight. He said: Did I not say to you that I know from Allah what you do not know. [Qur'an, 12:93-96]

What is understood from these verses is that the Prophet Jacob (s) was blind and that his son Yousuf sent him his shirt and asked the one who brought good news to wipe his father's face with the shirt in order to recover his sight, and this actually happened.

Despite our deep faith that Allah the Almighty is able to make the Prophet Jacob (s) recover his sight without the shirt of Yousuf (s), able to make water gush out of the rock, and the sea to split without the stick of Moses and able to restore to life the killed one without hitting him with some pieces of the cow,[1] Allah the Almighty has made a means for all that to happen to make people understand what means and intercession are from the law of Allah to His people, and not polytheism as the Wahhabis and their followers claim.

Allah says:

This is Our book that speaks against you with justice; surely We wrote what you did. Then as to those who believed and did good - their Lord will make them enter into His mercy; that is the manifest triumph. And as to those who disbelieved: What! were not My communications recited to you? But you were proud and you were a guilty people. [Qur'an, 45:29-31]

---

[1] In reference to these verses:
"And when you killed a man, then you disagreed with respect to that, and Allah was to bring forth that which you were going to hide. So We said: Strike the (dead body) with part of the (sacrificed cow), thus Allah brings the dead to life, and He shows you His signs so that you may understand." [Qur'an 2:73]

THE PROPHET ALLOWED SEEKING BLESSING AND TAUGHT IT TO HIS COMPANIONS

Let no one be deceived by the sayings of those who deny - who say that seeking blessing in things is a heresy invented by some companions or some of their successors. They say that out of ignorance or fanaticism to new Wahhabism which is itself a heresy that accuses Muslims of polytheism just due to a false doubt the Wahhabis themselves have created.

The Messenger of Allah (s) acknowledged on many occasion what his companions did, seeking blessing in certain things and he recommended them to do that. After that, the companions competed among themselves to do it

Al-Bukhari in his Sahih has mentioned a tradition narrated by Adam from Shu'bah from al-Hakam that Abu Juhayfah said, "*The Messenger of Allah (s) went out with us at midday. He was brought some water and he performed wudhu' with it. People began taking from the remaining water of his wudhu' and wiping themselves with it. The Prophet (s) offered the Noon Prayer in two rak'as and the Afternoon Prayer in two rak'as, and there was a stick in front of him. Abu Musa said, 'The Messenger of Allah (s) called for a vessel of water with which he washed his hands and face and ejected (from his mouth) in it and said to them (his companions), 'Drink from it and pour on your faces and necks.*"[1]

Al-Bukhari mentioned another tradition in his Sahih clearer than the previous one. He mentioned that Abu Musa (may Allah have mercy on him) said, "*Once, I was with the Prophet (s) while he was in al-Ja'rana (a place) between Mecca and Medina, and Bilal was there with him. A nomad came to the Prophet (s) and said to him, 'Would you not carry out to me what you have promised?'*

---

[1] *Sahih al-Bukhari*, vol. 1 p. 59. Section of Wudhu

The Prophet said, 'Be delighted!'

The nomad said, 'How much you said to me - be delighted (with good news)!'

The Prophet (s) came to Abu Musa and Bilal while somehow angry, saying, 'He rejected the good news. You both come to me!'

They came to him. He called for a vessel of water. He washed his hands and face in it, and then rinsed out his mouth in it and said, 'Drink from it and pour on your faces and necks and wait for good news!' They took the vessel and did so. From behind a curtain, Umm Salama (the Prophet's wife) called out, 'Leave some of it for your mother!' And they left some to her."[1]

These true traditions on seeking blessing do not show that the Prophet (s) approved of the matter, but rather it was he who ordered his companions to do it after he had washed his hands and face and rinsed out his mouth with the water. Then, he asked them to drink and pour on their faces and necks from that water. He gave them good news that they would receive goodness by the blessing of that water with which the Prophet washed his hands, face, and mouth and Umm Salama (the Prophet's wife) asked to leave some of that water for her to be blessed with. So where are the Wahhabis from these facts? Or are there locks on their hearts!

---

[1] *Sahih al-Bukhari*, vol. 5 p. 199. Chapter Maghazi.

MUHAMMAD IS A HUMAN NOT LIKE OTHER HUMANS, BUT AS CORUNDUM AMONG GEMS

Once again, we say to all people that the Prophet Muhammad (s) is the best of all creatures and no one from the children of Adam can be compared to him. He is the master of them all. Despite whatever may be said about his human aspect, Allah has purified him from every impurity and vice.

Traditionists have mentioned that he had qualities that no one from the human beings ever had. The examples on that are too many; flies never ever sat on him, a cloud always cast shadow over him, earth swallowed all his excrements, the scent of musk emitted from his holy body was such that Abu Bakr said when he was laid out dead, "*May my father and mother die for you! How good you smell whether you are alive or dead!*"

When I read these traditions that I have already mentioned and believed in their reliability, I understood from them what others might not understand. I would not deny anyone to drink from the remainder of the Prophet's washing water, because the Prophet (s) is not like any other human being; he is like corundum among other gems.

Which one of us may willingly drink from water with which someone else has washed his hands, face and mouth? In addition to that, we fear that microbes and diseases that may come from dirt and filth. Our souls detest that, especially when we see with our eyes what is done to the water.

Yet unless we have believed and are certain that the Prophet (s) has been purified from all dirt, microbes, and bad smells and that his body is pure and immaculate, we shall not perceive these traditions. And if the loyal companions did not have that deep faith in these facts, they would not compete with each other to drink the remainder of the used water from Prophet's washing, to an extent that they struggled for it. In fact, the loyal companions knew the facts about the Prophet (s) that others did not know. The remainder of the washing water in which the Prophet (s) had washed his hands, face and mouth did not suffice for them.

We shall mention here more than that which human souls can bear to heat.

Al-Bukhari has mentioned in his Sahih a long story from which we shall take the theme that concerns our study. He said, *"...then Urwa began glancing at the Prophet's companions and he said, "By Allah, the Messenger of Allah (s) did not expectorate, except that it (his extract) fell in the hand of one of them (willingly) and he (a companion) rubbed it to his face and skin. When he (the Prophet) ordered them, they hurried to carry out his order, and when he performed the wudhu', they quarreled with each other to get (the remainder of the water of) his wudhu'..."*[1]

Al-Bukhari also mentioned a tradition narrated by Urwa that al-Musawwir and Marwan which said that the Prophet (s) came out to them at the time of Hudaybiyyah... and he mentioned the tradition, *"the Messenger of Allah (s) did not expectorate, except that it (his extract) fell in the hand of one of them (willingly) and he rubbed it to his face and skin..."*.[2]

This leads us to say that the great companions (may Allah be pleased with them) would not do that, unless the Prophet (s) kept silent when they did it, or rather approved it for them.

There is no doubt that the companions saw charismata because of this act, such as recovering health and soundness, goodness, prosperity and cure of diseases; otherwise, they would not massage their faces and skins with Prophet's pituitrin.

To confirm what we say, we quote this tradition from Sahih al-Bukhari, to show people the falsehood of Wahhabism. The tradition reads, *"Once, the Messenger of Allah (s) went out in the midday to the desert. He performed wudhu' and offered the Noon Prayer in two rak'as and the Afternoon Prayer in two rak'as, and in front of him*

---

[1] *Sahih al-Bukhari*, vol. 3 p. 254.
[2] *Ibid.*, vol. 1 p. 70.

there was a stick...Awn added that his father Abu Juhayfa said, "Passers passed behind it (the stick). And then people got up and began taking his (the Prophet) hands and massaging with them their faces. I took his hand and put it on my face. It was colder than ice and better (in its scent) than the scent of musk."[1]

---

[1] *Sahih al-Bukhari*, vol. 4 p. 229.

SEEKING HEALING BY THE PROPHET'S BLESSING

There is no doubt that the Prophet Muhammad (s) cured patients by his touching, water of *wudhu'*, saliva and other things.

Muslim has mentioned in his Sahih and al-Bukhari as well that Sahl ibn Sa'eed (may Allah be pleased with him) said, "*On the Day (battle) of Khaybar, the Messenger of Allah (s) was heard saying – 'I will give the banner to a man at whose hands Allah will grant victory. He loves Allah and His messenger, and Allah and His messenger love him.' That night people remained in suspense, wondering to whom among them the Prophet (s) would hand the banner. They all looked forward to it. Next day he (the Prophet) asked where Ali (as) was, and it was said to him that he had sore eyes. The Prophet (s) spat in Imam Ali's eyes and he recovered as if he had never suffered any pain. Then the Prophet gave the banner to Ali who said, 'Should I fight them to be like us (Muslims)?' He (the Prophet) said, 'Go on until you arrive in their field, and then invite them for Islam and tell them of their obligations. By Allah, if Allah guides by you one man, it is better for you than to have red camels (abundant wealth)'.*"[1]

Al-Bukhari has said too, "*I heard as-Sa'ib ibn Yazid saying, 'Once, my aunt took me to the Prophet (s) and said to him, 'O Messenger of Allah (s), this son of my sister has fallen.' He rubbed my head and prayed Allah to bless me. Then, he performed wudhu' and I drank from the water of his wudhu'…*"[2]

He also said, "*I heard Jabir saying, 'One day, the Messenger of Allah (s) came to visit me when I was ill of insanity. He performed wudhu' and poured on me from the water of his wudhu' and I became sane. I asked him, 'O Messenger of Allah (s), with whom*

---

[1] *Sahih al-Bukhari*, vol. 4 p. 20.
[2] *Sahih al-Bukhari*, vol. 1 p. 56, 57.

shall my inheritance be with, for I have neither parents nor children?' Then, the verse of obligations (inheritances) was revealed."¹

Surely, the Messenger of Allah (s) was in such a position to Allah that he made a blind man recover his sight by his saliva and a mad one recover his sanity by the water of his *wudhu'* and that his companions massaged their faces and skins with his pituitrin seeking health and soundness.

It has been mentioned in traditions that Huthayfa ibn al-Yaman had a pouch with which he cured patients and that whomever he put the pouch on was cured. People were very influenced by him until his news reached the Prophet (s) who sent for him, asking, "*Are you seditious O Huthayfa?*" He replied, "Certainly not O Messenger of Allah (s), but I have kept the stone that once had harmed your foot. I put it in a piece of cloth, and now I cure patients by it."

The Prophet (s) said to people, "*If you trust in a stone, it shall benefit you.*"²

We do not mean by these traditions that we place trust in jugglers and swindlers, or that we do not believe in scientific medicine. How would that be when we always depend on the Prophet's saying, "*Bring a physician to him, because Allah has created the disease and created the cure to it*"?

And this does not mean that Muslims only depend on supplication, amulets, the Qur'an, blessing and other things that are familiar in all Muslim countries for treatment. We quote these evidences just to argue against the Wahhabis who deny all these things and consider whoever believes in them as a polytheist.

Surely, the companions had their justification in seeking blessing and *tawassul* in the Prophet (s), because they lived with him and saw his miracles and charismata which astonished them and filled their selves with reverence and hope.

Biographers, who were interested in the Prophet's miracles, have mentioned all the miracles mentioned in the Qur'an of the prophets

---

¹ *Sahih al-Bukhari*, vol. 1 p. 56, 57.
² I do not remember the source of this tradition, but I have heard it from our teachers in Tunisia.

who had preceded him, such as healing the patients, the blind and the lepers, giving life to the dead, the coming down of food from the heaven, talking with animals and many other signs.

We shall mention only one or two traditions from al-Bukhari and let researchers themselves read what scholars have written on this matter.

Qatada narrated that Anas said, "*A vessel was brought to the Prophet (s) while he was in az-Zawra. He put his hand inside the vessel and water began gushing out from between his fingers. All people performed wudhu (from that water)". Qatada said, "I asked Anas how many men there were and he said that they were three hundred or about three hundred men.*"[1]

Jabir ibn Abdullah narrated, "*On the day of al-Hudaybiyya, people felt thirsty. There was a pot before the Prophet (s). He performed wudhu'. People hurried towards him, and he asked, 'What happened to you?' They said, 'we do not have water to perform wudhu' or drink, except this water before you.' He put his hand in the pot, and water began gushing out between his fingers like springs. We drank and performed wudhu'."...I asked how many ones they were and he said, 'If we were one hundred thousand, the water would be enough. We were fifteen hundred men.*"[2]

Alqama narrated that Abdullah said, "*One day, we were with the Messenger of Allah (s) on a travel. We ran out of water. He (the Prophet) said, 'Bring me a little of water.' They brought him a vessel having a little water. He put his hand inside the vessel and said, 'Come on to the pure, blessed (water) and blessing is from Allah!' I did see water spring between the fingers of the Messenger of Allah (s)...and we did hear the glorifying (tasbeeh) of food while it was being eaten.*"[3]

---

[1] *Sahih al-Bukhari*, vol. 4 p. 170. chapter - The signs of prophethood in the book "The beginning of creation".
[2] *Ibid.* p.171
[3] *Ibid.* p.172

WAHHABISM HAS HISTORICAL ROOTS

If we go back to our history and look up its painful events, some of those events shall attract our attention to reveal to us that Wahhabism,[1] which we have known in this century, had ancient roots since the very beginning of Islam. They were apparent at one time and hidden at another. One time they appeared daringly, and at another they time hid because of fear and dissimulation, until the time that Islam had regressed and its pillars and great personalities were afflicted. Then colonialism came to feed and strengthen this new thought.

The aim behind it was to destroy the sanctity of the Prophet Muhammad (s). Muslims, due to the colonialists' thoughts, sanctified two things - the Qur'an and the *Sunnah*. These are the two basic sources of the Islamic Sharia that was targeted by them.

They know that the speech of Allah can never be changed and distorted, because Allah, the Almighty has undertaken its preservation. But as for the Prophet's *Sunnah*, it is liable to distortion and fabrication. In fact, since the first day when the Prophet (s) left for the better world, disagreement took place among Muslims on the Prophet's *Sunnah*.

However, the colonialists perceived that the scholars of the nation had set right the *Sunnah* and collected its true and reliable traditions and put laws and rules to keep it safe from increase or decrease. Therefore, they thought of a satanic trick that might help them do away with the spiritual matters that were the most active factor in the life of Muslims. It was that whenever Muslims gave up on these spiritualties they would approach them step by step with unfaithful materialism, and then they would become like the scum of a flood.

---

[1] More more detailed information, please see *Wahhabism* by Ayatullah Ja'far Subhani at: https://www.al-islam.org/wahhabism-ayatullah-jafar-subhani

They looked for a Muslim man who had infinite ambition, and they discovered Muhammad ibn 'Abdul Wahhab, to whom Wahhabism is ascribed. They inspired in him from their spirit and convinced him that he was the savant of his age and that he had genius and intelligence that even the orthodox caliphs did not have. They showed him the violations of the caliphs against the clear texts of the Qur'an and the Prophetic *Sunnah*, especially the objection of Umar ibn al-Khattab to the Prophet (s) during his life. They convinced him that Muhammad was a human being who was fallible; that he committed many mistakes and that some people had to correct him. This was a proof of his (the Prophet's) weakness. They aroused his greed to the rule and to prevail over Arabia first and then all over the Arab and Muslim world.

Wahhabism was established on these concepts - trying their best to degrade the Prophet (s) and slighting his importance, until their scholars openly said, "*The man has died.*" And their head said, "*Muhammad is just a worn-out rope that neither does any benefit nor harm, and my stick is better than him because it benefits and harms.*"

Sayings like that were said at the time of al-Hajjaj ibn Yousuf ath-Thaqafi who himself said, "*Woe to them! They circumambulate a worn-out rope. If they circumambulated the palace of Ameerul Mu'minin Abdul Melik ibn Marwan, it would be of use to them.*"

In fact, nothing made al-Hajjaj and the vicious Umayyad rulers so daring, except for the daring of Umar ibn al-Khattab who said in the presence of the Prophet (s), "*This man (the Prophet) is raving. The Book of Allah is sufficient for us.*"[1]

In this very impudent saying, there are all the meanings that the Wahhabis try their best to confirm and fix in the minds of people. They say that Muhammad has died and is no longer but a part of history. Whoever supplicates through his means is as if he worships him and makes a partner in deity. This is not a new concept; it has a root in history. Abu Bakr said openly before people, "*O people,*

---

[1] *Tarikh al-Tabari* vol.3, p. 173. *Sahih Muslim* vol.3, 1959. For more details of this incident, read '*Black Thursday*' by the same author available at: https://www.al-islam.org/black-thursday-muhammad-al-tijani-al-samawi

whoever worshipped Muhammad – so Muhammad has died, and whoever worshipped Allah, Allah is alive and will never die."[1]

What was the reason for Abu Bakr to say so while he certainly knew that no one of Muslims worshipped Muhammad at all? Did Abu Bakr believe that some Muslims actually worshipped Muhammad? If it was so, then why did Muhammad keep silent before those people, or why he did not prevent or scold them or even kill them?

I have been convinced that they (Abu Bakr, Umar...etc.) had the same thoughts that the Wahhabis have today. It means that they could not bear to see people sanctify and honor the Prophet (s). It made them angry to see people hurry and fight with each other to get the remainder of the Prophet's water of *wudhu'* to massage their faces and skins for blessing and to be closer to Allah by loving him and his progeny. All that created a reaction among the people of Quraysh who began hating Muhammad (s) with no guilt being committed by him.

The chief of Quraysh Mu'awiyah ibn Abi Sufyan revealed what was hidden in their chests when al-Mughirah suggested to him, "*O Ameerul Mu'minin, would that you be kind to your cousins of the Hashimites! By Allah, nothing has remained with them that you may fear. And this may cause you good mention.*"

Mu'awiyah said, "*How far! The man of Taym*[2] *ruled, wronged and did what he did. By Allah, as soon as he died, his mention died with him. People may remember him and just say: Abu Bakr. Then the man of Adiy*[3] *ruled for ten years. As soon as he died, his mention died with him. People may remember him and say: Umar. Then our brother Uthman ruled. He did what he did and people did to him what they did. As soon as he died, his mention and what happened to him died with him. But the man of Hashem,*[4] *everyday his name is announced five times (I witness that Muhammad is the Messenger of*

---

[1] *Sahih al-Bukhari* vol.6, p. 17.
[2] It was the name of Abu Bakr's tribe.
[3] The name of Umar's tribe.
[4] The tribe of the Prophet (s); Hashim was the great grandfather of the Prophet.

Allah (s)). So which mention will last after this? May their mention be buried!"[1]

It was Wahhabism in its prettiest clothes and clearest tongues. It plotted yesterday and is trying now to execute the plot for today and tomorrow.

They desired to put out the light of Allah with their mouths but Allah will perfect His light, though the unbelievers may be averse. [Qur'an 61:8]

---

[1] Mentioned by ibn Abil al-Hadid in his book *an-Nasa'ih al-Kafiyyah li man Yatawalla Mu'awiyah*, quoted from *Tarikh al-Tabari* and Ibn Athir.

WAHHABISM PROHIBITS VISITING OF GRAVES

One of the heresies widespread in the present time is the prohibition of visiting of graves by women. When a Muslim woman goes to perform the Hajj, they (Wahhabis) do not permit her to visit the Baqee' Graveyard or any other graveyard there. The Wahhabis prohibited this thing and still prohibit it with no any evidence except fanaticism.

Muslim has mentioned in his Sahih, Chapter of Funerals, that Aa'isha once asked the Prophet (s) what she should say if she visited graveyards, and the Prophet (s) said, "*You say: Peace be on you, O peaceful people! You are from the foremost and we, if Allah wills are from the following and may Allah forgive the first and the last.*"[1]

Al-Bukhari has mentioned in his Sahih that Anas ibn Malik said, "*One day, the Prophet (s) passed by a woman crying at a grave. He said to her, 'Fear Allah and be patient!' She said, 'Be away from me! You have not been afflicted as I have.' She did not know him. It was said to her that he was the Messenger of Allah (s). She came to his house and did not find doorkeepers. She apologized to him that she did not know him before. He said, 'Patience is (required) but at the first shock'.*"[2]

There are too many traditions about this subject in the books of the Sunni and the Shia, but the Wahhabis deny and pay no any attention to them.

When I argued with one of the Wahhabis about these traditions, he said to me that they were abrogated. I said, "In fact, the prohibition is that which was abrogated, because the Messenger of Allah (s) said, '*I had prohibited you from visiting the graves, but now you visit them, because they remind you of death*'."

He said, "This tradition means men and not women."

---

[1] *Sahih Muslim* vol.2, p.669, *hadith* no.103
[2] *Sahih al-Bukhari*, vol. 2, p. 79, Chapt. 'Visiting of Graves, Funerals.'

I said, "It has been proved in history and to the scholars from the Sunni that Fatima az-Zahra' (sa) visited her father's tomb every day, and she cried there and said, '*O father, calamities have been poured on me that if they were poured on days, they would turn nights.*'[1] It is well known in history that Imam Ali (as) built her a special house called 'the house of sorrows' where she spent most of her time weeping."[2]

He said, "If we suppose that this narration it true, it concerns Fatima alone."

Unfortunately, this blind fanaticism! How can a Muslim imagine that Allah and His messenger prohibit woman from visiting the grave of her father, mother, brother, husband, or child where she may pray Allah to have mercy and forgive them and where she may grieve for them through tears of mercy and remember death and afterlife like a man does?

This is an injustice against a woman which Allah never pleases to do or does, neither does His messenger or any man of a sound reason.

---

[1] *Tarikh al-Khamis* vol.2, p. 173

[2] *Bihar al-Anwar* vol.43, p. 177

THE AHLUL BAYT AND A MODERN MUSLIM

The jobs of the present age have occupied most of man's time and not left for him any free time. In the age of the Mission - the first age of Islam, jobs were limited in that a man was a farmer, a trader or a manufacturer. These three jobs gave man enough free time to practice his worships as he liked and at their specified times. When the time of prayer came even if a Muslim was in the place of his work, he stopped working to offer the prayer with a tranquil soul.

As for today where governments have employed most of people for assured and defined salaries and for several hours, people are not allowed to stop working in order to offer the prayer. A student, teacher, manager, physician, nurse, worker, soldier, policeman, officials in companies, factories, and mines, the guards of borders, officer in a weather station or airport...etc. do not find free time to offer the prayer in its five prescribed times.

I myself suffered this problem when I was a teacher. My soul was upset and my conscience was confused as time did not permit me to offer the prayer in its specified time. I often missed the *Dhuhr* (midday), *Asr* (afternoon), and *Maghrib* (time of sunset) prayers especially during winter. I often offered the four prayers (in addition to *Isha* - evening Prayer) altogether in the night. Sometimes, I went back home very tired so that I could not offer them, or I offered them in spite of me.

I discovered that many Muslims gave up prayer for the reason that they were psychologically stressed, hoping that chance might permit them to offer this obligation later. Because of this, dislike came to some people who saw that the prayer was like a nightmare, which affected their ease. They began criticizing Islam of being a religion of fatigue, difficulty and hardship, and saying that Christianity had relieved its followers from many ties where they pray only one time a week; on Sunday which is a holiday.

How often the missionaries struck the right cord before a Muslim youth, claiming that their religion (Christianity) would keep pace with civilization at all ages! They say that prayer once a week and fasting (abstaining from eating meat only) for only three days in a year make their religion a religion of love and peace.

How much did these propagandas attract the Muslim youth, who suffered, in their early childhood from the pressure of parents to perform *wudhu'* and prayer, to a terrible degree in some families? You see that some parents, especially unlearned ones, want their children to be exactly like Rabi'ah al-Adawiyyah[1] if they are females and like Ahmad al-Badawi if they are males. They wake them up before the dawn and tire them with prayers. They watch them day and night, and blame and punish them severely for everything. They beat them sometimes just because they forget something. They send them to government schools and burden them with duties, until they become boring, and then hate the religion while they are not yet adolescent. I do not say except what I have already seen. I saw many children from my relatives, who offered the prayer under pressure; give up the prayer when the authority of parents was no longer over them, or when they were far from the family and its ties.

Many times, I tried to convince some parents from my relatives not to beat or force their children to offer the prayer and that they must treat them kindly and leniently, to endear the prayer to them and not to make it as a nightmare to them, but I often faced their saying that the Prophet (s) had said, "*Beat them (children) to offer the prayer when they are seven years old (or ten years in some traditions)*".

In this way, the Muslim youth lose their prayer and give up on their religion, even if they do not follow the missionaries. In addition to that, the television, games and many other things take the youth away from the remembrance of Allah.

---

[1] An exemplar in faith and piety.

THE SOLUTION IS IN THE AHLUL BAYT'S SCHOOL

Whoever observes the school of the Ahlul Bayt (as), concerning the Islamic education, shall find sufficient solutions that Allah the Almighty has legislated for His people to make religion easy for them and within the reach of everyone - young or old.

Allah the Almighty says:

He has not laid upon you any hardship in religion. [Qur'an, 22:78]

Allah desires ease for you, and He does not desire for you difficulty. [Qur'an, 2:185]

Allah does not impose upon any soul a duty but to the extent of its ability. [Qur'an, 2:286]

TO RELIEVE FROM HARDSHIP

This is the general rule in Islam; every hardship is kept away, every difficulty is disliked, and every strait is prohibited. If it is so, then what is the strictness there for, that which we find in the books of jurisprudence among all Muslims?

If a Muslim reads some chapters on *wudhu'* or *ghusl* (ritual wash or bath), he feels that jurisprudents have added difficulty to the easiness, and imposed on man more than his capacity.

It is known in the school of the Ahlul Bayt (as) through traditions narrated by them from their grandfather the Prophet Muhammad (s) that "*Wudhu' is two washes and two wipes; to wash the face and the hands, and to wipe (with the wet remaining in the hands) the head and the feet.*"

THIS IS THE WUDHU'

As we have said before and in order to make it easy for Muslims, Allah the Almighty has imposed *wudhu'* on Muslims before offering the prayer. Allah says:

O you who believe, when you rise up to prayer, wash your faces and your hands as far as the elbows, and wipe your heads and your feet to the ankles. [Qur'an, 5:6]

Then, *wudhu'* is to wash the face and two hands and to wipe the head and the two feet. As we see, it is easy and accessible with no any difficulty or hardship. If a Muslim is at home or traveling, in an airport or a railway station, this *wudhu'* shall not embarrass him at all; he just turns on the tap and washes his face and hands, and then he turns off the tap and wipes his head and feet with the wet of his hands. He may not take off his shoes except in the place of prayer if it is near, and then he wipes his head and feet.

But, if the *wudhu'* is as described by (Sunni) jurisprudents who say:

1. To wash the hands to the wrists three times
2. To rinse out the mouth three times
3. To wash the nose three times (by inhaling and ejecting out)
4. To wash the face three times
5. To wash the right hand three times and the left hand three times
6. To wipe all the head
7. To wipe the two ears
8. To wash the right foot three times and then the left foot three times

It shall be of difficulty and hardship, especially to the youth when they are in travel. It is difficult to wash the feet in winter and then to wait until they dry in order to put on the socks.

What is important in this matter is that the school of the Ahlul Bayt (as), that do not rely on personal opinions nor on misinterpretation before clear texts, acts according to the Holy Book and the pure *Sunnah* of Prophet. The *wudhu'* that the Shia follow is the *wudhu'* that Allah has ordered Muslims in the Holy Qur'an and it is the *wudhu'* that the Messenger of Allah (s) and the infallible imams of his progeny did practice.

May Allah have mercy on Abdullah ibn Abbas who often said, "*I do not find in the Book of Allah except two washes and two wipes, but you insist on following the rule of al-Hajjaj.*"[1]

Muslims today, especially the learned youth, have to go back to the right way of Islam with its simplicity and ease to make people love and wish for the religion. How often the Prophet (s) announced before Muslims, "*Make it easy and do not make it difficult! Do not make (people) alienated from the religion!*"[2] And he often said, "*Do not make it difficult for yourselves, lest Allah makes it more difficult for you as He did for the Children of Israel.*"[3]

How many people, who escaped from the prayer because of *wudhu'* or they offered the prayer but with *tayammum*[4] for fear of water which caused them prurigo in the hands and toes of the feet,[5] recovered soundness and became tranquil with the *wudhu'* of the Ahlul Bayt (as), they recovered soundness!

---

[1] *Musannaf 'Abd al-Razzaq* vol.1, p. 38.

[2] *Sahih al-Bukhari* vol.1, p. 27.

[3] *Sahih Muslim* vol.2, p. 1105. *Sunan Abu Dawood* vol.4, p. 276, *hadith* no. 4904.

[4] Ritual purification with sand, soil, or dust instead of wudhu' when there is no water.

[5] In the school of the Ahlul Bayt (as), one can practice tayammum even if water is available when he fears from a disease, or what may lead to or complicate a disease as narrated from Imam as-Sadiq, "...soil is one of the two purifying things".

THIS IS THE PRAYER

The prayers in the school of the Ahlul Bayt (as), are offered in three times instead of five times:

One time for the *Fajr* (dawn) Prayer

One time for the *Dhuhr* (midday) and *Asr* (afternoon) Prayers

One time for the *Maghrib* (time of sunset) and *Isha'* (evening) Prayers

We have written a separate chapter in our book "*To be with the Truthful*"[1] to prove the legality of these three times from the Holy Qur'an and the pure Prophet's *Sunnah*; therefore, we do not want to expatiate or repeat what we have already said. Let whoever wants to see the details refer to that book.

Anyhow, we want here to explain the wisdom of Allah in gathering between the times of the prayers in this way. As we have said in a previous chapter (the Ahlul Bayt and modern Muslims) most of whom are employees who form three thirds of a society, do not offer the prayer or offer it lazily and unwillingly, or offer it with difficulty and hardship. This is because they know that it is not permissible for them (in the view of religion) to leave the work during the time of work, for which they receive wages, in order to offer their prayer.

We have nothing to do with those, who cry out in the mosques calling people to leave their jobs at the times of prayers even if it costs them to lose their jobs, because Allah - as they claim - is the One Who provides His servants with sustenance, and not the employer or the owner of the factory.

What is odd is that these very imams, who bear this thought, contradict themselves in the same subject. Once, I heard one of them praising Umar ibn al-Khattab and saying, "One day, our master Umar came into the mosque and saw some man offer the prayer before the coming of people. The second time, he came and found

---

[1] https://www.al-islam.org/be-with-truthful-muhammad-al-tijani-al-samawi

him offering the prayer. In the third, he (Umar) asked him (the man), "Who spends on you?"

The man said, "My brother spends on me."

Our master Umar said to him, "Get out of the mosque! Surely, your brother is better than you are. The sky does not rain gold or silver."

When I was alone with the imam (of the mosque) I, said to him, "Did you not say a month ago, 'Allah is the One Who provides His servants with sustenance, so leave your work in order to offer the prayer'?"

He looked at me with a smile and said, "For every occasion there is a certain saying! My first saying was from the Qur'an, and my second saying was our master Umar al-Farouq's. My first and second sayings are both true..."

I said, "May Allah reward you with good! I have benefited from you."

We come back to the subject of the wisdom of Allah behind the gathering of prayers in one time. We say that Allah is the Wise, the All Knowing, the Creator of everything, who knows the past, the present, and the future; nothing is hidden from His knowledge. He has known that in some certain time people would be confined to their jobs that would limit their freedoms and times, and since Muhammad (s) was the last of prophets, His law would be valid until the Day of Resurrection and be within reach of all human beings. The wisdom of Allah provides for ease and relief for people who abide by religion. Therefore, Allah recommended His messenger to offer the Dhuhr and Asr Prayers in one time either by advancing the Asr Prayer or delaying the Dhuhr Prayer, and offer the Maghrib and Isha' Prayers together either by advancing the Isha' Prayer or delaying the Maghrib Prayer[1] and to teach his nation this way in order to relieve them from hardship.

---

[1] This advancing and delaying is from the beginning of the Zuhr Prayer's time to the last of the Asr Prayer's time, and the same thing is to the Maghrib and Isha' Prayers. But as for one who has enough free time, it is recommended for him to offer each prayer in its time.

The Messenger of Allah (s) did what he was ordered to do. He led congregational prayers in Medina many times in this way, and when he was asked why, he said, "*in order not to make it hard for my nation or in order not to embarrass my nation*".[1]

Ibn Abbas said, "*The Messenger of Allah (s) offered in Medina seven (rak'as) and eight (rak'as); the Dhuhr and the Asr prayers (together) and the Maghrib and Isha' Prayers (together).*"[2]

This is the wisdom of Allah the Almighty and this is the prayer of the Messenger of Allah (s) according to the order of his Lord, in order not to cause the nation any hardship. Then, why do we refrain from this way in offering the prayers, when it is easy and possible for all people; employees, workers, students, soldiers...etc.? There is no job in the world that may disturb these times and there shall be no excuse for any Muslim after that.[3]

It is well known that the labor law in the world limits the hours of work to eight hours a day into two periods - the first one from eight o'clock AM to the midday, and the second from two o'clock PM to six o'clock PM, where there is a break of two hours for rest at midday. In this case, a Muslim can offer the *Dhuhr* and *Asr* prayers during this time of rest before coming back to his work. Thus, he offers the *Dhuhr* and *Asr* prayers in their right times and comes back to his work with a tranquil mind and a pleased conscience.

If the work is continuous for all day as in the mines and some other factories - the labor law determines the work in seven continuous hours including a break of half an hour for rest. A company may manage the work by dividing the workers into three groups alternating each other in this way:

1. A group works from 7 o'clock AM to 2 PM
2. A group works from 2 PM to 9 PM
3. A group works from 9 PM to 4 AM

---

[1] *Sahih Muslim*, vol.1, p. 490, *hadith* no. 708. The book of Prayer, chapter Combining the two prayers.

[2] *Sahih al-Bukhari*, vol. 1 p. 143, 'Book of Timings of Prayers.'

[3] There is a saying by our *ulama*, "whenever the conditions of something are too many, the chance of its availability is too little"; therefore, make it easy so that you may get it!

By this Divine wisdom of the times of prayers, all groups can offer their prayers in their right times without any difficulty or embarrassment, and no one after that may say that he cannot find time for the prayer or that he missed the right time of prayer.[1]

By this, we follow the Holy Qur'an and the Prophet's *Sunnah* in offering the prayers in their times, for the prayer is a timed ordinance for the believers. At the same time, we keep away from ourselves and from others any hardship and embarrassment. Perhaps, most of the youth who give up the prayer, may return to it when they know that Allah the Almighty has permitted it in this way, and the Messenger of Allah (s) and his progeny (peace be on them all) had offered it in this way.[2]

---

[1] Of course, we do not talk about the very special cases that may force workers to work for ten continuous hours or more that is called "overtime". Such workers, as well, can offer the prayers if they want, for the wudu and the offering of the Midday (Dhuhr) and Afternoon (Asr) prayers take about six minutes. Do these workers not go to the WC? Does this not take time?

[2] In many cases, the prayer can be offered according to the conditions of those cases; a traveler in the airplane can offer the prayer while sitting in his chair, a patient, who cannot move, can offer it while lying down, a handicapped person can offer it in the way possible to him, and so on.

THIS IS THE ZAKAT

The school of the Ahlul Bayt (as) (Shiism) is different from the other Islamic creeds who believe in the obligation of the *zakat* but not the *khums*. They see that *khums* is required only in the booties of war.

As for the Shia, they believe that zakat is obligatory and *khums* is obligatory too in all what a Muslim gains in a year. According to the Prophetic *Sunnah*, *zakat* is obligatory on the following things:
1. Gold and silver coins
2. Livestock - camels, cows, sheep, and goats
3. Four yields - wheat, barley, date, and raisin

If we ponder on these mentioned articles of *zakat*, we see that they do not satisfy the need of building an integral Islamic society that looks forward to development, in keeping its pace with modern times, getting rid of poverty and neediness, assuring of safety and good living, building of hospitals, universities, streets and highways, assuring of good abodes, enough salaries for unemployed people or those disabled by diseases, old age or any disability.

It is known among all nations that the wealthy class forms not more than twenty percent of a nation, the middle class that hardly satisfy their needs may form fifty percent, and thirty percent of people are poor and needy, who are in terrible need of any help.

If we rely only on the *zakat* in those afore mentioned items that the Prophet (s) had mentioned and with the defined value of 2.5%, it shall be not enough to satisfy the needs of people and the requirements of the age.

One, who has thousands of olive trees, shall say: '*zakat* is not obligatory on me, because the Messenger of Allah (s) has not mentioned olive among the yields included in *zakat*.' The same can be said about many other yields such as tons of fishes taken out of the sea by modern tools. One, who has thousands of poultry, does not have to pay *zakat* as well. One, who has many real estates, also does not have to pay *zakat*. If we suppose that all these people were convinced to pay the *zakat*, they shall not pay more than 2.5% of their properties, which is a very little amount which neither fattens nor avails against hunger!

As for the *khums* that Allah the Almighty has imposed on Muslims when saying:

And know that whatever thing you gain, a fifth of it is for Allah and for the Messenger and for the near of kin and the orphans and the needy and the wayfarer. [Qur'an, 8:41]

We have talked about this verse in details in our book "*To be with the Truthful*". Whoever wants more details let him refer to this book. We do not want to convince people that the Umayyads misinterpreted and annulled this verse and limited its rulings to the booties of war only, rather we want to show what the Ahlul Bayt (as) did in this concern, and the Ahlul Bayt (the people of the house) are more aware of what there is in the house! They did according to the Holy Qur'an and the Prophet's *Sunnah* and said that Muslims must pay the fifth of whatever they gain within a year.

If we think deeply through a simple mathematical operation, we shall clearly see the great difference between the reality that Muslims live today and the theory that has not been applied except to a very small group of people, and in a disorderly way.

Let us take an example - a Muslim who has ten thousand dinars. If this Muslim follows the rulings of the Sunni, he shall pay the *zakat* from his wealth at a percentage of 2.5, which is two hundred and fifty dinars, but if he follows the rulings of the Shia, he shall pay the fifth of his ten thousand dinars, which is two thousand dinars. When this Muslim pays the *zakat* according to the Sunni, nine thousand and seven hundred and fifty dinars shall remain with him, but when he pays the fifth according to the Shia, eight thousand dinars shall remain with him.

On this basis, a poor Muslim among the Sunni gets two hundred and fifty dinars for his living of a year, whereas a poor Muslim among the Shia gets two thousand dinars a year. The difference between the two poor Muslims is too big.

If the *zakat* of the Sunni suffices for the living of one poor Muslim, the *zakat* of the Shia suffices for the livings of eight poor Muslims.

If we compare between a rich Muslim and a poor one among the Sunni, we shall find the following account; 9750 in opposite to 250, which is a very weak proportion, forming one of forty. It means that if the poor Muslim has one loaf of bread, the rich one has forty loaves.

In comparison between a rich Muslim and a poor one among the Shia, we shall find the following account; 8000 in opposite to 2000, which is a reasonable and acceptable proportion, forming one of four. It means that if the poor Muslim has one loaf of bread, the rich one has four loaves.

In another word, a poor Sunni Muslim has one share, whereas a rich Sunni Muslim has thirty-nine shares. The difference between the two is too immoderate, and this is what Allah has warned us of when saying:

So that it may not be a thing taken by turns among the rich of you. [Qur'an, 59:7]

Indeed, in this case, the rich who form only twenty percent of the nation possesses ninety-five percent from the general wealth, and the rest of people possess five percent from that wealth. As for a Shia poor Muslim, he has one share from every four shares, and this difference, though it is big, is not so immoderate. The rich here possess seventy-five percent of the wealth, whereas the poor possess twenty-five percent of that wealth.[1]

---

[1] What confirms this fact is that many Sunni economists say that the proportion of 2.5% of the zakat is no longer sufficient to meet the increasing expenditure where the different needs of man have become much more than his needs in the past. In this concern, they think that they must not follow the very literality of the Qur'anic texts concerning the political and economic affairs!!! Refer to *An Introduction to the Islamic Economics*, by Dr. Abdul Aziz Fahmi, p. 163.
Instead of accusing the texts of being insufficient - and this is from the daring things that the Sunni are blamed for, where they claim that the

In addition to that, Islam encourages voluntary charities. In fact, Islam imposes on Muslims some other obligatory charities like the *zakat al-fitr* (after fasting in Ramadan), sacrifices in the Hajj, penances and some vows. Islam also gives a legal ruler the right to take from the rich and give to the poor in some necessary circumstances, or put it in the public treasury.

However, the reality is other than what Allah has mentioned in the Qur'an and what the Prophet (s) and his progeny did. You see that the wealth of the Muslim nation is in the hands of the rich who are very few, but they possess everything whereas the poor, who are the great majority, have nothing.

The communist blocs knew this phenomenon in the Muslim world; therefore, they attacked it very easily by attracting its learned youth in the colleges and universities, using the theory of the distribution of wealth among all individuals.

Most of the Muslim youth believed in communism and denied their religion and beliefs. They began blaming and criticizing their fathers and grandfathers. In fact, Islam met a very dangerous affliction from communism that destroyed it from inside at the hands of its own learned youth. These very Muslims fought against Islam when they got the reigns of authority, and then they affected their people too much.

If we were not safe from communism, we have to blame the first Muslims who distorted the rulings of Allah and caused the affairs of the Muslim nation to get to where Muslims are in now with their poverty, underdevelopment, ignorance and blind fanaticism. There is no power save in Allah, the Most High, the Most Powerful!

Qur'an and the Prophet's *Sunnah* do not include all rulings, and so they (the Qur'an and the *Sunnah*) need other tools and analogy!!"
And if they had referred it to the Messenger and to those in authority among them, those among them who can search out the knowledge of it would have known it" - these are the Ahlul Bayt (s). So, the right solution is to add the khums to the zakat and not limit it to the booties of war only. In this way, Muslims shall be prosperous.

TEMPORARY MARRIAGE AND ITS IMPORTANCE

One of the most dangerous problems that destroy human societies is the problem of sex. As it is well known, sex is the basic factor that makes life continue as willed by Allah the Almighty Who has made masculinity and femininity in everything - man, animals, plants...etc.

Allah says:

And of everything We have created pairs that you may be mindful. [Qur'an, 51:49]

And Allah has made wives for you of your kind, and has given you children and grandchildren from your wives. [Qur'an, 16:72]

In order that life continues, male and female must marry and produce offspring. This is the norm of Allah in His creation. For marriage and production, Allah has created this unruly instinct in man and woman equally that each gender wishes and longs for and yearns to have sexual intercourse with the other to satisfy his or her lust. In this way, an ovum is pollinated by a sperm and a fetus is formed that develops until it becomes adult to repeat the same role, and thus life continues.

And He it is Who has created man from the water, then He has made for him blood relationship and marriage relationship, and your Lord is powerful. [Qur'an, 25:54]

The Islamic Sharia has put conditions and limits for this instinct in a way that not all people may bear. Islam has prohibited sexual intercourse, except by lawful marriage in order to preserve honor, lineage, offspring and dignity of man.

The sexual lust may be awakened in a young boy and a young girl in their early years when they are not more than ten years old. In the west, these young boys and girls may practice sex easily and without limits because the western peoples think it is a natural instinct, not having any problem with this. Therefore, they encourage it and pave the way for early mixing between boys and girls or that parents may practice sexual intercourse before their children to make them be used to seeing their parents naked, besides observing other behaviors that open wide the door to adultery before young boys and girls. In many instances, a girl would have lost her virginity before she is fourteen years old. This is very common there; to a degree that when a man gets married to a woman and finds her still a virgin, he is astonished and considers that woman to be unnatural or savage.

For Muslims, the matter is totally different. There is no room for uncovering private parts before children at all. There is no place for mixing between males and females, except within certain limits conditioned by the required veil of woman. Add to that the moral and psychological education that children receive from parents, especially girls from mothers. Thus, girls grow up with shyness and fear of sex, bearing in mind that their virginity is the criterion of their chastity, abstinence, honor and perfection of body.

Most of times, a young woman may come to the marital house while she knows neither much nor little about sex, and perhaps the husband may be so too. This is if they live in a Muslim society that follows the actual laws of Islam, or we may say 'the ideal Muslim society' that seems to be imaginary, because it is very difficult or somehow impossible to be applied, as it is not possible to suppress this instinct in males or females anyhow.

However if we try to ignore this instinct, we shall not be successful most of times. When the genitals and glands of a male and a female develop, they feel the desire to have sex. They shall practice sex in one way or another, however much the parents try to watch over them. There is no doubt that males and females shall find an opportunity to meet, and in the least boys may practice sex with boys and girls with girls. Certainly, this is a dangerous matter, having bad effects and psychological diseases that may be a main reason for destroying the family, which then leads to the corruption of entire society.

Western societies have exceeded all the limits in practicing sex, until people there have become like animals in satisfying this unruly lust, which is considered there as a conceded right of male and female and a part of their freedom even if they are married and living with their spouses. As they think, a husband has to regard the feelings of his wife if she wants to satisfy her lust with whomever she likes, and a wife has to regard the feelings of her husband if he wants to do the same with any woman other than his wife.

However, in the Arab and Muslim societies, we are very immoderate in the matter of sex to the extent that we have burdened our societies with psychological complexes, sexual suppression, secret practices and yearning for woman with fatal lust as that of animals.

WOMAN IS WRONGED AMONG US

Woman, in the Arab and Muslim societies, has been wronged in general, since the day when she was buried alive until today.

Muslims have not understood until now that woman has body and soul just like man; she has intellect, heart, feelings and instincts. Man cannot claim that he has honor and dignity, except that woman can claim this too. Allah says in the Qur'an:

O you men, surely We have created you of a male and a female, and made you tribes and families that you may know each other; surely the most honorable of you with Allah is the one among you most careful (of his duty); surely Allah is Knowing, Aware. [Qur'an, 49:13]

So their Lord accepted their prayer: That I will not waste the work of a worker among you, whether male or female, the one of you being from the other. [Qur'an, 3:195]

Of course, we do not deny that Allah the Almighty has given man a degree over woman for leadership and constancy, but it has nothing to do with preference at all. Allah the Glorified says:

They (women) have rights similar to those against them in a just manner, and the men are a degree above them, and Allah is Mighty, Wise. [Qur'an, 2:228]

The wisdom of Allah has determined that man and woman are equal in rights and duties, but a degree has been given to man over woman in leadership, because Allah has given man more power and strength and made him responsible for guarding and protecting woman. When a woman feels fear and fright, she hurries to seek protection of her man or husband. Therefore, Allah has imposed fight and *jihad* on man and exempted woman from that. In fact, Allah has imposed on man to fight and be martyred for the sake of woman. Allah the Almighty says:

How should you not fight for the cause of Allah and of the feeble among men and of the women and the children... [Qur'an, 4:75]

This is what I have understood from the Holy Qur'an. It does not mean that Allah has preferred man to woman; certainly not! There may be a man better than one thousand women, and there may be a woman better than one thousand men!

We must take the Messenger of Allah (s) as our exemplar. He treated woman in a way that the history of humankind has never known better than. Despite the fact that some of his wives hurt him, he never hurt any one of them at all. He always ordered Muslims to be good to women. Nevertheless, some bad spirits of the pre-Islamic era have remained among Muslims until now. You may hear that some man has divorced his wife because she did not bear a male child. Until now, they raise from the Qur'an only this motto "*and beat them*", besides their sayings that "*woman is the seed of Satan*", "*she is sedition*", "*she is shame*", "*she is scandal*"...etc.

Woman among Muslims has remained underdeveloped and ignorant. She has no right to learn and study. Some people do not agree with her leaving her father's house, except to the house of her husband or to her grave.[1]

---

[1] There is no doubt that a jurisprudent or a preacher is the son of his milieu and society. He carries out his mission within the reality he lives in; therefore, he does not tire himself to show the ruling of Allah, face new changes, and keep to justice. He may not observe whether people in that society are excessive or wasteful. For example, is woman wronged, or she is given her full rights?

Let us not rely on some weak traditions that do not fit our milieu and social backgrounds. A jurisprudent may not talk about the essence of hijab (Islamic veil), learning of woman, mixing (of males and females), the influence of the TV...etc, but he does not wake up, except when he is shocked by changes, sudden events and the cultural invasion of the west against us, and then he behaves as a surprised one; either he clings to his heritage and fanaticism, or gives a fatwa in a hurry and after sometime, hesitating between nomadism and modernity, open and closed society!

Some men claim and repeat false traditions before learned men and women that the Messenger of Allah (s) has said, "*The best thing for woman is that she should neither see a man nor let a man see her.*"

What kind of mentality is that, which contradicts what has been mentioned in the Holy Qur'an, concerning the freedom of woman and her rights equal to man's? Otherwise, what is the meaning of this saying of Allah:

Say to the believing men that they should lower their looks and guard their private parts; that is purer for them; surely Allah is Aware of what they do. And say to the believing women that they should lower their looks and guard their private parts and do not display their adornment except what appears thereof. [Qur'an, 24:30-31]

This is very clear evidence on the freedom of woman in going out of her house as man does, and that she is ordered to lower her gaze and observe her modesty exactly as man is ordered to do.

Yes! The mentality of the pre-Islamic age has prevailed to some extent in the Arab and Muslim societies. Muslim men have exploited the degree that Allah has given them over woman to give themselves all the rights and deprive woman of all her rights, leaving her with nothing.

I would not go far if I say that the main reason behind our underdevelopment is our injustice against woman and closing the doors before her - no learning, no culture, no communication, no association, no going out and no right to choose her spouse. Until recently, woman is married without her choice. In fact, how can she choose while she does not know any man?[1]

---

[1] The books of history and biographies mention that women came to the meeting of the Prophet (s) and asked him to find them good husbands. Once, some women came to the Prophet (s) and said to him, "*We cannot be alone (to talk) with you in your meeting of men...*" He assigned to them an appointment in the house of someone, and then he went to them at the appointed time and place.

Thus, a woman may find herself, in the night of wedding, before a man in age that of her father and she can do nothing except to submit unwillingly, and then it is said to her, "this is what Allah has determined for you; therefore, you have to be patient!" Then, she becomes like a productive milk cow that has nothing to do, except to give birth, suckle, and bring them up because her husband likes to have many children!

Detest and hatred may rise and grow between the two spouses, because the husband is too old and may not understand the needs and feelings of the young wife, and most of the time, he leaves her alone, suffering the pains of the instinct and lust. And since the husband is jealous of her young wife, he tries his best not to let her see any man and not to let any man see her.

However, the sexual lust defeats everything and this woman falls in the first opportunity, as a reaction against suppression and deprivation. Consequently, unlawful relations come out. Forbidden fruit is sweet! Many a woman has a lover, and many a man has a lover or lovers and many children are born at the expense of others! Then doubts, troubles, problems, quarrel and lastly divorce comes about. The society is corrupted and high values are replaced by disorders, treasons, adultery, vices, and all sins. Unfortunately, this is what actually happens in our societies nowadays. Therefore, we must face these painful facts and not overlook them or bury our heads in sands like an ostrich.

Since the first day when I understood Islam and became certain that it is the best law at all, I called in meetings, conferences, and publications for the liberation of woman for making her learned and erudite. Surely, woman is the half (or more) of society, and when half of the society is paralyzed, the body of the nation shall not be able to carry out its functions and will die little by little.

The Prophet (s) permitted women to do some works. He said to the wife of Abdullah ibn Mas'ud, who was forced to work to spend on her husband and children, *"...you shall have reward for your spending on them, so spend on them!"* There are too many examples concerning the affairs of woman, showing her freedom and rights.

Another injustice of our society against woman is that we have thought of the lust of man only and found effective solutions for it, in order to "close the door of excuses". Therefore, we have built public places for men to satisfy their desires whenever they like, and with no denier or objector! Rather, it seems that the matter is too natural to the extent that sometimes a brother may meet his brother, or some man may meet his nephew or another relative there in that place, and he may feel proud and victorious, because that place is a proof of manhood where no one can enter it except one who is manly!

If such a man, who feels proud before his fellows that he has gone to such place and been acquainted with different women, comes back home and sees his sister look at passersby in the street from the window, shall turn the house upside down and beat that poor sister until she bleeds![1]

Why did jurisprudents think of the satisfaction of man's lust and they did not think of the satisfaction of woman's lust if they were just?

I do not call for the liberation of woman, as the case is in the corruptive West - where people do not believe in values and good morals and they believe in freedoms only. I call for the liberation of woman within the limits that Allah and His messenger have determined such as hijab, abstinence, modesty and chastity and beyond that she is free to do, as her brother does in her father's house and as her husband does when she is married. If we actually do that, we shall save ourselves and our society from corruption, vices and underdevelopment.

There is no doubt that jurisprudents must have thought of that, but they regarded it unlikely to find public places for women to satisfy their lusts, because this is a thing impermissible. They might deduce differently that from the fact that Islam permits man to marry one, two, three or four women at the same time, but prohibits so for

---

[1] Some Sunni jurisprudents gave a fatwa that one, who looks at a foreign (non-mahram) woman, is to be whipped (one hundred whips), relying on the saying of the Prophet (s), *"The two eyes may commit adultery"*, mentioned by Ahmed ibn Hanbal in his Sunan and by at-Tabari in his al-Kabeer from Abdullah ibn Mas'ud.

women in order to preserve lineages and children because woman is the one who bears and gives birth and not man.

However, fact is that this instinct is always vital in woman. Therefore, sufficient solutions must be found to preserve woman's dignity, honor, and entity exactly like that of a man.

Has Islam ignored this fact? Has Islam permitted for man what it has not permitted for woman?

The Prophet (s) talked much about the subject of sex and gave sufficient solutions to keep the Muslim society safe from corruption and sin. He said, "*O youths, whoever can afford to get married let him get married, because it is better in lowering the (unlawful) gaze and better in being chaste. Whoever is not able to let him fast, for it shall be a protection for him.*"[1]

It is a sufficient solution for the youth, who can afford to get married. Through marriage, the youth, males or females, can satisfy their sexual lust whenever it is required and save their selves from erring. The problem is only with those who cannot afford to get married. At the time of the Prophet (s) also when marriage was so easy and simple and did not cost much, there were young men who could not get married. Then how is it not going to be more of an issue nowadays when marriage has become too difficult and costly for many reasons?

From among these reasons is that young men and young women keep on learning until the age of twenty-five, and after that, they look for a suitable job that may assure their living. Then, they must prepare a house with its furniture in compliance with the requirements of the modern ages that have become necessary. One may be, at least thirty years old to be able to get married.

A young man and a young woman, who can biologically get married in the tenth or twelfth year of age, cannot actually afford to get married, except in the age of thirty. Then, what do they do during all these long years? If we say that they have been so abstinent and chaste and have not thought of sex at all, we may be liars to ourselves, for they are human beings and not angels; especially in

---

[1] *Sahih al-Bukhari*, vol. 7, p. 3. Book of Marriage.

this age where mixing is something very natural everywhere. A male student mixes with a female one in the university. In fact, since primary school until high education, there is mixing between males and females which often occur away from parents and observers. A girl may live with her boy classmate for nine months, but she does not live with her family except for three months. So what happens there?

The answer is well known by the students themselves and by their teachers, and by everyone who works inside or outside his house.

TEMPORARY MARRIAGE IS THE VERY SOLUTION

We have discussed the wisdom of Allah when we talked about the offering of two prayers at the same time and said that Allah is kind to His people; He has created them, and so He guides them to what benefits them because He is Beneficent, Merciful. And since Allah is kind to His people, so He always wants ease for them. He says:

Should He not know what He created? And He is the Knower of the subtleties, the Aware. [Qur'an, 67:14]

How can a reasonable one imagine that Allah has created man weak and created in him the sexual instinct that he is terribly excited and then He determined severe punishment on him by either whipping or stoning when he would satisfy this unruly instinct?

Can we convince others to embrace Islam when we show these rulings and then we say that Allah is merciful to His people, Allah wants ease for them, He does not impose on man what he cannot bear or that He has not made in religion any embarrassment or hardship?

Before we try to convince others, can we convince ourselves with this justification? Certainly not!

The sexual intercourse may be practiced without raping, violence or force, but with mutual love, satisfaction, and agreement between a man and a woman where there is no harm against anyone and that precaution is observed so that pregnancy and birth do not take place. Should such a man, who satisfies the desire of a woman whose abstinence and chastity prevent her from committing adultery, be killed? We must think deeply on this subject, especially when we see the injustice of our societies against woman.

All that does not let inside me a bit of doubt that Allah the Almighty, Who has permitted a sick one or a traveler not to fast in the month of Ramadan and to offer the half of prayers, or to offer the prayer while sitting or lying down in some cases, Who has permitted

Muslims to perform *tayammum* with earth when there is no water, Who has permitted a faithful to pretend unfaith in some cases to preserve his life, properties, and honor, and has permitted Muslims to sleep with their wives in the nights of Ramadan, because He knows that it is too difficult for man and woman to abstain from sexual intercourse for a month that He has said,

It is made lawful for you to go in unto your wives on the night of the fast. They are raiment for you and you are raiment for them. Allah is Aware that you were deceiving yourselves in this respect and He has turned in mercy toward you and relieved you. So hold intercourse with them [Qur'an, 2:187]

So if it is so, how would Allah ignore the sexual lust that He Himself has created and is aware of its ferocity and bad results which might destroy societies?

Allah has created woman for man and created man for woman for the sake of tranquility and peacefulness. Allah the Glorified says:

And one of His signs is that He created you from dust, then lo! you are mortals ranging widely. And of His signs is that He created mates for you from yourselves that you may find rest in them, and He ordained between you love and mercy; most surely there are signs in this for a people who reflect. [Qur'an, 30:20-21]

These verses talk about men and women altogether; Allah has created both man and woman from earth, and made one as a mate to another so that each may find peace and tranquility with the other.

Thus, Allah must put a solution to this instinct so that both the male and the female live a pleasant life full of love, mercy and tranquility.

All Muslims have agreed that Allah had mercy on his people, men and women, when He permitted for them the temporary marriage. This mercy came down while Muslims were in utmost need of it. The great companions, who were examples in faith and piety, could not be patient with their sexual desires. They complained to the Prophet (s) and asked him to permit them to castrate themselves.

Al-Bukhari has mentioned in his Sahih that Qays ibn Abdullah (may Allah be pleased with him) said, "*We were with the Messenger of Allah (s) in a battle, and there were no women (wives) with us. We said, 'O Messenger of Allah (s), can we castrate ourselves?' He prohibited us from doing that. Then, he permitted us to marry women (in temporary marriage) for a garment (as simple dowry), and then he recited:*

O you who believe! do not forbid (yourselves) the good things which Allah has made lawful for you. [Qur'an, 5:87][1]

Praise be to Allah! Glorified is He! How kind and merciful He is to His people!

The Prophet (s) prohibited his companions from castration and permitted them for temporary marriage. He prohibited them from forbidding temporary marriage because it is from the good things that Allah has permitted for them. This is clear evidence on the mercy of Allah to His people, lest they harmed themselves by castration which was prohibited.

Therefore, sexual desire is a nature in man that must be satisfied and not suppressed, because its suppression causes psychological and bodily diseases. Men (and woman) have to satisfy this desire within the legal limits that Allah has determined and the Prophet (s) has declared to Muslims.

This great mercy (temporary marriage) that Allah had given to His people and all Muslims acknowledged its lawfulness in the Holy Qur'an were prohibited later on. Most people claimed that it had been prohibited by the Prophet (s).

We say to these people that this claim cannot be accepted by sound reason, because this gift of Allah was permitted to solve the problem of the sexual desires for a Muslim man and a Muslim woman. Then, is this problem no longer available so that this permission has to be annulled? Or does the Prophet (s) have the right

---

[1] *Sahih al-Bukhari*, vol. 6 p. 66.

to prohibit what Allah has permitted? Is there one thing in the Islamic Sharia that Allah had permitted for His people and then He prohibited it?

By Allah no! There is nothing of that at all. May Allah have mercy on Ameerul Mu'minin (as) who said:

Temporary marriage is a mercy that Allah has given to His servants. Were it not for the prohibition of Umar, no one would commit adultery except a wretched one![1]

In this discussion, we do not want to prove the legality of temporary marriage, for we have already proved that in our book '*To be With the Truthful*', but we want to say that the Ahlul Bayt (as) have said it is lawful until the Day of Resurrection, quoting their grandfather the Messenger of Allah (s). We say that the Ahlul Bayt (as) have done Muslims great favors, which has preserved their

---

[1] *Sharh Ma'ani al-Athar* vol.3, p. 26. Also refer to *Temporary marriage* by Abdullah al-Fakiki, and *To be with the Truthful* by Muhammad al-Tijani al-Samawi (the author of this book) where he mentions the sources of this tradition. From among the books that have been written on Temporary Marriage is *al-Fusool al-Muhimmah* by Sayyid Sharafuddeen al-Aamili, Juristic Questions by the same author, *al-Bayan* by Sayyid al-Khoei, *al-Ghadir* by Allama al-Amini, *Mut'ah* (temporary marriage) in Islam by Sayyid Husayn Mekki, *Temporary Marriage* by Sayyid Muhammad Taqi al-Hakim, *Temporary Marriage in Islam*, by Sayyid Ja'far Murtadha, and the introduction of *Mir'atul Uqool*.

It is said that Imam Malik had permitted temporary marriage. Refer to *al-Hidayah fi Sharh al-Bidayah*, p. 385, Poulaq Press, printed with *al-Fatth al-Qadeer*. It is also said that Ahmed ibn Hanbal had permitted it with necessity; refer to *Tafsir ibn Kathir*, vol. 1 p. 474, and some other companions! There are traditions narrated from Ibn Abbas, Ubay ibn Ka'b, Mujahid, Sa'eed ibn Jubayr, ibn Mas'ud, as-Sadi and others who agreed when reciting this verse: *And those of whom you seek content (by marrying them) TO A FIXED TERM. [Qur'an, 4:24]*. There are about more than twenty traditionists and exegetes from the Sunni who have said that temporary marriage is lawful.

religion and high values that keep pace with all ages and face all challenges.[1]

In the end, Muslims shall find no way that leads to the best, except by the way of Ahlul Bayt (as) and no school that complies with modern ages and overcomes all challenges, except the school of Ahlul Bayt (as) that have been based on the Qur'an and the Prophet's *Sunnah*. Allah says:

Is He then Who guides to the truth more worthy to be followed, or he who himself does not go aright unless he is guided? What then is the matter with you; how do you judge? [Qur'an, 10:35]

---

[1] Since the matter of sex brings societies heavy burdens, some Sunni *ulama*, after having found that temporary marriage is a lawful way to solve many problems, began permitting it to their youth, but under different names and with different facades!

TEMPORARY MARRIAGE WAS LEGISLATED FOR WOMAN'S WELFARE

Temporary marriage is a divine mercy that Allah has endowed on His servants. It is for the welfare of men and women with no difference. However and as we have said before, men have absolute freedom and they can enjoy themselves in the public places that are founded for this purpose and protected by the law. Moreover, men have the right to marry two, three or four wives at the same time; therefore, sexual pleasure is available to them wherever and whenever they like.

On this basis, I can deduce that temporary marriage which Allah has permitted, is to make the rights of a woman to be equal to the rights of a man in this aspect, because this kind of marriage does not prevent woman from getting married to more than one man and even to many if she observes the *iddah* and the other conditions of this marriage. The only difference between man and woman in this regard is that man can get married to four women at the same time, but woman cannot get married even to two men at the same time. This is because of the reason that we have mentioned before that there is a possibility that the sperms of two men may gather in the womb of one woman, and then it is not known which man is the father of the child created in the woman's womb, whereas this is impossible for the man who has many wives.

This is the rule of Allah that we find even in tame animals that live with us. If we put a ewe with two rams, there shall be a bloody quarrel leading to the death of one of them. If we suppose that both rams copulate with the ewe, then we are not certain which of them impregnates the ewe. If we put one ram with a herd of ewes, there shall be no quarrel, and we are certain that all the born sheep are children of that ram. What we say about rams and ewes can be said about hens and cockerel, rabbits, camels, cows, goats…etc. Allah says:

There is no animal that walks upon the earth or a bird that flies with its two wings but (they are) genera like yourselves. [Qur'an, 6:38]

Once, someone said to me, "If the matter is so, then a sterile woman can get married to two men at the same time, because the cause has fallen off."[1]

I said, "This is not possible, because the Islamic rulings are not limited to causes that when a cause has fallen off, the ruling is annulled. If we say that the cause of the prohibition of wine is the loss of one's reason where Allah says,

O you who believe, do not go near prayer when you are intoxicated until you know (well) what you say. [Qur'an, 4:34]

Then, is the one who is not intoxicated after drinking a cup or two of wine, not subject to this ruling?

Certainly not, O my friend! That substance whose much quantity causes intoxication, the little of it (even one drop) is also unlawful.

And if we say that the cause of the prohibition of pig is impurity and filthiness, then will eating its meat be lawful when it is sterilized and all microbes are removed!?

The rulings of Allah do not rely on only one cause. There may be many causes that no one knows except Allah the Almighty. Therefore, we must be satisfied with the rulings of Allah and accept them willingly and submissively, because Allah does not want for His people except what brings them good and prosperity. Allah says:

---

[1] The matter is not material only. Today, science shows us a quick result whether there is pregnancy or not, but the matter is related to moral and spiritual things; the material purity of the womb is not the basis. For example, the woman, whose husband divorces her after he has not slept with her for a long time that may be years for some reasons, has to undergo the iddah since the first moment of divorce.

Is it then the judgment of (the times of) ignorance that they desire? And who is better than Allah to judge for a people who are sure? [Qur'an, 5:50]

That is Allah's judgment; He judges between you and Allah is Knowing, Wise. [Qur'an, 60:10]

Therefore, Muslims have to be submissive and obedient.

Allah says:

It behaves not a believing man and a believing woman that they should have any choice in their matter when Allah and His Messenger have decided a matter; and whoever disobeys Allah and His Messenger, he surely strays off a manifest straying. [Qur'an, 33:36]

On this basis, believing men and believing women have to accept the decree of Allah concerning the matter of temporary marriage and to thank Him for this mercy, especially woman whom Allah has given through this marriage all the rights, whereas man only has the right to accept or not.

In the continuous marriage, man has "the right of bed" that whenever he asks her wife to sleep with, she has no right to refuse. A husband has the right to sleep with his wife whenever he likes. She even has no right, legally, to fast recommendable fasting (not even in Ramadan) except by his permission. Allah says:

Your wives are a tilth for you, so go into your tilth whenever you like. [Qur'an, 2:223]

Man has also been given the right to divorce his wife. Allah says:

O Prophet! when you divorce women, divorce them for their prescribed time (iddah). [Qur'an, 65:1]

Man also has been given the right to return his wife (to marital life) before the end of the *iddah*. Allah says:

Their husbands have a better right to take them back in the meanwhile if they wish for reconciliation. [Qur'an, 2:228]

Man has the right too to divorce his wife three times (trio-divorce). Allah says:

Divorce may be (pronounced) twice, then keep (them) in good fellowship or let (them) go with kindness...and if he divorces her (for third time), she shall not be lawful to him afterwards. [Qur'an, 2:229-230]

Man has been given the right to marry more than one wife (at the same time). Allah says:

Then, marry women as seems good to you, two and three and four. [Qur'an, 4:3]

However, in temporary marriage everything is in the hand of woman; she is the one to decide. She recites the wording of the marriage contract, and man only accepts or refuses. Woman is the one who determines the period of this marriage, and consequently determines her divorce with no condition or tie. She has the right to put any condition she likes against man. She may say to the husband, for example: On condition that you do not leave me all this time and do not marry other than me. Or she may say: on condition that you do not have sexual intercourse with me, or on condition of sexual intercourse but to ejaculate out of the womb lest I bear. Or she may say: on condition that we spend the honey-moon in Holy Mecca.

In temporary marriage, woman can stipulate whatever she likes. Allah says:

Then as to those of whom you seek content (by marrying them), give them their dowries as appointed; and there is no blame on you about what you mutually agree after what is appointed; surely Allah is Knowing, Wise. [Qur'an, 4:24]

It suffices woman as honor that she can marry herself in temporary marriage without the permission of her guardian (her father for example). In another word, it is woman who gets married to man in this kind of marriage.

TEMPORARY MARRIAGE AND ITS BENEFITS

Unfortunately, Muslims do not look at this marriage except by the eye of criticism. They do not discuss except its negative points, which are very little, and do not see its positive points which are very many.

In fact, everything has negative and positive points. As this kind of marriage was not practiced since the time of Umar ibn al-Khattab, who prohibited it with no any legal cause, so people consider it as adultery and they look at it disgustingly. This does not mean that it is disgusting, but because people have neither known nor practiced it.

It is like the offering of two prayers at one time, or like the *khums*, or wiping the feet in *wudhu'*. Despite that they have been available in the Holy Qur'an and despite that the Prophet (s) has practiced and ordered Muslims to practice them, most of people are ignorant of them. Muslims find them strange for nothing, but just because they are not familiar with them in their daily life. You see that they do not find adultery as strange as they find temporary marriage strange!

A young woman often tried to incite some young man to commit adultery with her. When he refused and suggested that they should get married in temporary marriage, she refused and said that she did not know this kind of marriage.

If you argue about the matter of temporary marriage with Sunni scholars and prove its legality with irrefutable proofs from al-Bukhari and Muslim and when they are embarrassed before the evidences, they say that this marriage is a kind of humiliation to woman. When you prove to them the opposite, they begin talking nonsense and say: will you marry me your sister or daughter in temporary marriage?

They speak with the mentality of domination over woman. They often say that woman cannot marry herself (to someone by her will) and that her marriage is in the hand of her guardian. They think that woman is like a cow that is sold and bought, and that she has no right to choose her husband. Indeed, this is the very humiliation to woman and not her temporary marriage.

Temporary marriage is a mercy from Allah for woman and it is not a kind of humiliation. She has the full right to refuse temporary marriage and no one can ever force her to accept it. If they think that this kind of marriage is humiliation to woman, then what do they say about polygamy where another fellow wife or other fellow wives are brought home inspite of her presence and without her agreement or willingness to participate with her in everything; her husband, her house, and later on the inheritance?

Is this worse or that when her husband gets married for a short period (temporary marriage) to some woman who shall share with wife, besides that this wife may not know anything at all about that marriage, which shall end soon, and about that second wife, who shall leave back for her own life?

We have said before that temporary marriage within its legal conditions and limits is for the advantage of woman and not for her disadvantage. As temporary marriage is not obligatory and as it cannot be imposed on anyone, man or woman, against his or her will, so what for is all this nonsense, defamation and accusation?

I am so sorry for this afflicted nation that claims the love to the Prophet's progeny (as), while it contradicts them in all rulings which they narrated from their grandfather the Prophet Muhammad (s) and did according to these rulings. Despite that Ja'fari School (Shiism), which is the jurisprudence of Imam Ja'far as-Sadiq (as), is taught in al-Azhar University in Cairo, many people because of fanaticism, still doubt it and doubt it belongs to Imam Ja'far as-Sadiq (as).

It is certain that the twelve infallible imams (as), at the head of whom is Imam Ali (as), called among people for the legality of temporary marriage and said that it was a mercy for people. Abdullah Ibn Abbas, as well, often said to people that temporary marriage was lawful. Muslims were divided into two parties; one of minority who followed and did according to the doings of the Ahlul Bayt (as), and the other one of great majority who followed the caliphs (but not Imam Ali as) and companions.

Matters have remained until now as they were before; the followers of the Ahlul Bayt (as) see temporary marriage as lawful, and the followers of the caliphs see it as unlawful.

After all and as we offer this study, we do not want to force anyone to accept it. People are free to choose what they see as true, but we have to uncover the hidden facts so that the truth becomes clear and shiny before whoever intends and looks for it.

In our view, temporary marriage has many benefits:

If a male student and a female student, who live together throughout the school year while they are in the age of intensity of sexual passion, get married temporarily, they shall be in intimate companionship and association even if they do not have sexual intercourse when they both agree to this condition.

This may last for the period of their study, and after that, they can decide either to separate, or conclude a contract of continuous marriage if they want. In fact, the first marriage shall give the two spouses more chance to know each other in the best way and shall be able to get over all the obstacles that may face them in their continuous marital life.

This marriage shall give them relief, peace and tranquility and make them proceed with their studies easily. Their relation shall be lawful and honest and shall make their consciences satisfied and pleased and consequently Allah will be pleased with them. They shall be safe from troubles and suspicious looks of other students, who when they know about this marriage shall stop to trouble them.

On the other hand, if a female student moves from one young man to another, having in her handbag tens of love letters from this and that besides the contraceptives for fear of pregnancy and scandal and if young men move from one girl to another to taste the honey of each one, as bees tasting flowers, and play with the fates, futures and feelings of those girls, paying no any attention to the honor, dignity, and feelings of their families, and when those girls finish their studies and return to their homes followed by suspicions and accusations that shall cause them tens of complexes arising from the leaving of those traitors who promise and after satisfying their desires, leave those deflowered girls alone to be later on filled with rage and spite against the society and to try avenge for themselves by every means - it shall be found not strange by those pretending scholars!!!

A traveler, who travels for a long period away from his home and wife, may be able to be patient (with his sexual desire), but if not, he has to get married in temporary marriage to assure his ease, tranquility, and faith. His wife may agree willingly when she knows that her husband has followed the lawful way and kept away from unlawful ways. A wife knows her husband well and shall prefer him to be in the house of an honest and upright woman, who gets married to protect her honor and honesty and make use of Allah's mercy rather than to look for a prostitute in a street every day who takes his money and gives him fatal diseases after having slept with other men many times on the same day. Surely, there is nothing of that in temporary marriage, as one from among its conditions is that the woman having married in temporary marriage has no right to remarry except after having undergone all the *iddah* of her first marriage which is a period of two menstruations or two months for a woman in menopause.

Temporary marriage can solve the problem of a spinster who has not married for one reason or another. Islam permits her to satisfy her desire in this lawful way.

Temporary marriage also solves the problem of a widow who does not want to marry in continuous marriage for the sake of her children or any other reason.

How often it happens in our Arabic societies that a beautiful woman falls in love with a teenager or a young man in the age of her son. This woman may sleep with this teenager and remain doing so secretly in unlawful association. Temporary marriage makes their association lawful and preserves their honor and dignity.

A woman, who is afraid to travel alone or that some countries may prevent her from traveling except with a *non-mahram*, can conclude a contract of temporary marriage just for the purpose of travel. Marriage in this case can be without sexual intercourse.

A man, who has a female servant at home, is not permitted by Islam to touch any part of her body or look at her while unveiled, and her full veil may embarrass her when doing her job in the house and before her master. This man can conclude a contract of temporary marriage between his young son[1] and the servant inasmuch as for the period of her employment, and thus she becomes his daughter-in-law who is *mahram* to him. In this way, there shall be no problem or embarrassment.

A young woman, who remains alone for hours in the house of a man for learning special lessons or a foreign language, or any other reason, can conclude a contract of temporary marriage with that man to avoid that forbidden privacy, about which the Prophet (s) said, *"No man and a woman are alone in privacy except that Satan becomes the third of them."* In this way, this privacy shall be lawful and the woman can put off her hijab before her teacher or shake hands with him. However, she can stipulate any condition she wants.

There are many other cases where temporary marriage becomes mercy for people lest they commit sins, which may cause the society much corruption and many physical and psychological diseases. Temporary marriage, in many cases, is the only solution to save society from these diseases and to preserve honors, lineages, dignities, and nobilities.[2]

Say: Surely Allah does not enjoin indecency; do you say against Allah what you do not know. [Qur'an, 7:28]

---

[1] The boy may be no more than some years, and it is not intended in such a marriage that the sexual intercourse happens, but it is just to make lawful through this marriage what is unlawful without it. This does not mean to make lawful what Allah has prohibited, for this is of disbelief, but to follow what the Sharia may permit. Shaking hands with a non-mahram woman is not lawful, but it becomes lawful after a legal contract of marriage with that woman.

[2] When I was preparing a thesis for higher studies in one of the Sunni colleges, I heard one of the female officials of the college blaming a teacher why he did not visit her the last night where she had prepared a gateau and been waiting for him. The teacher was trying to apologize.
I say: if there is no contract of continuous marriage or temporary marriage, then what shall be the legal excuse for them to meet and mix as man and woman?!!

Surely Allah enjoins the doing of justice and the doing of good (to others) and the giving to the kindred, and He forbids indecency and evil and oppression; He admonishes you that you may be mindful. [Qur'an, 16:90]

THIS IS AL-MAHDI

Muslims in general in the past and the present believe in the Savior who shall bring back to them their glory and honor and repair what tyrants and oppressors have corrupted and destroyed, and restore to them their religion. This savior and reformer is Imam al-Mahdi (as), about whom the Prophet (s) gave good news when he said, *"If nothing remains in this life except one day, Allah will prolong that day until al-Mahdi, who is from my progeny and whose name is like mine, shall appear to fill the earth with justice and fairness after it shall have been filled with injustice and oppression."*[1]

This Savior of Mankind, who will complete the mission of the prophets and messengers in the earth so that the Light of Allah is perfected at his hands, is the center of the attention of all three major religions; Judaism, Christianity and Islam. The Jews, Christians and Muslims all are waiting for him and claim him to be from them according to their many traditions about him.

Since we believe definitely that Islam is the last of religions and that there shall be no prophet after Muhammad (s), so we are certain with not a bit of doubt that al-Mahdi is from the progeny of the Prophet Muhammad (s) and he is the last of the twelve infallible imams, behind whom Jesus Christ (s) will offer prayer as a kind of honoring and glorifying.

In this quick discussion, we do not want to study everything about al-Mahdi, because the history and the Prophet's traditions in this context has already been talked about in our book – '*To Be With the Truthful*'.[2] Besides this many books, theses, and encyclopedias have been written on al-Mahdi (s). We only want to show the belief of the Ahlul Bayt (as) where they stand alone away from the rest of

---

[1] Refer to *Al-Jam' bayna as-Sihah as-Sittah* (gathering between the six Sahihs), chapter - Signs of the Day of Resurrection and *al-Aqa'id al-Islamiyyah* (Islamic beliefs), by Sayyid Sabiq.

[2] https://www.al-islam.org/be-with-truthful-muhammad-al-tijani-al-samawi

Muslims in rulings and beliefs that comply with the challenges of the world and in fact, they may precede challenges sometimes.

The Jews, Christians and Muslims have been overcome by materialism to an extent that they have gone away from religion and been affected by atheistic, materialistic, and secularist doctrines, in a way that spirituality has become too weak in them. Therefore, they are looking for solutions, which they do not find anywhere except in the divine good news.

Moreover, the violent wars that have exhausted humankind, especially the poor and the weak everywhere in the world, who die of hunger in millions, while tyrants and oppressors compete with each other to possess the most fatal weapons and to occupy nations by all means - cultural, economic and technology. Were it not for the hope of a better future with justice, peace and noble life that man looks forward to, there would be no meaning or sense in this life. And were it not for the belief of Muslims in Allah, Who has promised to support His religion to prevail over all religions when saying: *He it is Who sent His Messenger with guidance and the religion of truth, that He might cause it to prevail over all religions, though the polytheists may be averse. [Qur'an, 9:33]*

Were it not be for this faith, despair would fill their souls and they would be losers! It is this faith that fills souls with energy, vitality, the love of life, expectation of a better future, and the waiting for deliverance, because after hardship there shall come ease.

This is al-Mahdi (as) - who is the hope of Muslims, or in fact the hope of all humankind. The belief in al-Mahdi (as) is not a matter of mocking. Allah the Almighty says:

Say: O my servants! who have acted extravagantly against their own souls, do not despair of the mercy of Allah; surely Allah forgives the faults altogether; surely He is the Forgiving, the Merciful. And return to your Lord time after time and submit to Him before there comes to you the punishment, then you shall not be helped. And follow the best that has been revealed to you from your Lord before there comes to you the punishment all of a sudden while you do not even perceive. Lest a soul should say: O woe to me, for what I fell short of my duty to Allah, and most surely I was among scoffers. [Qur'an, 39:53-56]

"THEN I WAS GUIDED" IS THE AHLUL BAYT'S BOOK

The Ahlul Bayt (as) have well known charismata even in these days. How often that we hear from here and there that some charismata have happened to some of the Shia, or that they have seen some charismata somewhere by virtue of the Ahlul Bayt (as). It is not something strange, for the Ahlul Bayt (as) are the infallible Imams of guidance, leaders of people and suns in darkness.

Even if Umar ibn al-Khattab did not know the actual significance of the Ahlul Bayt (as) in his time, he himself led us to their great position with Allah when he prayed to Allah by means of al-Abbas, the Prophet's uncle, who was not of those from whom Allah had kept impurity away and purified through thorough purifying.[1]

Al-Abbas (Prophet's uncle) was not of those upon whom Allah had ordained blessings as He had ordained on His prophet. He was not of those for whom Allah had imposed love on all Muslims. He was not of those whom to Allah had bequeathed the knowledge of the Book. He was not of those whom Allah had greeted in His Book when saying:

"Peace be on Aal Yasin," [Qur'an, 37:130]

He was not of the infallible imams for whom the Messenger of Allah (s) had imposed on the nation, guidance to follow them and ride aboard their ship. He was not of those who had inherited the knowledge of the Prophet (s).

Nevertheless, Allah responded to Umar, because he beseeched Allah by means of a relative of the Prophet (s). If he had beseeched Allah by means of Ali, Fatima, al-Hasan, and al-Husayn, he would have seen greater wonders and the blessings of the heaven. The earth would have come down to them, and they would have eaten from above their heads and from under their feet.

---

[1] The Prophet (s) and his progeny who were the ones referred to by the Qur'anic verse of Purification.

What is important is that Umar revealed to us something very important and he uncovered to us what was concealed. The fact is that kinship to the Prophet (s) has charismata which can be ignored by no one. The relatives of the Prophet (s) are those people who if they ask Allah, He will respond to them immediately in everything. Therefore, when Umar saw absence of rain and felt that there might be famine to threaten Muslims with destruction, he resorted to the kinship of the Messenger of Allah (s), and then it rained by the will of Allah to honor the kinship of the Prophet (s).

Where are the Wahhabis when they see these irrefutable proofs and where are the Muslims who have kept themselves away from knowing the truth?

Sheikh Jallool al-Jaziri (may Allah have mercy on him) was one of the *ulama* of Zaytoona (University) in Tunisia. By the favor of Allah, he arrived at the truth and turned to be Shia. He wrote his last book in which he discussed the event of al-Ghadir and paid homage to Ameerul Mu'minin Imam Ali (as), the virtues of the Ahlul Bayt (as), and their charismata. He told me that once Tunis faced lack of rain and famine until all people were about to die. The people of Tunis offered the prayer for rain many times, but the sky abstained from giving them even a drop.

When the lands became too dry, people went complaining to one of the righteous, who was Allama Sheikh Ibrahim ar-Riyahi, and asked him to pray to Allah so that He might respond to him. The Sheikh said to them, "Gather with me one hundred men from the *Ashraf*,[1] so that I will offer the prayer for rain with them." One hundred *Sharifs* came to him, and before finishing the prayer, and though it was very hot, the sky rained heavily. It rained for three days and all valleys overflowed until people were afraid of drowning.[2]

---

[1] Ashraf in Tunisia are the sharifs or sayyids who are the descendants of the Prophet Muhammad (s) via Ali and Fatima (peace be on them).
[2] Sheikh Jallool al-Jaziri mentioned in his book "al-Fawa'id al-Fakhira Lezad ad-Dunya wel Aakhira - the excellent benefits for the provision of this life and the afterlife", p. 78, quoting *Tarikh* (history of) *Ibn Dhayyaf* that once when the epidemic (plague) spread in Tunisia, the *ulama* met in the

When I was guided to the Ahlul Bayt (as), thanks be to Allah, and wrote my first book '*Then I was Guided*', I did not imagine that it would receive all this reception and fame.

By the way, it would be not useless to mention here an anecdote that my dear friend and great scholar Dr. As'ad Ali, who was a great man of letters, once told me when I visited him in his house in Mazza in Damascus. As we were talking, among a group of his disciples and friends, he reminded me of something that delighted me too much. He said, "I read your book 'Then I was Guided' and know its secret."

I asked with astonishment, "What is the secret of the book?"

He said, "When you came in to visit our master (Imam) Musa al-Kadhim (s) and said, 'O Allah, have mercy on him if he is from the righteous', he did according to the saying of Allah

"And when you are greeted with a greeting, greet with a better (greeting) than it or return it" [Qur'an, 4:86]

And, he greeted you better than your greeting to him. When you greeted him, saying, 'O Allah have mercy on him', he greeted you with better than your greeting, saying, 'O Allah, guide him (to the right path)!' So Allah responded to him and guided you, and after that came this book, and this was the secret of its success."

This is a fact which I have believed in and it has entered deep into my heart. I have believed that the Ahlul Bayt (as) were the secret behind the success of the book without doubt. I met no one who showed to me other than his admiration of the book. The book has been published more than twenty times and translated into seventeen languages in the world. Thousands of Muslims everywhere in the world were guided to the truth by this book, especially in Africa where there were no Shia and Muslims lived there without sectarian backgrounds.[1]

Zeytoonah Mosque and decided to gather forty sharifs who all had the name Muhammad and to pray Allah to save them from that plague. They gathered the forty men by whose means Allah saved people and the plague vanished.

[1] In Iraq and Iran, people narrate many true stories about the charismata of the Ahlul Bayt (s) that have actually taken place. The visitors, students, and

scholars from India, Pakistan, Afghanistan, and other places, who have visited or come to study and live near the shrines of the Ahlul Bayt (s) and been blessed by their holy tombs, also narrate such stories.

"THEN I WAS GUIDED" IN THE COURT

Believing that "people are on the religion of their rulers" and taking the Messenger of Allah (s) as my exemplar that he had sent many letters to the kings of his time inviting them to Islam; an idea came to my mind.

In his somehow similar letters to the kings of his time, the Messenger of Allah (s) had said, "*Be Muslim and you shall be safe and Allah will reward you twice, but if you turn your back, the sin of the magi shall be on you.*"

This is evidence that "people are on the religion of their kings" that if the kings believe, people believe, if they disbelieve, people disbelieve, and if they become polytheists, people become polytheists too.

The idea that preoccupied my mind was to send copies of my book '*Then I was Guided*' to the Arab kings and presidents accompanying them with friendly letters befitting their positions so that they might remember (Allah), for surely their reminding would benefit the believers! Since they are at the head of the countries of this nation, so they are the men of power and authority, and their responsibility for the fate of people and the fate of the Muslim nation is a very great responsibility. "*Every one of you is a shepherd (responsible) and every one of you is responsible for his herd (subjects)*" as the Prophet (s) said.[1]

Believing that the successful ones in this life and the afterlife are the true believers who do good, enjoin each other with truth, and enjoin each other with patience, and that "*No one of you is a true believer until he wishes for his brother what he wishes for himself*", and "*if Allah guides by you one man, it is better to you than the world and all that there is in it*"...for all that, I sent copies of 'Then I was Guided' to King Hasan the Second of Morocco, President ash-Shathli bin Jadid of Algeria, President Zainul Abedin bin Ali of

---

[1] *Sunan Abu Dawood* hadith no. 2928

Tunisia, President Mu'ammar al-Qadhdhafi of Libya, King Husayn bin Talal of Jordan and his brother (heir apparent) Hasan bin Talal, and to King Fahad ibn Abdul Aziz of Saudi Arabia.

I sent each book with a special dedication and a letter of high reverence by registered mail. The copies of the book were received by all consignees. I knew that from the receipts I received from the post office that had the signatures of the secretaries of all the kings and presidents I sent the book to. I waited too long for the replies, but I received none except one reply from Zainul Abedin bin Ali the president of the Republic of Tunisia, who expressed to me his sincere thanks.

Once in a press conference in India when I mentioned this story, I was asked, "Do you think that President Zainul Abedin has read your book?"

I replied, "The president is so busy that he has no time to read a book, but if he has read it, he is thanked for that, and if not, he is excused. The important thing is that he was the only one, from among the kings and presidents to whom I sent the book, who replied to my letter."

While waiting for the replies and before receiving the reply of President Zainul Abedin, I traveled to Tunisia and there were two hundred copies of *Then I was Guided* with me in my car. At the port, the custom officials hesitated to detain the copies of the book. They sent for their boss, who said when he saw the book, "Is this the Green Book?"

I said, "Its color is green, but it is not the Green Book of al-Qadhdhafi."

He said to me, "Do you not know that letting books pass in this quantity is forbidden and it requires a permit of import?"

I said, "O brother, this is my book and I am its author. I have offered a copy as present to his Excellency the President."

He took a copy of the book and compared the name of the author to the name in my passport. When he became certain, he said to me, "I too want you to give me a copy as gift."

I said, "With great pleasure! What is your noble name?"

As I was writing a dedication to him, he was signing the permit.

I arrived in Tunis, the capital and gave some copies as present to some of my friends there. Then I traveled to my birthplace the city of Qafsah, where I met my relatives and old students. After two or three days, half of the copies were distributed.

I thought of my traditional opponents too, and gifted each one a copy of the book with a dedication by name and with some nice words of courtesy, out of my belief in the saying of Allah:

And not alike are the good and the evil. Repel (evil) with what is best, when lo! he between whom and you was enmity would be as if he were a warm friend. [Qur'an, 41:34]

I said to myself that they might be guided to the truth and leave fanaticism, or at least they might refrain from troubling me.

Then, I traveled to some neighboring towns and villages and distributed the rest of the copies. Nothing remained with me in my car except three or four copies that I kept for what would be later on.

President Zainul Abedin returned the glory of the Zeytoonah University and it was reopened after it had been closed for thirty years. He sent government delegations to each district to appoint the director, whom the people of the district chose to manage the branch of the Zeytoonah University there. Unfortunately, the one who was chosen in Qafsah and his appointment was celebrated, was the most spiteful one to me and to the Shia.

This man seized that opportunity and gave the copy that I had sent to him to the commissioner of the district, accusing me with dangerous accusations. The commissioner of the district gave permission to the governor to arrest me, take back all the copies of the book that I had gifted and sent to people. Those who would be found to have the book were called in order to be questioned and a report was to be written on the case.

The agents of police and security forces began carrying out the orders and looking for me everywhere. At that time, I was a guest at one of my friends, who was a manager of a big department. My son-in-law came to me there in a hurry and told me about the matter. He suggested that I should go immediately to the borders and leave the country. I thanked him for his feelings towards me and said to him, "If I do that, I shall give them an excuse against myself. I will wait for them with all courage, for I have nothing to fear of, nor have I done anything that I may regret."

The agents of the security forces came and took me with them to the police station. There, questioning and argumentation began with the chief of the chief inspector with some of politeness and respect until the governor arrived. As soon as the governor saw me, he shouted at me, "Do you want to make a revolution in this peaceful country? Do you think that we are in Iran here?"

He turned to inspector and said to him, "This master has brought three thousand copies of a book full of blasphemy and brought one hundred millions of money to distribute them among people, inciting them to revolt and rebel."

I said to him with challenge, "Firstly, my book is not a book of blasphemy nor does it call for revolt. If it was so, I would not present a copy of it to his Excellency President Zainul Abedin, nor would I come to Tunisia at all. Secondly, if I have brought three thousand copies, I would have to come with a big truck to carry them. The car, which I have come with, is now detained with you. You can fill it yourselves to see how many copies it may contain. Thirdly, you say that I have distributed one hundred millions of money among people. I daresay and insist on you to bring even one man, saying that I have given him even one fil. After all, I did not come to the country stealthily or by force. I came in a lawful way and was searched like the rest of people. If I had one hundred millions, they would not let pass without a permit. Surely, you are more aware of these affairs than I am."

Finding my speech reasonable, he asked me, "How many copies of the book have you brought?"

"Twenty copies", I replied.

He said, "Give me two hundred names of the persons whom you have given copies of your book."

I said, "This is not possible, not because I refuse to give you the names, but I really do not know them. For example, from among them there are some of my students, whom I have not seen for ten years or more; I know them by the face and do not remember their names."

After consultation, they decided to set me free that night, but to come back to them the next morning. Early in the morning, I came to them at the appointment. They made me ride in a car accompanied by two men from their agents. We went to the neighboring villages in order to take back the copies of the book from the houses that I knew. On the way, I discovered that my two companions were mustabsir[1] (Shia).

One of them said to me, "Professor, have you forgotten me? Do you not remember me? I was one of your students in the seventies in the Preparatory School of Teachers. Last night I did not sleep, for I took your book from the (police) station and read it all. I swear by Allah that I am like you (Shia)." The second said, "I, too, read your book two days ago when one of my friends brought it to me. It opened my heart to many things that I doubted before and could not find convincing answers to them except in your book. Now, I am a Shia."

We all laughed for that chance and did not feel the distance. In three days and from many villages, we collected copies of the book as possible as we could. According to the orders, the Security Force agents delivered a summons to everyone who was found to have a copy of the book.

I met the commissioner and after a short talk, he said to me, "They frightened me of you and said that you are an extreme Shia and are financed by al-Khomeini. They said that you say it is permissible to marry one's sister."

I laughed saying to myself, "Now, I know my friend!" I told him that the matter was the matter of suckling and it was mentioned in the same book. He smiled and took out a copy of the book from his drawer, saying to me, "What you said is true, but I blame you, because you have not offered me a copy of the book. If you did since the day of your coming to Qafsah, nothing would happen. However now, the case is out of our hands. It is in the court that shall decide

---

[1] *Mustabsir* is a term used to refer to a Sunni who willingly turns Shia.

on the matter. After that, you come to us to give you back your passport to travel with peace."

I understood from this man's speech that they, after having become certain about my innocence of all rumors and having known through the detained documents that the president had received my book from Paris, moved the case to the court to only see if the contents of the book was dangerous to the regime or religion.

I went to the court after having known from the Shia agents that all the persons, who were questioned, did not say about me except good. The questions that they were asked are as the following:

1. What is your relation with Dr. al-Tijani?

   The answer was either "my teacher" or "my friend".

2. Did he give you money?

   The answer was "No, I have never received even one *cent* from him."

3. Did he ask you for money?

   The answer was "No at all! He never asked anything from me".

In the court, I requested to meet the vice-president. After his permission, I went in to him. I saw a copy of my book on his table with a piece of paper inside it. I said, "Sir, I am the author of the book. I have come to Tunisia for one week, but now I am detained since a month without any guilt. I am very worried about my wife and daughters who are alone in Paris."

He interrupted me, saying, "The book must be read first and then the judgment will be announced. I have read about one third of it and inshallah I shall finish it tonight. Tomorrow, the judgment will be given on it."

I said, "Sir, I do not ask from you anything, but to act quickly."

He said, "Come to us tomorrow afternoon!"

The next day, I went there and was surprised by the vice-president who received me at the door and embraced me very warmly, saying, "I believe in everything in this book, O Doctor!"

My eyes were filled with tears and I did not believe what my ears heard. He said to me, "Please, come in! We will write down the judgment for you. If you had spent millions to make public your book, it would not have been made public, as it has become now. Some of my friends called me from Tunis asking me for your book, which has been called "Salman Rushdi al-Qafsi (of Qafsah)"

I sat down, praising Allah and thanking Him too much for His favors and assistance to me in the same court in the matter of suckling, and then in the matter of the book where they had intended evil against it, but it changed into good.

Mr. Vice-president wrote down the judgment and gave it to the clerk to type it with a typewriter. He ordered his clerk to release the detained copies of the book, and then said to me, "I would ask Your Honor for ten copies of the book to offer them to my friends. If you like, we can give the rest of copies back to their owners from whom they were taken."

I said, "I myself will do that after receiving the judgment."

Some officials came to me asking for the book. I gave the Vice-president what he wanted and distributed more than ten copies in the court.

Mr. Vice-president gave me the judgment after having signed it himself. He ordered his clerk to carry the rest of copies to my car. Then, he gave me my passport and took leave of me.

I left, being so delighted and happy. I gave back the copies of the book to their owners, putting in every book a copy of the judgment. Thus, the book was circulated even in coffee-houses with no fear or embarrassment.

Since forbidden fruit is sweet, this temporary detainement made the book so famous and caused an intellectual revolution to some people. Because of this, many people turned to be Shia.

And Allah turned back the unbelievers in their rage; they did not obtain any advantage and Allah sufficed the believers in fighting; and Allah is Strong, Mighty. [Qur'an, 33:25]

When I went back to Paris, I found among the letters that had come to me the letter of Mr. Zainul Abedin bin Ali, the president of the Tunisian Republic.

Really, I cannot hide my interest and pride in the charisma that I have seen and am still seeing by the virtue of the Ahlul Bayt (peace be on them).

The last of our prayer is that praise be to Allah, the Lord of the worlds, and blessings and peace be on the noblest of prophets and messengers, our master and guardian Muhammad and on his pure, immaculate progeny.

Muhammad al-Tijani al-Samawi

the Tunisian

REFERENCE BOOKS

1. *Fear Allah* by Dr. Muhammad al-Tijani al-Samavi
2. *Islam and the Arab civilization* by Muhammad Kurd Ali
3. *Know the Truth* by Dr. Muhammad at-Tijani al-Samavi
4. *Imam as-Sadiq as known by the West* translated by Dr. Nooruddin Aal Ali
5. *Imam as-Sadiq, the Inspirer of Chemistry* by Dr. Muhammad Yahya al-Hashimi
6. *Al-Bidayah wal Nihayah* by Ibn Athir
7. *The History of the Arabs* by Philip Hatti
8. *Tabyin al-Haqa'iq* (showing the facts) by Az-Zuray'ee
9. *Tafsir Ibn Kathir* by Ismail ibn Kathir
10. *The Present Time of the Muslim World*
11. *The Crusades* by Borgia
12. *The Lives of the Companions*
13. *School Journey* by Sheikh Muhammad Jawad al-Balaghi
14. *The Excellences of our Civilization* by Dr. Mustafa as-Siba'i
15. *The Arabian man and civilization* by Anwar ar-Rifa'i
16. *Rawdatu Nadhar* by Ibn Qudama
17. *Temporary Marriage* by Sayyid Muhammad Taqi al-Hakim
18. *Temporary Marriage in Islam* by Sayyid Ja'far Murtadha al-Aamili
19. Sa'd as-Sa'ud
20. *Sunan Abu Dawood*
21. *Sunan Ahmad ibn Hanbal*
22. *Al-Sunan al-Kubra* by Imam al-Bayhaqi
23. *Dala'il an-Nubuwwah* by Imam al-Bayhaqi
24. *Trends of History in Qur'an* by Sayyid Muhammad Baqir as-Sadr

25. *Sunan ad-Daraqutni* by Abul Hasan al-Baghdadi al-Daraqutni
26. *As-Sira al-Halabiyyah* by Al-Halabi al-Shafi'i
27. *As-Sira an-Nabawiyya* by Ibn Hisham
28. *Conditions of Ijtihad* by Dr. Abdul Aziz al-Khayyat
29. *The Shia in Islam* by Allama Sayyid Muhammad Husayn Tabataba'i
30. *Sahih al-Bukhari*
31. *Sahih al-Tirmizi*
32. *Sahih Muslim*
33. *As-Sawa'iq al-Muhriqah* by Ibn Hajar al-Shafi'i
34. *Al-Ghadir* by Allama al-Amini
35. *The Dawn of Islam* by Ahmad Amin
36. *Al-Fusool al-Muhimmah* (important chapters) by Sayyid Abdul Husayn Sharafuddin
37. *Al-Fawa'id al-Fakhirah lizad ad-Dunya wal Aakhira* by Sheikh Jallool al-Jaziri
38. *The Book of Mut'ah* (temporary marriage) by Sheikh Abdullah al-Fakiki
39. *Kanz al Ummal* by al-Muttaqi al-Hindi
40. *Lisan al-Arab* by Ibn Manzur
41. *Ansab al-Ashraf* by Yahya al-Baladhuri
42. *Lisan al-Mizan* by Ibn Hajar 'Asqalani
43. *What the World has lost by the Declination of Muslims* by an-Nawawi
44. *Mut'ah* (temporary marriage) *in Islam* by Sayyid Husayn Makki
45. *Al-Bilad* Magazine
46. *Introduction to the Islamic Economy* by Dr. Abdul Aziz Fahmi
47. *Mustadrak al-Hakim* by Al-Hakim Nishapuri
48. *To be with the Truthful* by Dr. Muhammad al-Tijani al-Samavi
49. *Muqaddimah* by Ibn Khaldun

50. *Multaqa al-Abhur* by Ibrahim al-Halabi
51. *Al-Manaqib* by al-Khawarizmi
52. *Al-Mawahib al-Ladumiyyah* by Muhammad al-Zurqani
53. *Mizan al-I'tidal* by Muhammad ibn Ahmad Dhahabi
54. *An-Nasaa'ih al-Kafiyyah leman Yatawalla Mu'awiyah* by Ibn Abi al-Hadid
55. *Nayl al-Awtar* by Al-Shawkani
56. *Al-Huda ila Din al-Mustafa* by Sheikh Muhammad Jawad al-Balaghi
57. *Al-Isabah fi Tamyiz al-Sahabah*, by Ibn Hajar al-'Asqalani
58. *Tarikh al Kabir* by Imam al-Bukhari
59. *Tarikh al-Khamis* by Husayn ibn Muhammad Diyarbakri
60. *Al-Muwatta* by Imam Malik
61. *Al-Mu'jam al-Kabir* by Tabarani
62. *Musannaf 'Abd al-Razzaq* by 'Abd ar-Razzaq as-San'ani
63. *Tazkiratul-Khawas* by Sibte Ibne Jauzi
64. *Musnad Ahmad* by Imam Ahmad Ibn Hanbal
65. *Al-Hidayah fi Sharh al-Bidayah* by Imam Malik
66. *Wafa' al-Wafa' bi Akhbar Dar al-Mustafa* by Al-Samhudi Al-Shafi'i
67. *Sharh Ma'ani al-Athar* by Ahmad ibn Muhammad Tahawi
68. *Kashf al Khafa* by Isma'il ibn Muhammad al-Jarrahi
69. *al-Imamah wa al-Siyasah* by Ibn Qutaybah al-Dinawari
70. *Tarikh al-Khulafa*, by Jalaluddin Suyuti
71. *Al-Durr Al-Manthur Fi Tafsir Bil-Ma'thur* by Jalaludin Suyuti

www.ingramcontent.com/pod-product-compliance
Lightning Source LLC
LaVergne TN
LVHW091716070526
838199LV00050B/2419